THE FUTURE OF BEHAVIOURAL SCIENCE

According to 250+ Experts

Merle van den Akker

BRISTOL
UNIVERSITY
PRESS

First published in Great Britain in 2026 by

Bristol University Press
University of Bristol
1-9 Old Park Hill
Bristol
BS2 8BB
UK
t: +44 (0)117 374 6645
e: bup-info@bristol.ac.uk

Details of international sales and distribution partners are available at bristoluniversitypress.co.uk

DOI: 10.51952/9781529244618

British Library Cataloguing in Publication Data
A catalogue record for this book is available from the British Library

ISBN 978-1-5292-4459-5 paperback
ISBN 978-1-5292-4460-1 ePub
ISBN 978-1-5292-4461-8 ePDF

Cover design: Liam Roberts Design
Front cover image: Adobe Stock/Shawn Hempel
Bristol University Press uses environmentally responsible print partners.
Printed and bound in Great Britain by CPI Group (UK) Ltd, Croydon, CR0 4YY

Bristol University Press' authorised representative in the European Union is: Easy Access System Europe, Mustamäe tee 50, 10621 Tallinn, Estonia,
Email: gpsr.requests@easproject.com

FSC
www.fsc.org
MIX
Paper | Supporting responsible forestry
FSC® C013604

Contents

About the Author

Merle van den Akker is a behavioural scientist and Senior Product Manager at the Commonwealth Bank of Australia, where she applies behavioural science to financial decision-making at scale. Her research spans consumer finance, investing behaviour, and the design of effective behavioural interventions.

Merle has spent years making behavioural science accessible – through writing, and hundreds of interviews with leading scientists from academia, industry, and policy. That archive of conversations is the foundation of this book.

This book brings together more than 250 voices in behavioural science, reflecting her belief that the field is best understood not through a single lens, but through the diverse experiences of those shaping it.

Acknowledgements

This book would not exist without the generosity, openness, and intellectual curiosity of the many behavioural scientists who agreed to be interviewed. To each of you: thank you. Thank you for your time, your candour, and your willingness to reflect not just on your successes, but also on the uncertainties, challenges, and turning points that shaped your journeys. This collection is a direct result of your contributions.

I am especially grateful to those who engaged more than once, who continued the conversation over time, and who supported this project beyond their own interviews. Your enthusiasm for the field and for sharing it with others has been both motivating and deeply appreciated.

To my colleagues and collaborators, thank you for continuously challenging my thinking and sharpening my work. And allowing me the time to take on this project next to my many other projects!

To my friends and family, thank you for your support, patience, and encouragement throughout this process. Writing a book alongside a full-time role and ongoing research is no small undertaking, and your understanding made it possible. And the fact that you weren't tired of hearing about it after months and months is admirable to say the least.

And finally, to the readers: whether you are new to behavioural science or have been part of the field for years, I hope these interviews offer something of value; insight, inspiration, or simply a sense of connection to a broader community of people trying to better understand human behaviour.

Preface

This book began as an excuse. Or perhaps more charitably, as a project: an interview series launched in 2019 to learn from people much further along the behavioural science journey than I was. At the time, I was a PhD student trying to understand what it meant to work in the field, what skills were needed, what paths were possible, and what behavioural science might become.

What started as 12 interviews, six by me and six by my former classmate, the brilliant Etinosa Agbonlahor, now Chief Executive Officer (CEO) of Decision Alpha and formerly at Fidelity and Commonwealth Bank, grew into over 250 conversations spanning academia, policy, and practice. It was never meant to be a book. But over time, patterns emerged. Recurring hopes for the field. Persistent blind spots. Calls for rigour, relevance, and reform. This book gathers those themes, not as a transcript of the series, but as a critical synthesis of what we learned, and where we might go next.

It is important to say clearly: this is not a book about what behavioural science is. It is about what it could become. The field is still defining itself, and that process is not passive; it is something we actively shape, with every project, paper, and conversation. Therefore, if you are reading this, maybe you are already part of that future. Or maybe, like me when I began, you are still figuring out your place in it. Either way, I hope these chapters leave you feeling more informed, more connected, and above all, more excited about the road ahead.

The journey behind the book

The interviews that gave rise to this project were never uniform. Some were academic debates about methods and measurement. Others were candid stories of failure, wrong turns, or unexpected lessons. A policy maker in Latin America spoke about testing interventions in under-resourced contexts; a corporate consultant shared frustrations about trying to maintain rigour in a fast-paced commercial environment; an academic reflected on watching their most-cited paper fail to replicate. Taken together, these stories were not just about behavioural science as a discipline but about behavioural science as a community.

That community is broader and more diverse than I realized when I began. There are the pioneers who brought experiments into economics or introduced psychology into public policy. There are the institutional builders, who set up behavioural insights teams within governments, Non-Governmental Organisations (NGOs), or firms. There are critics who remind us of blind spots and biases. And there are the students and early-career researchers who are impatient for change, who want a field that is credible, global, and just.

The interviews did more than fill my notebooks. They shifted my perspective on what this field is for. Again and again, I heard that behavioural science is not just a set of tools, but a responsibility. When we study human decision-making, we are not neutral observers. We make choices about what questions to ask, which methods to use, whose behaviour to examine, and whose voices to amplify. These choices shape the science we produce and the societies we help build.

The stakes

That realization matters because the stakes are high. Behavioural science now finds itself applied in contexts as varied as pension enrolment, climate change, digital privacy, vaccine uptake, and financial inclusion. In each of these domains, the science carries weight, shaping policies, technologies, and lives. But with influence comes responsibility. If our methods are narrow, our claims overstated, or our evidence fragile, the damage is not just academic. It risks undermining trust in the entire field.

This book, therefore, does not shy away from criticism. It looks honestly at the problems behavioural science has faced: the replication crisis, the overreliance on Western, Educated, Industrialized, Rich, and Democratic (WEIRD) samples, the tendency to privilege novelty over reliability, and the temptation to reduce complexity into neat nudges. But the purpose of critique here is not demolition; it is renewal. Loving a field does not mean ignoring its flaws. It means holding it accountable to its own promises.

What this book covers

The book is structured thematically, drawing on interview insights and academic research to explore big questions and thorny issues. We begin by unpacking the history of the field (Chapter 1), then turn to where things may have gone wrong (Chapter 2). We interrogate the mythology around nudge (Chapter 3) and confront our sampling and methodological biases (Chapters 4 and 5). We then discuss the replication crisis and the demands of scientific integrity (Chapter 6), followed by the ethical questions that affect us all (Chapter 7). Finally, we ask what skills the next generation of behavioural scientists will need, how we might foster them (Chapter 8), and offer advice for those who want to grow in the field, whatever shape that may take (Chapter 9).

Each chapter follows the same spirit: curious, critical, and occasionally confrontational. The tone is respectful and admiring, but not neutral. No book can represent the entire field; however, I have done my best to reflect what I heard and learned, and to present it with the clarity, humility, and hope that behavioural science deserves.

A future still being written

If there is a single thread running through this book, it is possibility. Behavioural science has never been a static field. From its roots in psychology and economics, it has borrowed ideas, adapted methods, and reinvented itself in response to new challenges. Today, it is in the midst of another transformation, shaped by debates about diversity, inclusivity, methodological pluralism, and the rise of data science and artificial intelligence.

These debates are not distractions; they are the future. They are signs of a field coming to terms with its influence and responsibility. They show us that behavioural science is not simply about what works, but about asking what should work, for whom, and under what conditions.

That is why this book insists on framing behavioural science not as it is, but as it might be. The field's future will not be secured by insights alone. It will be secured by people who pair influence with responsibility, evidence with humility, and ambition with care.

An invitation

So consider this an invitation. If you are a student, I hope this book helps you see the paths available to you. If you are a policy maker or practitioner, I hope it offers tools to ask sharper questions and design stronger interventions. If you are an academic, I hope it affirms the value of rigour while opening the door to new collaborations and methods.

Most of all, I hope it leaves you with a sense that you are part of something still unfolding. The work of behavioural science is not finished. Its boundaries are not fixed. Its future is not guaranteed. But it could become something extraordinary: a discipline that is credible, cumulative, inclusive, and worthy of trust.

Welcome, then, to the future of behavioural science, not as it is, but as it might be.

1

How Behavioural Science Came to Be

> I think behavioral science in general has done a lot of things right. It embraced a broader view of human behavior, compared to where most economists stood a decade ago.
>
> Stefano DellaVigna (2024)

Introduction

Today, more than 300 institutions are applying behavioural science in public policy across 63 countries, including over 200 government teams.[1] The open-access database 'Behavioural Teams' lists more than 900 entries globally, spanning academia, nonprofits, governments, and the private sector.[2] And academic training has kept pace: as of 2023, nearly 90 Master's and 80 PhD programmes with a behavioural focus are being offered around the world, from the UK to India to South Africa.[3]

On the surface, behavioural science is a success story: globally adopted, institutionally embedded, and even decorated with two Nobel Prizes: one for Daniel Kahneman in 2002 (with a nod to the late Amos Tversky), and one for Richard Thaler in 2017.

But success hasn't shielded the field from criticism. The concept of 'nudge', so central to its rise, has consistently come under fire. A 2021 meta-analysis found only small average effects.[4] A swift rebuttal followed, arguing that once publication bias is accounted for, there may be no effect at all.[5] And that's just nudging. Add in the broader replication crisis, and we start to see deeper issues. Especially when foundational claims struggle to reproduce.[6]

Behavioural science often insists that 'context is king'. So let's take that seriously. What was the context in which this field emerged? And how might that shape the assumptions, expectations, and limitations we still carry?

A brief history of behavioural science

Behavioural science may seem like a young discipline, but its roots run deep, and understanding how it emerged helps explain both its current strengths and its growing pains.

At the beginning, there was philosophy. Economics and psychology didn't start as separate fields; they grew out of the same philosophical tradition. Adam Smith, for example, is widely remembered for *The Wealth of Nations*, but his earlier book, *The Theory of Moral Sentiments*, was all about human empathy, social norms, and judgement. He even hinted at what we now call loss aversion, writing that 'we suffer more ... when we fall from a better to a worse situation, than we ever enjoy when we rise from worse to better'.[7]

Over time, economics carved out its own identity, pursuing the mathematical elegance of a natural science. That meant prioritizing models over messiness, and leaning into the now-famous figure of homo economicus: the perfectly rational, self-interested decision maker. Psychology, meanwhile, was finding its own footing. In the early 20th century, behaviourism dominated, focused on observable actions and avoiding any discussion of thoughts or feelings that couldn't be measured.[8] The human mind was treated like a black box: unknowable, and best ignored.

That approach didn't last. By the 1960s, psychology had entered its 'cognitive revolution'. Researchers began focusing again on memory, attention, and decision-making: the kinds of processes that shape real behaviour. At the same time, cracks were forming in the foundations of classical economics. Herbert Simon proposed bounded rationality: the idea that people don't always optimize, but instead do the best they can with limited information and mental resources.[9] In other words: humans are not idealized models. They're human. Stefano DellaVigna, Distinguished Professor of Economics at UC Berkeley, recalls an incredibly important educational moment: 'My philosophy of science teacher said: "there's one thing that is important above all, which is to not believe anything they'll tell you in the economics classes ... it's all totally wrong."' And dissatisfaction with the idealized models grew.

This shift came into sharper focus in the 1970s with the work of Daniel Kahneman and Amos Tversky. Their studies on heuristics, biases, and prospect theory didn't just challenge economic orthodoxy; they showed that systematic deviations from rationality were the norm rather than the exception. Their research sparked a new line of inquiry and inspired others across disciplines, and people were paying attention. People such as Cass Sunstein, the Robert Walmsley University Professor at Harvard Law, co-author of *Nudge*: 'I was motivated by dissatisfaction with the rational actor model, as used at the University of Chicago, where I started my career. I was keenly interested in a different approach, and in the early 1980s, I discovered Kahneman and Tversky, and also Thaler. That was a big revelation.'

Another leading figure in the field, Graham Loomes, Emeritus Professor at Warwick Business School, described reading their work as a turning point. 'I found myself duplicating most of the patterns of choice that violated Expected Utility Theory ... so there must be a rational theory to explain them.' That moment of recognizing one's own irrationality became a gateway for many into behavioural science.

Others followed. Richard Thaler bridged psychology and economics with concepts such as mental accounting. Scholars such as Colin Camerer, George Loewenstein, and Robert Sugden contributed to what became behavioural economics: a field that acknowledged real human behaviour, in all its flaws and patterns. But it wasn't always welcomed. In the 1980s, Colin Camerer, the Robert Kirby Professor of Behavioral Economics at Caltech, still recalls 'enormous hostility' from the traditional economists housed in one department over, even as interest was growing elsewhere.

But even so, by the late 1990s and early 2000s, behavioural science was gaining momentum. In academia, yes, but also in policy and practice. Nobel Prizes were awarded. Research funding grew. Public-facing books began reaching new audiences and became huge best-sellers. Think only of the massive impact *Nudge* had. And what had once been a fringe movement started slowly becoming foundational.[a]

From academia to policy

From Nudge *to the nudge unit: behavioural science gets institutionalized*

When *Nudge* landed in 2008, it did more than inspire readers: it opened doors. Within 2 years, the UK government commissioned a report on how the insights it popularized might be applied more systematically. Among those tasked with writing it was Michael Hallsworth, Chief Behavioral Scientist of the Behavioural Insights Team (BIT), the UK government's pioneering nudge unit: 'The attention that Nudge created meant the UK government wanted to know more about how it could be applied', he recalled. 'I was part of the team that was asked to meet that wish, and we produced the MINDSPACE report in 2010.'[10]

It was, in some ways, an unusual start. But *Nudge* had done more than give behavioural science a public face; it had made it politically useful. According to *The Independent*, David Cameron was so taken with Richard Thaler's ideas that he appointed him as an unpaid adviser to the Conservative Party, a role Thaler later said, 'he played for fun'.[11] This support helped pave the way for the creation of the BIT in 2010: a dedicated unit inside Number 10, led by David Halpern.

BIT's early work quickly drew attention. Trials on everything from tax letters to job centre nudges showed how small psychological tweaks could deliver measurable results at low cost. The team was producing results, and just as importantly, producing headlines. But they were also building infrastructure, publishing their EAST framework in 2017, expanding globally, and offering consulting and training. Their now-iconic EAST cards (a set of tactile prompts for designing behavioural interventions) were everywhere.

BIT soon became the template. It spun out from government in 2014 as a 'social purpose company', expanded into the US, Australia, and beyond, and began advising other governments on how to set up their own behavioural insight units (BIUs). According to their own reports, they have now published over 250 studies and worked with dozens of countries on policy design and evaluation.[12] In 2021, the organisation became a subsidiary of Nesta, but retained its identity and focus.

The mission, for David Halpern, Founding Director and former CEO of the BIT, has always been expansive: 'Working with an amazing team and with scholars from across the world, we've been really able to design and test a string of interventions using behavioural science to have a real impact in the world', he wrote in 2022. 'Increasing savings; Getting people back to work faster; Halving sugar in UK soft drinks; Supporting children to get better grades; Reducing gender inequalities in the labour market; Re-integrating ex-combatants; Combating disinformation. We've even managed to save some tigers! … Always more to do … '

BIT's success also made behavioural science something new: not just an academic field, but a professional identity. By 2018, over two dozen government departments in the UK had behavioural insight specialists or teams embedded within them, from Public Health England and Ofcom to the Financial Conduct Authority.[13] The model was being copied, and not just in London. Serene Koh, Director of the BIT in Singapore, described the moment she joined: 'I had been working in government for a few years … My then line manager encouraged me to read Nudge and to also attend the very first BX conference in Sydney in 2014 … and have been in love with it ever since.'

Beyond Whitehall: behavioural policy goes global

The UK's BIT may have captured the spotlight, but it was far from alone. From Washington to Wellington, a wave of governments began experimenting with behavioural science; not as a temporary policy tool, but as a core capability.

In the US, the shift was striking. In 2008, Barack Obama appointed Cass Sunstein as Administrator of the White House's Office of Information and Regulatory Affairs, the office responsible for overseeing all federal regulations. 'I feel most honored to have been able to work, with many others, in introducing behavioral economics to law and public policy', Sunstein later reflected. 'In that regard, my work in the White House was a blessing and a joy.'

Momentum built. In 2013, the White House launched the Social and Behavioral Sciences Team (SBST), a group of scientists embedded across government agencies. Then, 2 years later, a core group from the General Services Administration formalized into the Office of Evaluation Sciences (OES), which still operates today. Although the SBST's formal mandate expired in 2017, its influence endures through the OES and its collaborations with agencies such as the United States Department of Agriculture, the United States Department of Health and Human Services, and the Consumer Financial Protection Bureau.[14]

One of the earliest and most influential organisations outside government was ideas42, a nonprofit behavioural lab founded in 2008 at Harvard University. Originally an academic spinout, it grew into a global organisation applying behavioural science in areas such as financial inclusion, education, and health. As ideas42 co-founder and former Chief Innovation Officer, Piyush Tantia put it: 'I am most proud of having built ideas42, the first non-profit in this space focused on applying behavioral science to social good ... We have worked on hundreds of projects with partners across more than 50 countries.' But even so, he approaches the field with caution: 'Even with our success, I feel behavioural science has a long way to go before it is used widely.'

Australia moved fast as well. A Productivity Commission roundtable in 2007 had already explored behavioural insights in regulation.[14] By 2012, the New South Wales BIU (NSW BIU) was up and running, its most iconic work being the 'sludge audit', aimed at reducing friction and complexity in public services.[15] The Behavioural Economics Team of the Australian Government (BETA) followed in 2016, alongside state-level teams in Victoria and the Australian Taxation Office. The same year, BETA launched with a mandate to bring experimental methods into the heart of policy. Their work has spanned everything from retirement planning to cyber security and mental health.

Other countries took note. The World Bank's Mind, Behaviour and Development unit (eMBeD) was founded in 2015 following the *World Development Report: Mind, Society and Behavior.*[16] Since then, it has run over 100 behavioural science projects across 70 countries, many in the Global South.

The rise of behavioural science in lower-income settings was not just top-down, but also local. The Busara Center for Behavioral Economics, founded in 2015 in Nairobi, became a critical player in adapting behavioural research for non-WEIRD contexts. 'The thing that I'm most proud of is being a part of bringing behavioural economics and behavioural science into the non-WEIRD settings', said Chaning Jang, co-founder and former CEO of Busara, now CSO of Irrational Labs. 'Seeing the people that come through Busara and leave … evangelising both behavioural science and evidence-based policy.'

Steve Wendel, co-founder and Head of Methodology of sistemaFutura, previously at Busara and Morningstar, echoed the importance of that shift: 'The WEIRDness of our research … is something that I focused a fair bit on at Busara, along with many others. WEIRD people like me still shape the agenda … I'd love to see our field broaden.'

India, too, developed its own institutional muscle. In 2019, the National Institution for Transforming India launched its Behavioural Insights Unit (NITI-BIU), in partnership with the Centre for Behavioural and Social Change at Ashoka University. Its remit includes sanitation, nutrition, and maternal health, grounded in Indian social contexts.

In the Middle East and North Africa (MENA) region, Qatar's Supreme Committee for Delivery and Legacy, set up to oversee the 2022 World Cup, created the Qatar Behavioural Insights Unit (later rebranded B4Development) in 2016. 'Having set up B4Development … and establishing Nudge Lebanon one year later were the twin accomplishments I am proudest of as a behavioural scientist', said the founder of B4Development and Nudge Lebanon, now Lebanon's Minister of State for Administrative Reform. 'I want to see more countries do an executive order type of decision … mandating government agencies to inject behavioural science into their work."

It is important to note that these organisations were not mere copies of BIT. They were adaptations, blending local knowledge with global methodologies, and often pursuing broader development or equity aims. The field was beginning to diversify, not just geographically, but philosophically.

Behavioural Science Inc.

In-house innovators

The rise of behavioural science inside corporations rarely began with job titles or team mandates. More often, it started with a question: 'Why is this happening?' For many early practitioners, it was the experience of watching human behaviour defy conventional logic that prompted them to seek out new frameworks, and then bring those frameworks in-house.

'In the early 2010s, I started to hear clients talk about behavioural economics', recalled Matthew Battersby, who founded Hill & Knowlton's behavioural science team and is now Global Head of Research and Development at Reinsurance Group of America:

> No consultant wants to be in a situation where their client is talking about something that they don't know about. So, I took it upon myself to read the books and the papers that were around at the time. I realized quickly that not only was it something that was relevant for my clients as financial services businesses, but actually for us as a communications firm.

However, it wasn't until 2014, he explains, that

> it really took off ... I came across the fact that the London School of Economics had just launched their Executive Masters in Behavioural Science ... in a space of six weeks, I managed to apply, get accepted and get the backing from Hill & Knowlton to use this to set up a behavioural science team.

This type of self-initiated momentum is echoed across many founding stories. Rory Sutherland, Vice Chairman of Ogilvy and founder of its behavioural science unit, Ogilvy Change, had long felt there was a missing logic behind what consumers did:

> In my early days in advertising, I used to refer to 'that thing which has no name.' So frequently was I confronted with results to experiments in marketing which bore no semblance of standard economic logic, that I was convinced that there was a wholly missing science ... About ten years later, through becoming addicted to science and economics blogs, I finally discovered that there was such a science.

Ogilvy's behavioural unit was one of the first in the world, but it wasn't alone for long. Behavioural science was already taking root in financial services. 'I was given the wonderful opportunity in 2006 to found a permanent behavioural team at Barclays at a time when the field was still relatively young outside academia', said Greg Davies, Head of Behavioural Finance at OxfordRisk:

> I don't think anyone really knew what a behavioural finance team was going to do, but this was pre-crisis and we were given a lot of room to experiment in the first couple of years. Then after the financial crisis it became clear to everyone that human emotions were at the center of almost everything, and behavioural economics shot up in prominence.

By the mid-2010s, teams were popping up across financial institutions. For instance, William Mailer, Chief Behavioural Scientist at the Commonwealth Bank of Australia, described his experience leading behavioural science functions at PwC and later at the bank:

> I've set up two different behavioural units over the last ten years ... More recently I was approached to start a behavioural economics team for Australia's largest bank, with the purpose of improving financial wellbeing for customers. Now five years old, this team is one of the largest of its kind. We have partnerships with some of the world's leading behavioural science research groups ... and developed a number of banking innovations that have had a significant positive impact on the health of millions of Australians.

This relevance was even more pronounced in insurance, where the nature of the product: long-term, abstract, and often future-facing, presents a classic behavioural challenge. 'If you look at classic difficult behaviors, anything that involves short term pain for long term gain, life insurance is that', said Battersby. 'That is exactly what we're focused on all the time: how can we encourage you to pay a monthly premium for a benefit that will come hopefully distant in the future and won't come to you but to your family?'

The fintech sector echoed similar lessons. Steve Wendel, who began his career as a software engineer, was one of the earliest behavioural practitioners in the space:

> Many years ago, I was a software engineer and the first employee at a fintech startup named HelloWallet. Our product was beautiful and wonderful. But people didn't want to use it. So we tried to figure out why. I reached out to one of the early behavioral scientists, Jon Zinman, to learn more about the field ... I learned behavioral science on the job by talking to people like them ... Later I set up a group called the Action Design Network (now Bescy) to help promote applied behavioral science.

These applied roles weren't confined to finance and fintech. At Microsoft, behavioural science also entered through the side door. 'My time at Microsoft will always be what I look at as being a huge success', said Connor Joyce, Senior User Researcher at Microsoft:

> Just because I was Microsoft's first behavioral researcher. I was able to support a team that really didn't know exactly what they needed ... I laid out the insights to actions framework, which is the basis of really how I personally go to market with my message now in this field ... Because insights are not enough to get behavioral change.

Across sectors, a common theme emerges behavioural science wasn't 'implemented' so much as it was smuggled in, often by individuals who had seen the cracks in conventional approaches, and convinced their organisations to try something new. They started small: a single pilot, a better form, a shift in defaults. And over time, many of those pilots became permanent teams.

Importantly, and something we will revisit in Chapter 2, these internal teams didn't just apply academic theory. They adapted it. In a fast-paced commercial context, behavioural science had to be actionable, measurable, and credible. Teams built partnerships with universities, ran field trials, and linked insights to tangible business outcomes. But unlike the policy sector, which often retained a more centralized mandate, these corporate teams evolved in a fragmented and decentralized way, each one learning, iterating, and institutionalizing in its own context.

In-house behavioural science became a kind of lingua franca for internal change: bridging departments such as marketing, product, customer experience, and strategy. In many cases, these internal teams also became breeding grounds for future entrepreneurs and consultants, who would later go on to launch their own behavioural science firms (as we'll see next).

By the late 2010s, the question inside many companies had shifted from 'What is behavioural science?' to 'Where else can we use it?' And with that shift came a growing awareness that applied behavioural science wasn't just a passing trend; it was a capability, one that was here to stay.

Brains for hire

While in-house teams were quietly embedding behavioural science into daily decision-making, another kind of engine was forming: external consultancies built specifically to bring behavioural science to life across clients, sectors, and borders. These firms became the translators and evangelists of the field, operating at the interface of research, business, and behavioural design.

Some consultancies were born from entrepreneurial instincts. Michael Barbera, Chief Behavioral Officer at Clicksuasion Labs, began with a deep curiosity about customer behaviour:

> As I ventured through my entrepreneurial journey, my curiosity continued to circle back to customer decision-making, and I wanted a formal education in business. I began my academic journey studying business strategy and eventually discovered behavioral economics, and human judgment and decision making. This is where my passion for entrepreneurship met with my curiosity for human behavior. I wanted to combine the two and find ways to apply behavioral science to real-world challenges in marketing and communication. In 2014, I started a research firm, and seven years later … Clicksuasion Labs continues to be my happy place.

Others came from major players in advertising, such as Ogilvy Change, which operated an internal team and served as a launching pad for practitioners such as Jez Groom, later co-founder of Cowry Consulting, and Richard Chataway, now Director of Behavioural Science at Concentrix Catalyst. Their careers reflect a broader pattern: many behavioural consultancies are founded by people who first gained credibility within large institutions, before stepping out to build something of their own.

Communications and marketing are natural domains for behavioural science, so it's no surprise that the consulting world is peppered with firms offering specialized behavioural insights for persuasion, customer experience, or public engagement. 'Shortly after I caught the behavioural science bug', recalled Sameer Munshi, Head of Behavioral Science & Simulation at EY:

> I remember I spent the day after Christmas in the public library, working on a pitch to start a behavioral unit at EY. At this point, I had been exposed to behavioral science for maybe six or eight weeks, but I had read everything I could. So I worked on a pitch over the holidays so I could come back to the head of our business – I got her Paul Dolan's book hoping to get a little reciprocity – and just pitched her on the value I see of behavioral science for EY ... In 2021, they gave me the green light ... Fast forward three years and it's been a really exciting ride building out the unit here.

What's striking is not just how many firms emerged, but how diverse they are in focus and geography. According to the Applied Behavioural Science Association, more than 350 for-profit behavioural science teams now exist globally, from large consultancies to niche boutique agencies.[17] Some are deeply quantitative, focused on experimental design and data analytics. Others are creatively driven, working on nudging customers toward better choices through storytelling, framing, or branding. This diversity reflects both the field's breadth and its challenge: behavioural science is applied in so many ways; it can be difficult to define what counts.

As with in-house teams, many consultancy leaders came to behavioural science laterally: from strategy, policy, or economics. But they quickly saw that its value wasn't confined to a single industry. Elina Halonen, co-founder of one of the first dedicated behavioural science consultancies, now an independent behavioural strategist, reflected on how different things were when she entered the field: 'I'm pleased to have been a part of the early days of applied behavioural science – it was a much harder sell ten years ago when a lot of people didn't know about this field!'

Behavioural consulting also began to flourish inside the largest professional services firms. Deloitte, EY, PwC, and others now house behavioural science functions that support a wide range of client projects: from digital transformation to risk management. At PwC Australia, Eshan Motwani, now a Behavioural Economist at Google, recounted his own winding path:

> I started my career as a Public Policy consultant but it wasn't until a few years later that I finally got to apply my interest in Behavioural Economics … My career coach just so happened to be Jason Collins, who was looking to kickstart the Behavioural Economics Practice there. I asked (though I think he would say 'demanded') to be added to every pitch and project he was exploring … Jason then left PwC a few years later and our team leaders fortunately agreed to let me take over running the Behavioural Economics practice.

By the early 2020s, there was no longer a single template for behavioural science consulting. Some teams focused on government clients. Others built behavioural products. Still others embedded nudges into digital design, customer journeys, or culture change initiatives. But a throughline remained: behavioural consultancies offered speed, flexibility, and external credibility, making them ideal for organisations not ready to build internal capacity themselves.

They also served another critical function: spreading the gospel of behavioural science. Through white papers, applicable frameworks with cute mnemonics, public talks, and conferences, many consultancies became important nodes in the field's informal infrastructure; bridging academia and industry, the Global North and South, for-profit and social impact work.

Much like in-house teams, the best consultancies didn't just apply behavioural science; they shaped it. They developed new tools, tested theories at scale, and trained the next generation of practitioners.

And as behavioural science continued to gain traction in business, their role as standard-setters, and challengers, only grew.

Beyond the buzz: the aftermath of the hype?

Professor Stefano DellaVigna remarked at the start of this chapter that behavioural science has 'done a lot of things right', especially in how it 'embraced a broader view of human behavior, compared to where most economists stood a decade ago'. And he's right. The field has pushed disciplines to look beyond rational choice models, beyond theoretical preferences, toward people's real decisions in real contexts. That shift has changed government policy, financial services, health systems, and even the way we design websites. From niche to mainstream, the ascent of behavioural science seems all but assured.

And yet, success brings its own complications. With behavioural insight teams in governments around the world, corporate behavioural science divisions proliferating, a growing field of independent consultants, and an academic discipline evolving at pace; what could possibly go wrong?

Well, plenty, as it turns out.

One challenge is definitional: what is behavioural science, really? In public imagination, and all too often in policy maker expectations, it remains synonymous with 'nudging.' While the field has long since outgrown that label, many of its critics haven't. Popular articles continue to reduce the field to simplistic tactics, from *The Wall Street Journal*'s *The Problem with Behavioral Nudges*[18] to *The Guardian*'s piece lamenting that nudges 'can make you buy more carrots – but can't make you eat them'.[19] These critiques raise important questions. But they also flatten the field, ignoring its theoretical breadth and methodological complexity.

These public misperceptions aren't just abstract reputational issues; they shape the work practitioners are asked to do. As Amy Bucher, Chief Behavioral Officer at Lirio, observed, one of the hardest tasks in practice is helping stakeholders recalibrate their expectations. Too often, behavioural science is sold as magic: quick fixes that can shift behaviours overnight. 'I've sometimes found myself trying to reset expectations', she told me, 'with a prospective client or a cross-functional partner who thinks that every behavioral design project should yield dramatic results like some of the seminal work on default choices'. When those results don't materialize, the risk isn't just disappointment, it's disillusionment.

But the problem, as Bucher argues, isn't that behavioural science overpromises. It's that we too often allow others to misread what it is promising. 'We're selling a fundamentally incorrect promise', she explained.

> The truth is that people are complex and messy, affected by circumstance and time, and unique in hundreds of ways. The truth is that we have a deep and rich toolbox we can draw from to match whatever the individual or group we're working with needs, and that making the right selection gets easier over time as we have more effective methods and platforms to power our approach. The truth is that we've learned so much about what makes people tick and how to help them move toward their goals, AND we still have an incredible amount to learn.

In other words, the magic wasn't in the simplicity; it was in the complexity all along.

Conclusion

Ultimately, behavioural science is not a finished product. It's a work in progress. And that's why I wanted to include this chapter on behavioural science's history. This history isn't just a timeline; it's context. Behavioural science was born from dissatisfaction with overly idealized models, and from a desire to understand real people. That ambition is what drives much of this book: not just to critique where the field stands, but to ask where it could go. In Chapter 2, behavioural science can go as it deals with its remit will be addressed because both its academic and applied sides have developed completely differently, and problems have seemingly popped up on either side that are holding back the field.

2

Why Good Evidence Went Bad

> I think the field is on the upswing, but we're swinging on a pendulum. I think in the next few years there will be wider adoption of behavioral thinking and design throughout industry and society … but also a few missteps that will create a backlash and cause the pendulum to swing back a bit. That said, I know that 99.9% of the people working in the field are thoughtful, conscientious and filled with the best of intentions to improve people's lives … so whatever backlash may come will serve to strengthen our methodologies, connections, services and value.
>
> Jeff Kreisler (2020)

Introduction

When behavioural science first crossed the threshold from academia to policy and practice, it seemed to offer something rare: scientific insight with real world utility. Here, finally, was a field that could bridge the gap between how people should behave and how they do. Government agencies, financial institutions, tech firms and Non-Governmental Organisations (NGOs) all wanted in.

In Chapter 1, we saw how this momentum built. Behavioural insights teams sprang up in dozens of countries. Research gained Nobel recognition. Frameworks such as MINDSPACE and EAST gave civil servants a new language. The field had arrived.

But arrival is not the same as reaching one's destination. The speed and scale of behavioural science's adoption came with compromises. A field rooted in context began to treat universality as default. A discipline shaped by complexity started favouring clarity. And a method for understanding human behaviour became synonymous with a single tactic: the nudge.

This chapter unpacks the trade-offs behind that ascent. Not to diminish what behavioural science achieved, but to surface what got buried along the way.

What went wrong

The nudge narrative took over too quickly

If there is a single concept that launched behavioural science into the mainstream, it was *nudge*. Elegant, scalable, and politically palatable, it captured imaginations far beyond academia. Nudge wasn't just a technique; it was a brand. And like most brands, its simplicity became both its strength and its weakness.

What Thaler and Sunstein proposed in *Nudge* (2008) was intellectually modest and strategically ambitious: a set of small design changes, such as defaults, framing, and reminders, that could shift behaviour while preserving freedom of choice. 'Libertarian paternalism', they called it. And in a post-crisis policy environment starved of budget and public trust, it was exactly what governments were looking for.

As William Mailer, Chief Behavioural Scientist at the Commonwealth Bank of Australia, noted, 'Given that most of the important challenges we are all facing have human behaviour at their heart … there will be a strong, and likely increasing demand for quality behavioural insight and effective behavioural interventions across most organisations in the next ten years.' The message was clear: behavioural science offered a form of governance that could be effective without being invasive.

But with nudge as the field's calling card, it also became its constraint. Rather than being used as one tool among many, nudging was increasingly treated as synonymous with behavioural science itself. That identity was shaped not just by policy successes, but by media coverage, political enthusiasm, and procurement processes seeking low-cost, low-risk solutions.

Michelle Handy, Lead User Experience (UX) Researcher at UL Solutions, described the dynamic bluntly: behavioural science was often used to increase uptake or reduce drop-off for predetermined decisions. What stakeholders wanted wasn't better behavioural diagnosis, but faster compliance. In her words, clients were often more interested in 'a silver bullet' than a behaviourally grounded process. When she tried to explain that behavioural science wasn't just about tweaks but about interrogating the problem space, interest waned.

This performative application hollowed out behavioural science's purpose. Instead of shaping how problems were framed, it became a toolkit for modifying user response. Instead of surfacing blind spots, it was used to obscure them.

And it worked. At first. Organ donation defaults, tax reminders, pension enrolment tweaks: all produced measurable results. But those early wins created unrealistic expectations. As Amy Bucher noted, 'It's very hard to help clients see why the tool that was perfect for those contexts might not work elsewhere.' The result was a narrowing of both the perceived value and the actual practice of behavioural science.

Nudge was never meant to carry the weight of a field. But once it became behavioural science's most recognizable export, it distorted the landscape around it. As Enrique (Quique) Belenguer Saborit, Behavioural Economics Discipline Leader at Banco Bilbao Vizcaya Argentaria (BBVA) warns, one of the biggest challenges will be the scope and scale of the problems we study: 'One of the biggest challenges I see is making sure we're actually solving the right problems. Too often, behavioural science gets stuck in small-scale interventions – optimizing emails, tweaking messages – without looking at the bigger picture. We need to be thinking systemically, not just about isolated nudges.' What had been introduced as a proof of concept gradually became mistaken for the concept itself.

Nudge as a concept has both done great good and bad for the field, as Sam Moore, Senior Behavioural Scientist at Evidn, states:

> One challenge I often think about is how we move beyond RCTs and nudge-based interventions and take the broader psychosocial system of influences into account when understanding and changing behaviour.

> While there's no doubt the nudge movement has been incredibly influential and is important for certain problems, I think it can limit the scope of our field when addressing the more 'wicked' problems that society is currently grappling with.

The problem of WEIRD evidence

Behavioural science, in principle, is a field that prizes context. Its very foundation lies in understanding how people actually behave, not in theory, but in practice, in real world settings, under real world pressures. And yet, paradoxically, many of the field's most widely cited insights are drawn from an astoundingly narrow base: experimental samples overwhelmingly composed of WEIRD individuals: Western, Educated, Industrialized, Rich, and Democratic.

What began as a convenience has hardened into convention. 'The field is dominated by researchers from Western countries, particularly the US and Europe', noted Patrick Forscher, Senior Behavioral Scientist at Busara and former Director of its meta-research group, Culture, Research Ethics, and MEthods (CREME). 'As a result, the issues studied often reflect the concerns and interests of those regions.' That skew is not just a methodological footnote; it determines what kinds of behaviours are deemed worth studying, what kinds of interventions are prioritized, and ultimately, what kinds of 'truths' behavioural science chooses to tell.

This bias flows downstream into application. Policies that succeed in Boston are airlifted into Nairobi. Nudges trialled in Copenhagen are rolled out in Delhi. The problem here is not ambition; it is assumption. Specifically, the assumption that behavioural interventions, designed and tested within one cultural milieu, can operate seamlessly within another.

Chaning Jang, co-founder and former CEO of Busara, now CSO of Irrational Labs, who has worked extensively on behavioural science in low- and middle-income countries, put the issue plainly: it's not just who we're studying; it's who we're excluding entirely. In settings where social norms, religious values, and state infrastructures diverge sharply from Western baselines, many of the psychological assumptions underpinning common behavioural interventions simply don't hold.

This isn't just ineffective; it can be unethical. As Dilip Soman, Canada Research Chair in Behavioural Science and Economics at the Rotman School of Management, warned, 'I do think that as an academic field we need to better acknowledge the limited portability of our results, to not overpromise their universality.' But understanding when results will work requires not just replication, but representation, and that requires structural change.

At present, the incentives in academia point the other way. What gets rewarded is speed: studies that are fast to run, easy to publish, and statistically significant. Recruiting a hundred psychology undergraduates in Toronto or London meets those criteria. Building partnerships in Nairobi or Manila often does not.

Some organisations are pushing against this tide. Units such as the World Bank's eMBeD and research firms such as Busara are actively diversifying the empirical base. However, these remain exceptions in a field still tilted towards convenience over comprehensiveness.

If behavioural science claims to offer insight into human behaviour, then it must reckon more honestly with which humans it includes, and which ones it leaves out.

The replication crisis and fragile foundations

If the problem of WEIRD samples reveals whose behaviour we've studied, the replication crisis confronts a deeper question: how much of what we think we know actually holds up?

Since the early 2010s, psychology and behavioural economics have been rocked by failed replications: studies once considered foundational collapsing under repeated scrutiny. Concepts such as ego depletion, social priming, and even celebrated nudges have not just struggled to replicate; they've sometimes failed spectacularly.

For those in the field, the implications go beyond academic embarrassment. As John Beshears, Professor of Business Administration at Harvard Business School, put it, the issue is not only what gets published, but what gets rewarded: 'Sometimes, there's an overemphasis on "clever and cute" research rather than studies that address first-order, high-impact issues. Novel, quirky findings can be valuable, but the real goal should be applying behavioral insights to meaningful, large-scale challenges.'

Beshears's critique points to a system that prizes novelty over durability. Many early studies were statistically underpowered, and replication efforts have exposed just how fragile that empirical scaffolding really is. A 2022 meta-analysis found that average effect sizes for behavioural interventions, once publication bias was accounted for, were often negligible.[5]

The problem, as Daniel Read, Professor of Behavioural Science at Warwick Business School, argued in 2019, was never just methodological; it was cultural:

> We have consistently oversold our research, drawing conclusions based on small samples and ungeneralisable designs, we have kept almost countless 'uninteresting' failures to replicate in the file drawer, and we have engaged in a great deal of p-hacking without even realising that is what we were doing. My prediction is that when the dust settles, we will have far fewer phenomena in behavioural economics, and these will tend to be phenomena that match our intuitions. The 'sexy' counterintuitive findings that filled the journals for a while … will start to wither away – indeed that is already happening.

Read's reflection is sobering because it's systemic. The field mistook noise for signal, shaping agendas, policies, and reputations around effects that couldn't be trusted.

This erosion of confidence has practical consequences. When organisations adopt interventions based on flimsy evidence, results disappoint. Credibility suffers. Funding disappears. The fallout doesn't stay in the lab; it lands in boardrooms and government offices.

Dilip Soman warned of exactly this risk: 'I do think that as an academic field we need … to make it easier for users of our science to better understand when things will work and when it might not.'

But the kind of local validation Soman advocates for, testing results in real world settings, is time-consuming and expensive. For teams under pressure, it's often out of reach.

The replication crisis is more than a technical failure. It's a logistical constraint, a strategic liability, and, at times, an ethical reckoning.

Because when science claims the authority to shape how people think and act, that authority must rest on more than statistical chance.

Methodological homogeneity

Rigour has long been the watchword of behavioural science. It signals credibility, objectivity, and scientific seriousness. But somewhere along the way, rigour became synonymous with a narrow vision of validity, one where randomized controlled trials (RCTs) dominate to the exclusion of all else.

In many ways, RCTs earned their place. They offer clarity, control, and the promise of causal inference. For policy makers looking to prove 'what works', the appeal is obvious. However, as the field matured, the dominance of RCTs began to reveal its constraints. They are expensive. They are slow. They often unfold in artificial settings. And perhaps most crucially, they filter out the messy, structural complexity of real life.

As Sasha Tregebov, formerly Director of BIT Canada and now Managing Director at the BIT Americas, explained, the lived reality of applied behavioural science work is far less tidy than the literature implies: 'We are trying to do meticulous and creative experimental design, data analysis, and qualitative research, while also having deep expertise in behavioural economics, social psychology … the list goes on.'

Tregebov's account captures the stretch many practitioners feel, tasked with delivering robust insights under tight timelines and imperfect conditions. Yet the field's methodological culture continues to lean towards quantification, even when the questions at hand demand something else entirely.

In this landscape, qualitative methods: interviews, ethnographies, and participatory observation are often dismissed as soft or subjective. Yet they are uniquely equipped to surface context, culture, and lived experience: precisely the factors that often determine whether a behavioural intervention will succeed or fail. Still, they remain sidelined.

Kerstin Oberprieler, Behavioural and Gamification Design specialist, argues that this orientation limits not only how we measure, but what we celebrate: 'To advance as a field, we need more openness and transparency around what works and what doesn't, moving beyond only celebrating the wins.'

This lack of openness reflects a deeper discomfort with methodological pluralism. If outcomes must be countable, immediate, and replicable to be recognized, then entire domains of behavioural insight, particularly those that unfold over time or defy tidy measurement, are effectively rendered invisible.

It's no coincidence that disciplines such as UX research, design thinking, and service design have gained traction where behavioural science hesitates. These fields embrace user stories, open-ended data, and systems thinking. Their methods are often messier, but also more human.

The irony, then, is that a field born to explain real world behaviour too often flattens it. It treats context as noise, not data. And in doing so, it risks becoming a caricature of its own intent. The rise of artificial intelligence (AI) may intensify this flattening. Shane Timmons, Senior Research Officer in the Behavioural Research Unit at the Economic and Social Research Institute (ESRI), sees enormous promise in AI for scaling analysis and supporting experimentation, but he is wary of overreliance, particularly in the formulation of research questions and experimental design. Behavioural science has often advanced through creative reframing, not just cleaner execution. There is a risk that AI-generated designs become technically competent but conceptually homogeneous: efficient, replicable, and increasingly similar. If methodological convergence is already a concern, automation may quietly accelerate it.

If behavioural science is to remain useful, it must be more than methodologically pure. It must be methodologically honest, willing to ask not just what works, but why, for whom, and under what conditions.

Ethical drift and public trust

Of all the challenges behavioural science faces, few are as urgent, or as reputationally dangerous, as the ethical ambiguity surrounding its methods. Nudges are often effective because they're invisible. That subtlety makes them efficient, but it also raises uncomfortable questions about consent, autonomy, and transparency.

What happens when behavioural insights are deployed not to empower, but to manipulate?

This is no longer a hypothetical concern. In commercial settings, behavioural tools have been appropriated into dark patterns: design tactics that exploit cognitive biases to drive subscription opt-ins, data disclosures, and purchases users might not otherwise make.

Eshan Motwani, Behavioural Economist at Google, articulated the field's growing anxiety:

> I'm worried that our field's earned trust is going to be eroded by increasingly common and sophisticated dark patterns. It's not hard to find manipulative choice architecture, especially online. Dark patterns leverage Behavioural Economics insights to be more effective and exploitative so it's easy to see how the two can be confused.

Without ethical guardrails, behavioural science risks becoming indistinguishable from manipulation. Yet most interventions in digital spaces aren't governed by review boards. There are no shared standards for disclosure, transparency, or even basic accountability.

Sarah Osman, founder of Osman Advisory Services and a behavioural science consultant with over two decades of experience in global development, noted:

> I have come into organizations where there's been a social and behaviour change consultant before and I often struggle to understand where they were coming from; what standards they were using or abiding to. And I think it would just be a good thing if we have a standard that we're working with.

In public policy, the situation is not necessarily safer. During the early COVID-19 response, UK officials cited 'behavioural fatigue' to justify delayed lockdowns, a term that suggested scientific backing but lacked empirical foundation. The backlash not only undermined the public health response but also eroded trust in the field itself.

This trust deficit is now becoming more visible, especially in applied settings. As Emily Daniels, Senior Behavioural Researcher at Bupa, observed: 'Relatedly, there's a trust deficit. Some view behavioural science as optional or even akin to marketing gimmicks.

This is exacerbated by the replication crisis and a lack of transparency about failures.'

For a discipline that operates in the shadows of choice architecture, that loss of legitimacy is no small thing. Once trust fades, so too does the licence to operate quietly. The choice before the field is stark: codify ethical practice, or risk being seen not as a force for good, but as a tool of soft coercion.

A closing note: behavioural science is not a monolith

Behavioural science is often treated as a coherent field; its internal divergences tell a more fractured story. Academic and applied behavioural science have evolved under different constraints, incentives, and assumptions.

Divergent lineages

Academic behavioural science, particularly in psychology and behavioural economics, is built on journal-based incentives. Researchers succeed by publishing novel results, often under intense pressure to generate statistically significant findings. This has led to what Stuart King, founder of the behaviour change organisation BeeZee Bodies and a former public health policy lead at Public Health England, described as a shocking realization: 'I was horrified to hear that they [an academic] would never and had never applied their work outside of the confines of a research study. They were proud that they never engaged with practitioners, policy makers or professionals outside of academia.' For King, the gap wasn't just intellectual; it was existential. 'Some people are entirely comfortable theorising about human behaviour without ever actually engaging with the people they are attempting to understand.'

By contrast, applied behavioural science emerged in the margins of policy, marketing, and design. Practitioners were tasked not with theory building but with getting things done, often quickly, cheaply, and visibly. As Matt Baldwin, Director of Customer Experience at Hive and a former assistant professor at the University of Florida, put it, 'Academics sometimes think applied work is sloppy or unscientific, while practitioners feel that academia is too abstract and disconnected from reality. Bridging this gap requires humility on both sides.' Baldwin's diagnosis is generous, but it also names the mutual suspicion that has characterized much of the relationship between the two spheres.

These distinctions are not merely cultural; they are structurally embedded. As Sasha Tregebov already observed previously, applied behavioural scientists are expected to wear many hats, while often lacking the time, resources, or institutional stability that academia provides.

The five problems, differently felt

Therefore, both sides of the field do not only practice the discipline differently; they experience its core problems in fundamentally different ways.

Oversimplification through nudge is a distinctly applied problem. The nudge agenda offered policy makers a seductive promise: behaviour change without coercion, complexity, or cost. In the academic domain, nudges have always sat within a broader landscape of behavioural theory. However, in government and consulting contexts, they became the field's brand. The pressure to deliver tangible results with minimal friction encouraged a reductive application of behavioural insights, often at the expense of rigour or context. While academics may criticize this oversimplification, they are rarely the ones forced to produce change under real world political and organisational constraints. For practitioners, simplification isn't laziness; it's survival.

The WEIRD bias: studying Western, Educated, Industrialized, Rich, Democratic populations, is primarily an academic problem, embedded in how research is designed, funded, and published. Undergraduate psychology pools, journal conventions, and institutional location all skew the evidence base. In contrast, many applied teams, particularly in development or global policy, routinely work with non-WEIRD populations. But their insights rarely shape theory. While academics are beginning to acknowledge the limits of WEIRD data, applied practitioners often already work beyond those boundaries; they're just not recognized for it.

Methodological homogeneity is also skewed towards academia. The dominance of RCTs, while justified for causal inference, often sidelines qualitative methods and contextual insight. In applied settings, mixed methods are not an intellectual preference but a practical necessity. Interviews, observations, and rapid prototyping are tools for engaging complexity, not shortcuts. Yet academic hierarchies continue to privilege 'clean' experiments, often dismissing applied methods as anecdotal or insufficiently scientific. This has created an asymmetry: applied teams are methodologically plural out of need, while academia enforces narrow norms in the name of rigour.

Replication failures, paradoxically, are more visible in academia but more damaging in applied settings. It is academic studies that are failing to replicate, but applied practitioners suffer when those fragile findings collapse in real world use. A failed study may be a learning opportunity for an academic; for a practitioner, it can mean a cancelled programme, lost funding, or public backlash. The replication crisis may have started in the lab, but its consequences are most acutely felt outside it.

Ethical ambiguity, meanwhile, is sharper on the applied side. Academics typically work under ethics review structures, however imperfect. But many applied teams, especially in tech or consulting, face minimal oversight, even when deploying large-scale behavioural interventions. Without clear standards or institutional backing, the risk of ethical drift is significant. In this domain, academia may be more reflective, but it is practitioners who are most exposed.

Collaboration: hopes and frictions

Given these uneven tensions, calls for collaboration between academia and application are both necessary and fraught. In theory, the logic is obvious. As Wändi Bruine de Bruin, Provost Professor of Public Policy, Psychology, and Behavioral Science at the University of Southern California, put it, 'For societal impact to happen, behavioural science research needs to be conducted in collaboration with the practitioners and policy makers who could stand to benefit from the findings.' Such partnerships, she argued, 'make the research more practically useful, easier to implement, and more widely recognised'.

But in practice, collaboration is often constrained by structural inertia. Gareth Harvey, Behavioural Scientist at Severn Trent and former Director of Consumer Psychology at DECIDE, pointed out that while funding bodies preach the gospel of interdisciplinarity, they rarely reward it: 'From my experience interdisciplinary research is less likely to get funding and there are virtually no incentives for academics to work with companies. When academics do try and work with companies, you quickly find that the systems aren't in place to allow collaboration.'

Even when such collaborations do happen, they often depend on unusual individuals rather than supportive institutions. Grant Donnelly, Associate Professor of Marketing at The Ohio State University, who works extensively on field experiments, noted: 'These relationships take a lot of time to build trust, but I think the initial investment is worth it, because you can uncover some amazing insights about consumer behavior.' Trust, not theory, is often the real currency of collaboration.

There are encouraging models. Alex Gyani, Managing Director for Asia-Pacific (APAC) at the BIT, pointed to the UK's fellowship schemes as enabling better integration of research and policy: 'In the UK it's more common to have fellowships that allow academics to collaborate with, or fully transition into, government. This allows for a much better integration of ideas … This really helped my career, so I hope that these types of programs can help others.' And Kerstin Oberprieler envisioned a future in which collaboration becomes the norm:

> We'll likely see more collaboration across industries and disciplines, tackling challenges like climate change, public health, and social justice. I also see an increase in real-world experimentation and the sharing of both successes and failures. To advance as a field, we need more openness and transparency around what works and what doesn't, moving beyond only celebrating the wins.

But for that to happen, the field must reckon with its own internal fragmentation. Not just as an intellectual issue, but as a material one. Academic and applied behavioural science have grown under different conditions, serve different audiences, and respond to different logics. Collaboration will only thrive when those differences are named, respected, and accommodated.

Not a monolith, but a mirror

Behavioural science presents itself as a unified discipline, but in truth it functions more as a mirror: reflecting the competing demands of academia, government, business, and civil society.

This isn't necessarily a flaw. But it is a fact. Behavioural science does not need to become homogenous to be effective. It does, however, need to become more self-aware. The field must abandon the illusion of disciplinary unity and start building mechanisms that allow it to learn across its own fault lines.

That means shared spaces, not just for knowledge exchange, but for shared accountability. It means adjusting incentives so that rigour and relevance are not pitted against each other. And it means fostering respect, not the polite kind, but the structural kind, in which the constraints of one world are treated as valid in another.

The field's future depends on this. As Professor John Beshears reminds us, 'The real goal should be applying behavioural insights to meaningful, large-scale challenges.' That goal will not be reached by either academics or practitioners alone. It will require both, and the messy, productive, and occasionally uncomfortable dialogue between them.

Conclusion

Behavioural science arrived on the policy and practice stage with remarkable speed. It promised a new way of seeing human behaviour: one grounded in evidence, nuance, and humility about how decisions are made. But as this chapter has shown, speed came with simplification. The field's core problems: overreliance on nudge, WEIRD evidence, methodological narrowness, replication failures, and ethical ambiguity, are not incidental. They are consequences of how behavioural science was institutionalized, scaled, and sold.

Crucially, these problems are not evenly distributed. Academic behavioural science struggles with representation, methodological rigidity, and the lingering fallout of fragile findings. Applied behavioural science, by contrast, faces acute pressures towards simplification and speed, often at the expense of depth and transparency. Neither domain is immune, but they are vulnerable in different ways. That asymmetry matters. It means solutions must be tailored, not universal. And it means collaboration must begin not with consensus, but with clarity about difference.

However, despite this fractured landscape, there are reasons for cautious optimism. Across interviews and institutions, there is a shared sense that the field is maturing. The questions being asked today, about power, ethics, equity, and context, are more expansive than those that defined its early years. The challenge now is to ensure that maturity does not come too late.

As Jeff Kreisler, Head of Behavioral Science at JPMorgan Chase & Co, observed at the start of this chapter, the field is swinging on a pendulum, between influence and introspection, popularity and backlash. That swing is natural. But whether the next arc brings resilience or retreat will depend on how honestly behavioural science confronts its limitations, and how boldly it chooses to evolve.

That evolution begins with its most seductive promise: the nudge. In Chapter 3, how a concept designed to illuminate choice has sometimes obscured complexity instead is examined. How nudge became the shorthand for behavioural science is traced, as is what was lost, ignored, or excluded in the process. If behavioural science is to be rebuilt worthy of the problems it seeks to address, it must begin by questioning the very tool that first put it on the map.

3

Behavioural Science Will Be More Than a Nudge

> For many people outside the field, behavioral science means a few things, like nudges, and doesn't reflect the breadth and depth of what behavioral science has shown it can do.
>
> Kate Wolin (2020)

Introduction

What's the first thing most people learned to associate with behavioural science? For many, it's a urinal in Schiphol Airport. That now-familiar intervention, fly stickers applied to the bowl to improve aim and reduce cleaning costs, became a kind of origin myth: clever, cheap, and effective. Alongside examples like automatic organ donation enrolment or the Save More Tomorrow (SMarT) programme, it gave the impression that behavioural science was about minor tweaks that quietly nudged people into better decisions.

It was simple, scalable, and incredibly sticky, and that was precisely the problem. As Michelle Handy, Lead UX Researcher at UL Solutions, observed through her own work, the field quickly came to be seen as 'a silver bullet … very nudge-heavy, very easy, quick-fix focused'. Nudging wasn't just a technique; it was the identity of the discipline.

Rather than being used to interrogate problems, behavioural science was often applied after the fact, as a way to increase uptake or reduce drop-off. As several practitioners put it bluntly, their team was regularly asked to 'sprinkle some psychology' on top of a pre-approved idea, rather than shape it from the beginning.

This wasn't a fringe concern. Many of those working in the field now feel that behavioural science has been reduced to what Paulina Lang, Head of Behavioural Science at the MMR Group, described as a narrow 'collection of nudges', as though if it's not a tweak to choice architecture, it somehow doesn't count.

This chapter asks what happens when a complex, human-centred discipline gets reduced to a single tool in its toolkit. It explores how and why nudge came to dominate public and institutional thinking, and what we risk when we let it stand in for the field as a whole.

Because ultimately, this isn't just about how we frame behavioural science.

It's about whether the field can reclaim the breadth and depth Kate Wolin, behavioural epidemiologist, CSO, and Kellogg Adjunct Professor, describes. Or whether behavioural science will remain confined to the narrow toolkit others expect of it.

What we got, and what we lost

When *Nudge* appeared in 2008, it offered something governments and organisations badly needed: a way to influence behaviour without new laws, major spending, or political risk. In the aftermath of the global financial crisis, with institutions under pressure and budgets under strain, the idea that a subtle change in wording or a shift in defaults could produce significant results was immensely attractive.

This was not simply an intellectual development: it was a strategic one. Behavioural science entered the scene at a time when trust in expert-led, big-government policy making had been badly eroded. Governments needed a way to act without appearing heavy-handed. Thaler and Sunstein's concept of 'libertarian paternalism', nudging people in better directions while preserving freedom of choice, was a politically viable compromise. It allowed policy makers to intervene while still claiming minimal intrusion.

Michael Hallsworth, Chief Behavioural Scientist of the BIT, who was already applying behavioural economics in the UK government, recalled that Nudge didn't so much introduce new ideas as unlock demand. 'The attention that Nudge created meant the UK government wanted to know more about how it could be applied', he said. The *MINDSPACE* framework followed soon after, offering policy makers a structured behavioural toolkit. These tools quickly proved their worth: tax letters, pension defaults, and opt-out organ donation were not only effective but also simple to explain. Policy makers could announce them. Journalists could report on them. Citizens could understand them.

But the clarity and communicability of these early nudges came at a price. As behavioural science grew in prominence, it began to be treated less as a lens for inquiry and more as a menu of tweaks. Paulina Lang warned of an 'over-reliance on nudging', observing that many now 'think if it's not a nudge, then what else is behavioural science?' The field's visibility had skyrocketed, but its perceived scope had narrowed.

This narrowing wasn't just a matter of misunderstanding; it was structurally reinforced. As organisations and governments began procuring behavioural science services, they increasingly treated it as a deliverable: a 'nudge campaign' to be implemented, not a method of inquiry to reframe the problem. Elisabeth Costa, Global Chief of Innovation and Partnerships at the BIT, put it bluntly: 'You see it in policy making: plug in a social norm here, a friction there. But that's not what good behavioural science is.'

Michelle Handy described how, in many projects, the role of behavioural science had become purely instrumental. Stakeholders were enthusiastic at first; drawn to what she called the 'cool and sexy' image of behavioural science, but rarely willing to adapt their processes to benefit from it. 'They are not ready to change their existing ways of working or timelines', she explained. In most cases, what they really wanted was not a better understanding of behaviour, but a way to encourage compliance with decisions already made.

Too often, Handy said, her team was hired so stakeholders could just get 'some advice on how to get people to adopt their predetermined solution, instead of willing to examine the problem from a behavioral science lens in the first place.' And when she explained that behavioural science wasn't just about nudges or a silver bullet solution, but required a deeper diagnostic and experimental approach, stakeholders 'lost interest'.

Several practitioners echoed a similar frustration: behavioural scientists are often invited in after key decisions have already been made. 'Get us in earlier', is what Shane Timmons, Senior Research Officer in the Behavioural Research Unit at the ESRI and Adjunct Professor of Psychology at Trinity College Dublin, advises. When behavioural thinking is integrated at the design stage, it can anticipate structural problems rather than merely patch symptoms. But that requires organisations to see behavioural science not as a finishing touch, but as a diagnostic lens. But not every organisation is interested in doing that.

That disinterest speaks to deeper institutional incentives. As Scott Young, an independent adviser and educator and former Head of Private Sector at the BIT in the Americas, has outlined, many organisations resist behavioural science not because they doubt its value, but because it challenges established ways of working.[20] His research identifies three common barriers: the lack of a clear internal definition of behavioural science, fear that it will expose leadership blind spots, and discomfort with experimentation. In that environment, nudge: simple, fast, and depoliticized, offered a convenient workaround.

The more the field delivered on those terms, the more it became defined by them. Visibility increased, but the range of tools deployed shrank. Behavioural science came to be seen less as a process for investigating why people behave as they do, and more as a toolkit for subtly nudging them to behave differently. Amy Bucher, Chief Behavioral Officer at Lirio, described the challenge of resetting expectations: many clients, she noted, expected every project to yield the same dramatic results as the default effect in pension enrolment. 'It's very hard to help them see', she said, 'why the tool that was perfect for those contexts might not work elsewhere.'

What the field gained in legitimacy and institutional buy-in, it simultaneously lost in nuance and ambition. The systems that popularized behavioural science were also the ones that flattened it.

As Nick Hobson, the Managing Director at Influence at Work, put it, 'If all of behavioural science is the entire elephant, then nudging is the tail. We're missing out on the other 95%.' And yet, he added, that tail served its purpose. 'We needed nudging for the initial buy-in and proof of concept. But now that we have that, it's time to broaden our scope.'

The trouble with equating nudge and behavioural science

If behavioural science gained traction on the back of nudge, it has also become ensnared by it. As such, the broadening of our scope, as

Hobson suggests, isn't just a nice-to-have; it's increasingly a necessity. As the field became defined by its most digestible tactics, the risk wasn't only oversimplification. It was distortion. When policy makers, companies, or teams began to equate behavioural science with nudging, they weren't just narrowing its potential; they were undermining its purpose. Treating behavioural science as a grab bag of persuasive tricks doesn't just limit what we do. It changes how we are perceived, how our work is valued, and what problems we're even invited to solve, especially when nudge as a concept starts to run into issues.

Issues with libertarian paternalism

At first glance, the proposition of libertarian paternalism appears elegant: people remain free to choose, but are gently guided toward better outcomes. But in practice, many of these nudges depend not on choice, but on its absence: on inertia, cognitive shortcuts, or unthinking default acceptance. As several critics have pointed out, this raises uncomfortable questions. Is a nudge still libertarian if it is designed precisely to exploit the fact that most people won't notice or resist it? As the philosopher Luc Bovens has argued, the power of a default lies not in its appeal but in its invisibility.[21] When choice architecture guides behaviour without conscious awareness, the line between influence and manipulation becomes harder to draw.

Empirical evidence reinforces this point. Public acceptance of behavioural interventions is significantly shaped by perceptions of transparency and intent. When nudges are perceived as manipulative, especially those that leverage cognitive biases without explanation, they provoke backlash. As Darcie Piechowski, Global Performance Leader at IBM, put it, the ethical risk is not limited to malicious intent. 'Sometimes manipulation is intentional … but also sometimes it's unintentional, when you think you're doing the right thing.' That ambiguity, the space between helpful guidance and covert coercion, is precisely what worries both critics and practitioners.

The ethical discomfort intensifies in commercial settings. While a pension default may be justified by long-term welfare gains,[a] defaults used to extend free trials into paid subscriptions are more difficult to defend. And unlike in public policy, commercial nudging rarely faces ethical review. As behavioural science has proliferated into digital product design, loyalty marketing, and app engagement, the lack of formalized ethical standards has become more conspicuous. Unlike clinical research, behavioural science lacks institutional review boards, transparent consent mechanisms, or even a shared professional code. The result is a discipline whose public legitimacy may be growing, but whose ethical foundations remain precariously informal.

Recognizing these gaps, some in the field have pushed for frameworks that go beyond efficacy to address fairness, autonomy, and justice. Lades and Delaney's Fairness, Openness, Respect, Goals, Options, Outcomes, and Delegation (FORGOOD) framework offers one such attempt.[22] It asks not just whether a nudge works, but whether it works for the right reasons, for the right people, and under conditions they understand. As Bridgette Collado, Consumer Experience and Transformation Manager at Corewell Health, argued, ethical scrutiny should be approached not as a barrier to impact, but as a form of evidence generation in its own right: 'We need to start thinking about ethics like we think about evidence: as something to generate, not just assess.'

Issues with effectiveness

Yet the ethical tensions around nudge are not the only fault line. Its effectiveness has also come under sustained scrutiny. In recent years, the cumulative evidence around nudging has painted a more modest picture than early advocates suggested. While some interventions, like organ donation defaults or simplified tax letters, claimed to produce substantial gains, follow-up studies show diminished effects, if any,[23] and other nudges were found to produce underwhelming results from the start.

Meta-analyses reveal an average effect size far smaller than public discourse might suggest. One of the largest such studies, by Mertens et al in 2022, found a modest Cohen's d of 0.43,[b] with wide variation across domains.[4] More damningly, a reanalysis by Maier et al, later that year, argued that when publication bias was properly accounted for, the true effect size dropped to 0.11, verging on statistical insignificance.[5]

This was not just a scholarly debate. Around the same time, the earlier interviewed DellaVigna and Linos published results from over 120 field RCTs conducted by US government nudge units.[6]

Across more than 23 million participants, the median effect was a mere 1.4 percentage points; dramatically lower than the 8.7 points reported in academic studies. The implication was clear: the most high-profile nudges had been tested under ideal conditions, not real world ones. The hype had outpaced the data.

Behavioural scientists themselves were among the first to sound the alarm. As Umar Taj, Associate Professor of Behavioural Science at Warwick Business School and founder of Nudgeathon, noted, 'We as behavioural scientists know that those are the effects we are working with, but ... people outside of the field don't have those expectations.' When nudge becomes the public face of behavioural science, any underperformance is interpreted not as a failure of the tool, but of the discipline itself. And because nudge is often framed as low-cost, high-impact, scalable, and universally applicable, it carries a particularly high burden of expectation. When results fall short, disappointment is swift and reputationally damaging.

The case of COVID-19

The COVID-19 pandemic marked a pivotal rupture in the public image of behavioural science. Having risen to prominence on promises of low-cost, scalable, scientifically informed solutions, the field suddenly found itself implicated in one of the most high-stakes public health failures in modern British history. At the centre of this breakdown was the now-notorious term 'behavioural fatigue', used by UK government officials to justify delaying lockdowns, despite behavioural scientists themselves not endorsing, defining, or even recognizing the concept.[24]

Tara Austin, former Partner at Ogilvy and now Campaign Director at PAR.global was blunt: 'The pandemic was a good example of behavioural science used badly to dictate a strategy (without evidence) rather than inform.' The issue was not merely technical misapplication; it was representational overreach. Behavioural science had been sold, in some quarters, as a new governance orthodoxy, a smarter, leaner alternative to regulation or structural reform. But COVID-19 revealed the epistemic fragility of that positioning. The field promised certainty, and when it couldn't deliver, it was swiftly blamed.

A sentiment analysis by Sanders et al (2021) found that during the pandemic's first year, media coverage around 'nudge', 'Halpern', and the 'BIT' skewed decisively negative.[25] The very terminology that once conferred authority had become a liability. This reputational nosedive reflected a broader breakdown in trust: the idea that behavioural science was both too influential and dangerously naive. While behavioural scientists were actively running trials and advising on interventions, the public demand for definitive answers, clear rules, sharp timelines and causal clarity outpaced what the field could responsibly offer.

This episode is not a blip. It is the logical conclusion of a longer trend in which behavioural science has been oversold and under-supported. Rachel Altmann, CEO and co-founder at BeHive Consulting, captured the dilemma well: 'There's still a lot of research to be done; behavioural science is context specific, you can't just generalise things. Which is a problem if you also don't have the resources to do experiments for every single thing you need to know.' The gap between what behavioural science can rigorously do and what it is asked to perform has become a structural vulnerability. And this became really obvious during the pandemic; there was no language to talk about uncertainty. Which did nothing but make behavioural science look incompetent. As behavioural science, rooted in probabilistic reasoning and contextual specificity, was ill-matched to the crisis communication environment of a pandemic, where nuance was not just unhelpful but politically untenable.

The pandemic didn't just test behavioural science. It exposed the consequences of conflating the field with nudge, and of treating nudging as a proxy for institutional competence. 'We may need to think harder about where nudges are appropriate', said Liz Barker, formerly Director of Global Behavioural Intelligence at The Behavioural Architects and now a behavioural science PhD candidate at the University of Stirling: 'and where the benefit outweighs the costs … sometimes it may make more sense to use pricing tools, or taxation, or regulatory changes … We need a revolution.' That revolution never came. Instead, behavioural science, constrained by its narrow public image, was expected to supply answers it was never designed to provide.

The irony is that COVID-19 was not a behavioural science failure. It was a systems failure: of infrastructure, authority, and expectation. Teams often lacked the institutional mandates or resources to run timely experiments, or to scale promising interventions as Altmann highlighted. Behavioural scientists didn't ignore the complexity of the crisis; they weren't allowed the space to engage with it meaningfully. But because the field had positioned itself, too often, too confidently, as a source of low-friction certainty, the backlash was directed at them all the same.[26]

Nudge, in context

The lesson is not that nudges are ineffective or unethical. In the right contexts, with the right safeguards, they can be powerful tools. But when they are treated as synonymous with behavioural science, they shrink the field's intellectual and ethical horizons. They reduce a method of inquiry into a menu of fixes. They invite backlash when magic fails to materialize. And most dangerously, they displace more ambitious, systemic approaches to behaviour change; approaches that require time, experimentation, and institutional courage.

As Amy Bucher put it:

> Consider the conversation about whether nudging is a worthwhile approach to pursue, after several reviews found generally small effect sizes for particular nudges. Of course no single tactic, especially one as subtle as a nudge, is going to have a large omnibus effect size! Our work as behavioral scientists is to identify the right nudge for an individual, a behavioral target, and a context; A hammer is fantastic for pounding nails but terrible at turning screws, yet sometimes we measure the success of a tactic without examining the circumstances under which it works well.

Behavioural science must be understood not as a toolkit for compliance, but as a way of generating knowledge about how humans act, decide, and change. That means reclaiming its identity not through distancing from nudge, but through placing it back in context, as one tool among many, not the essence of the field.

Alternatives to nudge

Rather obvious to those who have been behavioural scientists for a while, but not only is nudge just a tool, it's one of many. Behavioural science has never been about a single tool. It is, by design, pluralistic; integrating insights from economics, psychology, anthropology, design, and data science. The debate is not whether one field is superior to the other, or whether one tool is superior to the others. It's how and when to use them together. And there are quite a few interesting extensions of and alternatives to nudge, for those who know where to look.

Nudge+

Nudge+, developed by Banerjee and John, is not a replacement for traditional nudge, but an evolution. It adds a reflective component, prompting individuals to actively engage with the behavioural cue rather than passively respond.[27] This preserves the efficiency of nudging while addressing concerns around manipulation, opacity, and autonomy.

The core idea centres around metacognitive awareness, making people conscious of how they're being influenced and offering space to evaluate that influence. For example, instead of simply defaulting to a vegetarian option, a nudge+ would pair it with a prompt: 'You're being offered the vegetarian meal because it's more climate-friendly. Would you like to stick with it or choose something else?'

This reflective design enhances both ethical legitimacy and impact. A large-scale UK study (n = 3,000+) comparing nudge, think, boost, and nudge+ found the latter generated the strongest intention to adopt climate-friendly diets.[28] Why? Because it didn't just cue action, it encouraged participants to consider their values before acting.

In obesity prevention, a classic nudge might default people into healthier options. A nudge+ might add a commitment device, like a self-pledge anticipating challenges (for example, late-night snacking). By surfacing intentions, it promotes agency.

The value of this approach goes beyond behaviour change. Nudge+ is transparent by design. It doesn't bypass awareness but elevates it; explicitly inviting resistance, reinterpretation, or modification. That's especially vital in ethically charged domains where consent and understanding are crucial.

Ultra nudge

Not all behavioural interventions are small. Some of the field's most impactful work comes not from tweaks to choice architecture, but from ambitious, resource-intensive programmes that scaffold complex behaviour change over time. Stefano DellaVigna recalls Richard Thaler referring to these as 'ultra nudges', although the term is debated. More accurately, they are large-scale, sustained interventions, still grounded in behavioural science.

A case in point is the Moving to Opportunity (MTO) programme. Launched in the 1990s by the US Department of Housing and Urban Development, the MTO was a randomized controlled trial testing whether relocating low-income families to low-poverty neighbourhoods improved long-term life outcomes.[29] Families received different housing vouchers, some with geographic restrictions and mobility counselling, others without.

The results were compelling. Children under 13 years old who moved to low-poverty areas saw lasting gains in education, income, and health. But the voucher alone wasn't enough; it was the surrounding support that made it work. Mobility counsellors helped families find housing and navigate barriers. Without that, many didn't use the vouchers. This is what DellaVigna means by 'ultra nudge': not a tweak, but a structure. Not cheap, but transformative.

What made MTO behavioural wasn't subtlety; it was recognizing lived constraints. The programme understood that decision-making under poverty is shaped by bandwidth, logistics, and chronic stress. By addressing those realities, it reflects behavioural science at its best.

As DellaVigna explained, these 'ultra nudges' represent the future:

> Not gimmicks, but guided support. Not minimalism for its own sake, but meaningful change. It's not cheap like a nudge. But think of the value in terms of happiness; just think of the earnings opportunities. So if we can do more, well, let's talk about what 'more' would be. It could be more out of the box. It could cost more. So I think that's the future, trying to be honest about the magnitude that one can get. That means finding out that some things are moderately effective, at a very low cost. And then let's keep going and find out what the things that are very effective could be.

This isn't abandoning behavioural science. It's fulfilling its promise.

Personalization

While early behavioural science focused on universal biases, modern approaches increasingly recognize the importance of individual differences. Nick Hobson put it succinctly: 'Our behavioural insights have been all about the E [environment] and no P [person]. It's always been about context, context, context. But it's (literally) half the equation. Once we begin accounting for individual differences, our behavior change interventions will be that much more impactful.' Much of the field has historically overlooked factors like personality, values, life stage, and cognitive style, all of which shape responses.

Evidence supports this. A landmark study by Shah et al (2023) on nearly 100,000 Mexicans found that a 'family security' message increased savings by 89 per cent for older adults but decreased them by 53 per cent for younger ones.[30] The average effect looked promising (+44.9 per cent) but concealed a polarising outcome. Age and life stage were key moderating variables. Still nudging, but no longer one-size-fits-all.

Other studies echo this. Schöning et al (2019) found that tailoring nudges to cognitive styles, for example, using graphics for visual learners, increased trust and reduced privacy concerns. In cybersecurity, impulsive users responded best to fast-action cues, while anxious users preferred step-by-step instructions. Personalization not only improved outcomes like password strength but also enhanced the perceived legitimacy of the intervention.[31]

In fintech, Canadian app users who received spending alerts tailored to their behaviour cut daily expenses by an average of C$ 8.15, far outperforming generic messages. It worked especially well for older, financially literate users new to the app.[32]

Still, personalization has limits. It demands granular data, poses privacy risks, and can't overcome basic knowledge gaps. As Colin Camerer, the Robert Kirby Professor of Behavioral Economics at Caltech, warns, not everyone moves: 'Personalization is important because one-size-fits-all interventions are so wasteful; a chunk of people won't budge, a chunk budge easily, and then there is a middle group who need just the right nudge.' In one education study, disengaged students were nudged to reflect more on math, but without the required baseline knowledge, performance didn't improve.[33]

Nor can personalization fix structural inequities. Even a precise nudge may fail if recipients lack the time, money, or capacity to act. Worse, it can backfire, evoking guilt or helplessness in sensitive areas like poverty, health, or climate change. Tailoring doesn't always mean empowering.

Yet, used thoughtfully, personalization enables behavioural precision. It rejects average treatment effects and asks: who benefits, who doesn't, and why? That's not just rigorous science; it's an ethical necessity.

Boosts

Among the most developed alternatives to nudge are boosts, a framework championed by Gerd Gigerenzer and Ralph Hertwig. Boosts don't steer behaviour in a set direction but instead equip people with tools, knowledge, and strategies to make better decisions themselves.[34] While nudges alter environments to guide behaviour, boosts improve individual competence, assuming poor choices often stem from misaligned or misunderstood information.

As Professor Gerd Gigerenzer, Director of the Harding Center for Risk Literacy and Director Emeritus of the Center for Adaptive Behavior and Cognition at the Max Planck Institute for Human Development, put it:

> Nudging is not about making people smart, but steers them to make choices that policy makers think they should make. Nudging has become a billion-dollar business, despite the 2022 meta-analysis by Maier et al. finding no evidence for nudging after adjusting for publication bias. Not in health, food, finance, or any other domain. We can do better by boosting.

His critique is both empirical and philosophical. Consider the widespread misinterpretation of probabilistic data, especially visible during COVID-19, when people had to interpret infection risks. Boosts like teaching natural frequencies (for example, '10 out of 100') significantly improved understanding among judges, doctors, and the public. These techniques are now part of medical curricula, enhancing diagnostic accuracy and reducing error.

Boosts operate from a different premise: whereas nudges accept cognitive limits as fixed, boosts treat cognition as improvable.[35] This leads to different designs: nudges are automatic and effortless; boosts require engagement and learning.

Evidence backs their durability. A Dutch study comparing a reframing nudge and a risk literacy boost on hospital hand hygiene found the nudge initially more effective (+35.8 per cent versus +21.4 per cent), but its impact declined post-intervention.[36] The boost's effect, by contrast, persisted and even grew (+2.6 per cent 1 week later). Boosts may therefore offer more lasting change, especially in institutional settings.

Similar findings came from financial decision-making trials in Serbia and the US. A numeracy boost teaching expected value led to better investment choices than disclosure nudges or social norm cues.[37] The boost had the greatest effect on participants who started with lower-quality decision-making, pointing to its potential in narrowing competence gaps.

Boosts aren't without challenges. They require effort, motivation, and a basic level of literacy. But this is also their ethical strength; they demand transparency and collaboration. As Elisabeth Costa notes,

> Another challenge is the framing debate – boosts vs nudges, i-frame vs s-frame ... We operate in complex systems. Sometimes an individual focus is right, sometimes a systems approach is better. We need both. Instead of arguing which is better, let's talk about when and how to use them effectively.

Boosts aren't a panacea, but they are a vital complement, especially where autonomy and long-term competence matter.

What behavioural science really is

For all the ways behavioural science has been mischaracterized, as a grab bag of nudges, a tactical compliance tool, or a shortcut to impact, the truth is both more mundane and more profound. Behavioural science is not magic. It is a method.

And it is already equipped with the tools we need to understand and shape behaviour in complex, context-rich environments. It simply hasn't always been allowed or resourced to use them.

Diagnostics

At its core, behavioural science is a way of asking questions. It begins not with solutions, but with diagnosis: what is the behaviour we are trying to change, and why is it happening (or not) now? As Sarah Kneebone, founder of Skyflower Solutions and former Education Manager at BehaviourWorks Australia put it:

> We mostly apply behaviour diagnosis and evidence review to generate audience insights and gather a detailed understanding of why a priority behaviour is or is not being performed. This allows us to co-design tailored, evidence-based, audience-informed interventions. We do sprinkle in some nudge-style tools to check for example the mechanics of the behaviour (is it easy to perform?, etc.), but by narrowing in, identifying a key target audience and investigating the drivers and barriers to them performing a single selected priority behaviour, we can be much more focussed and again increase the chances of success.

That analytical process: defining, observing, hypothesizing, testing, is what differentiates science from storytelling.

This is what makes behavioural science powerful: not its simplicity, but its rigour. And yet, as James Healy, founder of The Behaviour Boutique and former Principal for Human Capital Consulting at Deloitte, noted, it's precisely this scientific identity that has often been obscured by 'Jedi mind tricks' and 'gimmicky headlines'. 'Behavioural Science', he says, 'is about understanding that environment shapes behaviour – and proactively shaping environment to encourage and enable the behaviours that will deliver the outcomes we want'.

It is a way of seeing the world as it is, not as we assume it to be. And then, of changing it in ways that are thoughtful, tested, and human.

Experimentation

If diagnostics are the core, experimentation is the backbone. Without it, we risk building ideas on intuition and mistaking correlation for causation. As Laura de Molière, co-founder and partner at

Decision-Context, previously Head of Behavioural Science at the UK Cabinet Office, warns, there is a dangerous temptation in the industry to oversell simplicity: 'It's easier to sell when it sounds simple and powerful, but it's actually making our jobs harder … Clients expect immediate, miracle solutions, and when they don't see that, it damages the credibility of the field.'

True behavioural science is iterative. It proposes, tests, falsifies, learns. It rejects the idea of one-size-fits-all fixes. As Etinosa Agbonlahor, CEO of Decision Alpha and formerly at Fidelity and Commonwealth Bank, argued, the future of the field will hinge on rigorous testing: 'So no more lists of biases. It's going to be figuring out how we test and measure, because context matters a lot and will change things.'

Context, of course, is everything. A nudge that works in one setting may fail in another. An intervention that helps some users may alienate others. Without experimentation, we can't know which is which. We risk implementing ideas that 'seem like they should work' rather than ones that do.

Professor Susan Michie, Director of the Centre for Behaviour Change and Professor of Health Psychology at University College London (UCL), captures the stakes clearly: 'Everybody behaves, and everybody sees other people behaving … This can lead people to think we don't need more than common sense. But it's not true.' Behavioural science, like any science, is not obvious. Its insights must be tested. Its methods must be robust. Otherwise, we are just telling stories that feel right and calling them evidence.

Shane Timmons sharpens this point even further. Not all work labelled as behavioural science, he argues, truly follows the scientific method. Applying a well-known bias to a problem without testing or evaluation may borrow the language of the field, but it does not amount to behavioural science in its full sense. The discipline's distinctive contribution is not its catalogue of cognitive effects, but its commitment to systematic experimentation. Without that commitment to hypothesize, to measure, to potentially falsify, behavioural science risks becoming a persuasive narrative rather than an empirical enterprise.

Human-centred design

Experimentation alone is not enough. To understand human behaviour, we must also understand human lives. That's where human-centred design enters: as a vital complement to behavioural science's analytical tools.

Greg Davies, Head of Behavioural Finance at OxfordRisk, critiques the perception that behavioural insights are 'cute parlour games' that only ever 'seem only to tackle simple toy puzzles, and not address the complex systems in which all decisions are made'. And he's right too. Climate change, health inequities and political radicalization are not challenges that yield to reminders and defaults alone. They demand approaches rooted in empathy, lived experience, and systems awareness.

Human-centred design offers exactly that. Through methods like ethnographic interviews, participatory workshops, and journey mapping, it enables behavioural scientists to move beyond assumptions. It grounds hypotheses in the real constraints and trade-offs that people face. And it opens the door to deeper, more inclusive solutions.

This is not a departure from behavioural science; it is its fulfilment. It's how we ensure the problems we are solving are the right ones. That the interventions we build are responsive, not just clever. And that the field remains anchored in its founding mission: to understand behaviour as it actually unfolds, in the messy texture of real life.

Systems thinking and structural change

One of the most common criticisms of behavioural science is that it individualizes problems. It focuses on i-frame solutions (fixing the person) at the expense of s-frame ones (fixing the system). And this critique is not without merit.

Chater and Loewenstein have shown how nudge-led policy making can displace more effective structural reforms.[38] When people believe a problem can be solved cheaply, they become less likely to support higher-cost, systemic solutions, such as carbon taxes, regulation, or redistribution. And when behaviour is framed as personal choice, structural blame evaporates.

But this is not an indictment of behavioural science. It's a call to apply it more fully. The same tools used to test nudges can be used to test systems. The same lenses used to analyse personal decision-making can be used to diagnose institutional inertia. Behavioural science is not structurally apolitical, it has simply been applied that way.

Robert H. Frank, Professor of Economics at Cornell University's Johnson Graduate School of Management, put it: 'If you focus on climate change, the problem isn't that people aren't being environmentally conscious enough – it's that the important activities that give rise to carbon emissions aren't priced correctly.' Behavioural scientists should not shy away from these realities. They should confront them, armed with data, humility, and ambition.

The next iteration of behavioural science

Behavioural science has always been more than nudges. It is already a field of diagnosis, experimentation, learning, and design. It already spans the spectrum from individual behaviour to systemic reform. It already includes methods that are rigorous, reflective, and participatory. It already knows that people are not problems to be fixed, but humans to be understood.

The task now is to communicate this effectively to others, and to be honest about what behavioural science can and cannot do.

Towards a science beyond nudge

This chapter traced how behavioural science, once propelled into the spotlight by the success of nudging, has found itself constrained by it. Nudging helped behavioural science gain traction; it offered simplicity, visibility, and political viability. But the same features that made it appealing have also narrowed the discipline's perceived scope. As Richard Bordenave, Partner at Ipsos Strategy3 and former Chief Behavioural Officer at PRS IN VIVO, observed that the field now faces an identity crisis of its own making: 'creating silos, kicking out imposters, killing the fathers, looking very much inwards and desperately searching for recognition and a sense of purpose'. The risk, he argues, is existential: 'most people like behavioural science, but no one needs behavioural science'. Unless it can prove its added value, demonstrating how it improves on existing solutions, and when it should defer to alternatives such as regulation, taxation, or leadership reform, behavioural science will remain an appealing idea rather than a necessary one. The task, then, is not simply technical or evidential. It is strategic. To mature as a discipline, behavioural science must reframe its purpose, retool its methods, and reassert its relevance. The sections that follow suggest six ways of doing so.

Step 1. Reframing behavioural science as strategy

For all its visibility, behavioural science is still often misunderstood as a bag of tricks, a toolkit for quick wins, or a flavour of UX. As Rachel Altmann noted, 'we are still in a very early phase; we're still in the "educating our clients" phase, and this means that people don't necessarily accept behavioural science as a discipline on its own; people often see it as a nice to have. And a lot of people don't understand it', mistaking practitioners for designers or marketers. Behavioural science, in this view, is supplementary rather than foundational, an optional extra, not a core discipline.

This perception is the legacy of nudge: its simplicity made it appealing, but also easy to mischaracterize. What the field now requires is a repositioning, from behavioural science as implementation to behavioural science as insight. At its best, it is not a tactic but a diagnostic lens: a way to uncover friction, incentives, and mismatches between policy intent and lived experience. It can highlight, as the i-frame/s-frame debate reminds us, when the problem isn't behavioural at all.

Lena Belkor-Belogolova, Director of Insights & Analytics at the Scotts Miracle-Gro Company, described the discipline as still 'in the early stages', with many practitioners 'trying to figure out where we fit within industry incentives, and how we convince leaders that this matters'. That uncertainty is strategic as much as scientific. Behavioural science must learn to articulate its value as a way of thinking, one that adds clarity in complexity, not just marginal gains. This means resisting the temptation to overpromise. Contextual nuance, not generalized claims, is where the discipline's real power lies.

And crucially, this shift is only possible if behavioural scientists themselves are equipped to make it. Selling behavioural science as strategy requires practitioners capable of seeing the full picture, not just what people do, but why, when, and under what conditions they should be helped, left alone, or supported by other tools entirely.

Practical steps

- Shift positioning in client conversations. Practitioners should present behavioural science not as a bag of tricks for quick wins but as a diagnostic tool to understand underlying problems, emphasizing how it complements (or challenges) existing strategies.
- Use diagnostic frameworks early. Begin projects by mapping friction points, incentives, and system-level barriers rather than jumping straight into solution design. This shows stakeholders that the value lies in problem definition, not just in interventions.
- Educate leaders with real world examples. Case studies where behavioural insights redefined a problem, such as reframing tax noncompliance as system confusion rather than wilful avoidance, should be actively shared to demonstrate strategic value.
- Resist overpromising. Practitioners must be explicit about boundary conditions, explaining when behavioural science is helpful and when regulation, incentives, or system redesign may be more effective.
- Invest in practitioner training on strategic communication. Skills in framing, storytelling, and stakeholder management are essential so behavioural scientists can secure a seat at the strategy table rather than being called in to 'tweak'.

Reframing behavioural science as strategy won't solve every identity crisis the field faces, but it shifts the conversation onto firmer ground. By positioning itself as a diagnostic lens rather than a bag of tricks, the discipline shows its relevance not only in tweaking choices but in shaping how problems are defined and solved. Done well, this makes behavioural science less about novelty and more about necessity; an approach that earns its place at the strategy table rather than waiting to be invited.

Step 2. Professionalizing the field

As behavioural science gains visibility, it still lacks a coherent professional identity. Practitioners enter from diverse disciplines: psychology, economics, design, and marketing, often with uneven exposure to the applied research cycle. This has led to inconsistent standards, unclear boundaries, and variable quality. As Etinosa Agbonlahor put it, behavioural scientists must move beyond 'lists of biases' to develop the skills needed to design, test, and evaluate interventions rigorously. Knowing the literature, she said, is 'a great start, but a very poor finish'.

That 'finish' must involve more than quoting Kahneman. If the field is to mature, it needs shared expectations: a baseline of methodological competence, causal reasoning, and the confidence to say no, when behavioural science isn't the right tool. Agbonlahor suggests that future practitioners will have to be skilled technically: 'I see a future where you will not have any behavioural scientists who don't already have a strong data science background, because it's going to be impossible to effectively do behavioural science if you're not also running experiments and testing the impact of the recommendations you're making.' Academic rigour and data science, she argues, are not optional; they're foundational.

This professionalization demands infrastructure: defined competencies, recognized training routes, and clear accountability. Practitioners should know how to write a pre-analysis plan, run field trials, interpret nulls, and identify when behavioural tools fall short; topics explored further in the coming chapters.

But even strong skills aren't enough. As Steve Wendel, co-founder and Head of Methodology of sistemaFutura, previously at Busara and Morningstar, observes:

> Currently, a challenge we face is that the quality of work is very uneven across our field. In part, this arises from time pressure and the structural position that many behavioral science consultants are in. When we compete on price, we don't give ourselves the time and space we need to do high-quality work. And so we trap ourselves.

Without structural support, the field risks overselling its promise and undershooting its impact. To escape this trap, behavioural science must shift from being an outsourced solution to a recognized professional discipline. This means creating accreditation systems, embedding shared codes of practice, and ensuring continuous development. Only then will practitioners be equipped to move beyond short-term interventions towards lasting, systemic impact.

Practical steps

- Define a shared competency framework. Establish baseline expectations around research design, causal reasoning, ethics, and data analysis; therefore, practitioners entering from diverse backgrounds can meet the same professional standard.
- Develop accredited training pathways. Universities and other professional bodies should partner to offer standardized courses and certifications that integrate both methodological rigour and applied practice.
- Mandate continuing professional development. Practitioners should be expected to update their skills regularly, particularly in data science, experimental design, and ethical reflection, as part of maintaining professional status.
- Create peer-review structures in practice. Internal review panels or professional forums can provide feedback on proposed interventions, ensuring rigour before implementation.
- Embed behavioural science in institutions. Organisations should avoid outsourcing all behavioural work and instead invest in internal teams with career paths, training budgets, and structures for peer learning, building the field as a capability rather than a service.

Professionalization won't eliminate every gap or inconsistency, but it will set a higher floor. By defining shared standards, embedding ethics and methods training, and ensuring accountability, behavioural science can establish itself as a profession in its own right. This not only strengthens quality and trust; it also frees practitioners from competing on price and speed, allowing them to compete instead on rigour, relevance, and long-term value.

Step 3. Embedding experimentation as institutional muscle

One of behavioural science's greatest strengths, its foundation in experimentation, is also one of its most underused. Too often, this capability is treated as optional. Behavioural teams are asked to tweak, implement, or 'do something behavioural', but not to rigorously test, measure, or interrogate assumptions. In many organisations, experimentation remains siloed, under-resourced, or outsourced. In some, it's not considered at all.

This isn't just a missed opportunity; it's a strategic vulnerability. As Jez Groom, co-founder of Ogilvy Change and later founder of Cowry Consulting, put it,

> We're driving an agenda to make Behavioural Science more mainstream in business and building up capability in some of the biggest organisations in the world. In time, a lot of the smaller problems will be solved by people in these organisations and not specialist behavioural scientists. This will leave a far more gnarly challenge for practitioners …

To meet those challenges, behavioural science needs to be embedded, not as a one-off solution, but as a sustained organisational capability.

That means moving past the pilot mindset. It requires building internal capacity: cross-functional teams that bring together behavioural scientists, analysts, implementers, and delivery leads. It means designing systems to test hypotheses often and early, and cultivating environments where informed failure is not punished but valued. Just as crucially, it means shifting incentive structures away from rewarding only 'successful' results and toward recognizing good questions, valid tests, and honest interpretation.

Experimentation isn't a procedural step. Performed well, it reduces risk, informs design, and enables adaptive decision-making. Rather than gamble on untested assumptions, behavioural science offers an iterative model: test, learn, refine. As Adam Ferrier, Founder and Consumer Psychologist at Thinkerbell, puts it, the future lies in embracing 'measured magic', data-informed creativity that understands the value of rigour not as constraint, but as enabler. 'We're getting closer', Ferrier argues, 'to being able to see the short- and long-term impacts of marketing efforts … In ten years, I hope we'll see more of the industry embracing a "measured magic" approach.'

Experimentation, then, is more than methodological; it's strategic. The real shift needed is cultural: from delivering clever interventions to normalizing testing as the basis of good decision-making. When that happens, behavioural science moves from novelty to necessity.

Practical steps

- Normalize experimentation in decision-making. Organisations should adopt a 'test first' culture, requiring interventions to be trialled in controlled ways before full rollout, making experimentation a default rather than an add-on.
- Build cross-functional teams. Teams should integrate behavioural scientists, analysts, implementers, and delivery managers so that experiments are designed, executed, and applied effectively within operational contexts.
- Reward good questions and honest results. Incentive structures should be adapted to celebrate rigorous tests and valid null results, rather than only rewarding interventions that show positive effects.
- Invest in infrastructure for testing. This includes digital platforms for rapid A/B testing, data pipelines for evaluation, and knowledge-sharing systems so experiments feed into organisational learning.
- Train leaders to value iteration. Senior decision makers need to be educated on why 'failing fast' is beneficial, ensuring that experimentation is seen as reducing risk rather than slowing progress.

Embedding experimentation will not resolve every organisational challenge, but it will shift behavioural science from being a novelty to being a necessity. By making testing a routine part of decision-making, the field ensures that evidence, not assumptions, guides policy, strategy, and design. Over time, this builds not only better interventions but also more adaptive and resilient organisations.

Step 4. Playing the long game

'If behavioural science teams are just tweaking things at the margins – playing with wording or running isolated experiments – they won't last', warns Quique Belenguer Saborit, Behavioural Economics Discipline Leader at BBVA. 'But if they're solving big, strategic problems, they'll thrive ... Either we become indispensable, or we fade away.'

Assuming the groundwork has been laid; behavioural science reframed as strategy, grounded in rigour, and embedded through experimentation; the next challenge is sustaining that relevance. That means resisting the gravitational pull of marginal gains and fast fixes. If nudging opened the door, now is the time to step through it.

This requires going beyond the standard playbook. We need interventions that build the conditions for durable, meaningful change, not just short-term compliance. That means approaches that are effective, yes, but also legitimate, participatory, and designed with, not just for, users.

Alternative approaches, such as boosts, nudge+, ultra nudges, and personalization, offer promising directions. Each remains grounded in behavioural science, but each demand more from both practitioners and institutions.

They don't offer the quick thrill of an elegant nudge. But they deliver something more robust: interventions that last. They also counter the critique that behavioural science is manipulative or superficial. These approaches are transparent, respect autonomy, and can better withstand scrutiny.

Naturally, they're harder to implement. Boosts and ultra nudges require systems. Nudge+ demands openness about influence. Personalization needs data, infrastructure, and care. These aren't off-the-shelf fixes, and that's their strength.

The challenge, then, is not only designing better interventions but defending their value. That means communicating long-term return on investment (ROI), not only in behaviours changed, but in trust built, capability developed, and equity advanced.

Hybrid approaches show promise. A nudge gets someone to the gym; a boost helps them stick with it. This isn't about discarding nudges; it's about scaffolding them.

To sell the deeper value of behavioural science, practitioners must go beyond experiment execution. We must articulate the bigger picture: a more capable user, a better decision, a fairer system. And we must be at the table from the outset, not brought in to tweak, but to shape.

That is how we become indispensable. Not an add-on. Not a nice-to-have. Embedded.

Practical steps

- Develop dual metrics for evaluation. Every project should be assessed on both immediate outcomes (for example, response rates and sign-ups) and long-term persistence (for example, sustained savings and habit formation). Building these into evaluation frameworks makes durability visible and defendable.
- Build and circulate case studies of durable value. Document interventions where impacts lasted beyond the trial, such as boosts that helped people sustain healthier lifestyles, and use these to educate stakeholders about what good looks like.
- Incorporate trust and legitimacy into reporting. Beyond 'did it work?' evaluations should capture whether people found the intervention respectful, fair, and transparent; key measures of public acceptance.
- Train practitioners to communicate cost–benefit. Many decision makers look for ROI in financial terms. Practitioners must learn to frame benefits in economic, social, and reputational terms, showing how ethical and lasting approaches create wider value.
- Use hybrid approaches to demonstrate strength. Pairing nudges with boosts or system redesigns not only increases effectiveness but also shows stakeholders that behavioural science can deliver both short-term wins and sustainable outcomes.

Selling long-term ROI won't erase the appeal of quick wins, but it reframes the discipline's value. It makes behavioural science not just a tool for tweaking outcomes, but a partner in creating systems that endure. By proving its contribution to resilience, equity, and trust, the field secures its place at the strategic core of decision-making.

Step 5. Raising the floor: standards, transparency, and ethics

'Applied behavioural science is often the Wild West', Natalia le Gal, behavioural science consultant and founder of the consultancy Behava, noted, 'Unlike academia, which has strong ethical frameworks, applied work lacks consistency and accountability.'

As the field has grown in popularity, its foundations have remained patchy. Outside academic settings, norms such as preregistration, replication, and transparent reporting are inconsistently applied. Failed interventions are quietly shelved, success is often overstated, and standards vary widely depending on the client, budget, or team.

If behavioural science is to be taken seriously, it needs to raise its floor. Openly reporting null results should become standard, not a rare act of humility, but part of basic professional practice. More rigorous testing, clearer documentation, and consistent frameworks for evaluation aren't just good science; they're essential for credibility.

Ethical challenges are also evolving. As behavioural tools become more powerful, adaptive messaging, AI-generated nudges, personalized interventions; they raise deeper questions around consent, privacy, and legitimacy. Who gets nudged? Who decides the outcome? And where is the line between influence and manipulation?

Frameworks like FORGOOD help,[22] but only when applied in practice, not just referenced in footnotes. And practitioners must be prepared to ask the uncomfortable questions: not just 'does it work?' but 'should it be done?'

Behavioural science cannot afford to become a veneer for structural problems. Nudges that distract from systemic injustice, poor housing, underfunded health systems, precarious work, risk making the field part of the problem. Ethical behavioural science requires transparency, accountability, and the courage to say no.

Because if we don't define the limits of our tools, someone else will. And they may not be as careful.

Practical steps

- Normalize preregistration and documentation in applied work. Where feasible, intervention hypotheses, outcome measures, and analysis plans should be documented in advance, even if it's 'just' internally. This reduces hindsight bias and selective reporting.
- Create mechanisms for reporting null and negative results. Teams should maintain internal repositories (or anonymized shared databases) of failed or inconclusive interventions. Learning must be cumulative, not reputational.
- Adopt a standardized ethical review process for applied projects. Even outside academia, teams can implement lightweight ethics checklists addressing autonomy, fairness, data use, unintended consequences, and vulnerable populations.

- Clarify governance for adaptive and AI-driven interventions. When deploying personalized or algorithmically optimized nudges, define clear rules on consent, transparency, explainability, and escalation thresholds.
- Institutionalize 'should we?' alongside 'does it work?' Formalize ethical reflection in project gates. Before scaling, require a structured discussion of distributive impact, systemic implications, and alignment with institutional values.
- Separate behavioural insight from political cover. Establish guardrails preventing behavioural interventions from substituting for structural reform when root causes are systemic.

Raising the floor won't resolve every challenge, but it sets a baseline of professionalism. It builds trust by showing that behavioural science holds itself accountable, not just for its successes, but for its failures. In doing so, it signals that the field is ready to move beyond novelty, toward maturity.

Step 6. Advocate for systemic change when needed

Behavioural science has always focused on people, but too often, it has focused on the wrong ones. Rather than asking what's broken in systems, it has busied itself asking what's broken in individuals. This is no longer good enough.

Quique Saborit Belenguer offered a clear diagnosis: 'We need to take a broader view, looking at behavioural ecosystems rather than isolated interventions.' The field's fondness for tweaking choices at the margins, encouraging savings, gym visits, or recycling, is increasingly out of step with the scale of the problems it claims to address. Nudging someone to walk more won't heal a broken leg or rebuild a city without sidewalks. Prompting people to save for retirement is meaningless if wages don't cover rent. And reminders to lower the thermostat can't compensate for freezing homes with no insulation.

As James Healy puts it, behavioural science 'is about understanding that environment shapes behaviour and proactively shaping environment to encourage and enable the behaviours that will deliver the outcomes we want'. If that's true, then behavioural scientists must stop treating the environment as someone else's domain. Structural conditions are not footnotes to behaviour; they are often the root cause.

And here's the harder truth: when behavioural insights are used to gloss over policy failure, to push 'solutions' that bypass redistribution, regulation, or redesign, the field becomes complicit. There is a fine line between helpful pragmatism and strategic distraction. We must not cross it.

Because nudges won't save us from broken systems. And when those systems collapse, or simply fail to deliver, behavioural science will be one of the first in the firing line. 'Look', they'll say, 'it didn't work'. The backlash is coming. Not because the science is flawed, but because the field allowed itself to be the fig leaf. Let's not give them the story. Let's fix the systems.

Practical steps

- Conduct behavioural audits of major policies. Go beyond interventions to map where structural barriers, such as poor infrastructure or unfair incentives, make behaviour change impossible. Use these audits to inform policy makers.
- Partner with regulators and system designers. Work alongside city planners, finance regulators, or health authorities to integrate behavioural insights into system-level solutions, such as infrastructure reform or consumer protections.
- Train practitioners to spot systemic problems. Education and professional training should prepare behavioural scientists to recognize when behaviour is shaped more by systemic factors than by individual biases.
- Publish guidance on scope. Clear guidelines should help practitioners determine when behavioural science is appropriate, and when to defer to regulation, redistribution, or other systemic tools.
- Advocate publicly against fig leaf applications. Practitioners and professional bodies should call out cases where behavioural insights are being used to distract from deeper failures, positioning the field as a partner in reform, not a tool of avoidance.

Systemic change is never easy, and behavioural science cannot carry that burden alone. But it can help reframe problems, reveal hidden frictions, and support policies that address root causes rather than symptoms. By choosing to step beyond individual tweaks and engage with the environments in which behaviours occur, the field strengthens both its legitimacy and its impact. This shift will not transform behavioural science into a panacea, but it will ensure it is part of the solution, not a fig leaf for deeper failures.

Conclusion

Behavioural science began as a bold proposition: that understanding how people actually think, feel, and act could unlock smarter, fairer, more effective policy. But over time, that proposition was distilled into a single tool, nudge, and in doing so, the discipline narrowed its own horizon. It became, in too many rooms, the polite afterthought brought in too late, expected to deliver too much, and often used to paper over problems it should have been helping to diagnose.

This chapter has traced how that happened, and why it can't continue. Nudging helped behavioural science earn its seat at the table. But now, to stay there, it must evolve. That means expanding the field's toolkit. But more than that, it means expanding its role: from add-on to architect. From fixer to strategist.

As Elisabeth Convery, Principal Adviser and Head of Research (Asia-Pacific) at the BIT, put it:

> I think behavioural science has an image problem. The term 'nudge' has been both helpful and harmful ... It gives the impression that nudging is all we do – just tweaking small decisions at the last moment ... In reality, behavioural science has so much more potential. We can work at the systems level, designing upstream interventions that shape behaviour long before people even reach that last-mile decision point.

The goal, as she and others have argued, is not to discard nudging but to put it back in its place; one tool among many. Not a shortcut, but a starting point.

That requires rigour. It requires resistance to oversimplification. And it requires practitioners willing to fight for depth over decoration. But as we push back against simplification, there is also a risk that critique curdles into cynicism. As Shane Timmons cautions, scepticism is essential; cynicism is corrosive. Assuming that behavioural interventions are naive, manipulative, or doomed to fail may feel intellectually sophisticated, but it shuts down experimentation and halts learning. The more constructive posture is openness to new ideas, coupled with the discipline to test them properly. If nudge is no longer the answer to everything, the solution is not retreat; it is better science.

Behavioural science must be embedded early, used diagnostically, and applied in ways that are ethical, participatory, and testable. It must partner with design, policy, and systems thinking, not compete with them. And above all, it must stop apologizing for complexity. Good behavioural science is slow, iterative, and contingent. And that's not a weakness. It's a strength.

But the greatest threat isn't public misunderstanding. It's internal complacency. If the field keeps delivering clever tweaks to broken systems, it will keep getting asked for clever tweaks, and nothing more. As practitioners, we must be willing to say when nudging isn't enough. When the answer isn't a behaviour, but a structure. When the challenge isn't framing the message, but redesigning the rules.

And it means calling out when behavioural interventions are being used to paper over systemic failure. We can't let nudges, or any part of our toolkit, become an excuse not to fix the system. Because there will be plenty of eager-eyed journalists ready to write behavioural science's next failure story, regardless of whether the science deserved the blame.

So let's take control of the narrative. Let's be transparent about what behavioural science can't do; and louder about what it can. Not by narrowing the field to what's simple, but by embracing the full scope of what's meaningful.

Not just the tail. But the full elephant.

4

Behavioural Science Will Include Everyone

> I don't think we can ignore the topic of power: who controls the discourse? Who is setting the agenda? What voices aren't being heard? And why aren't we hearing other people, other voices? These are the questions we need to be asking ourselves. How inclusive is this profession? What are the topics we're not really talking about? We are at a really tricky point in the world. We need to figure out which ways that the wind is going to blow; towards a world which is more inclusive, multifaceted and allowing us to hear and be willing to hear different perspectives? That's the challenge and opportunity I see for behavioural science.
>
> Colin Strong (2024)

Introduction

Imagine being asked to perform a 5-minute job interview in front of three evaluators dressed in lab coats. You're not allowed notes or preparation. You must speak continuously, then count backwards from 1,022 in steps of 13. Make a mistake, and you start again.

This is the Trier Social Stress Test (TSST), a standard protocol in experimental psychology. Designed to trigger physiological stress responses, elevated cortisol, heart rate, and anxiety, it relies on two core elements: being judged and lacking control.[39] The test works remarkably well in Western settings, particularly with students. But in 2013, Busara tried to replicate it in Kenya, and it failed entirely. Instead of stress, participants responded with confusion, even laughter.[40]

Why? Because the cues embedded in the test were culturally irrelevant. Lab coats in Kenya signify butchers, not scientists. Public speaking is socially familiar, not threatening. The TSST's psychological triggers simply didn't translate.

This anecdote may be amusing, but it reveals a deeper issue within behavioural science: the field's persistent overreliance on WEIRD samples; those from Western, Educated, Industrialized, Rich, and Democratic societies.[41] These populations, often university students in the Global North, form the basis of much behavioural research. Yet findings derived from these narrow samples are frequently assumed to be universal.

As Colin Strong, Head of Behavioural Science at Ipsos UK and Professor of Practice at Nottingham University Business School, reminds us in this chapter's opening quote, the WEIRD bias doesn't just limit what we understand about human behaviour. It distorts it. This chapter explores how, and what we can do about it.

Built on white sand: how WEIRD samples shaped behavioural science

In 2010, Joseph Henrich, Steven Heine, and Ara Norenzayan published a landmark paper asking a deceptively simple question: 'Are the people who form the database of behavioural science actually representative of humanity?'[41] Their answer was unequivocal: no. Drawing on decades of empirical evidence, they showed that people from WEIRD societies are, in fact, psychological outliers across a wide range of domains. From visual perception and spatial reasoning to moral judgement, fairness norms, and notions of the self, WEIRD populations consistently behave differently from the vast majority of humanity.

These differences are not marginal. Consider the Müller-Lyer illusion, a classic visual task used for decades in cognitive psychology. Henrich et al compiled studies showing that American participants were among the most susceptible in the world to the illusion, while San foragers in the Kalahari showed almost no susceptibility at all.[41]

Or take fairness and cooperation: in economic games such as the Ultimatum Game, American adults typically reject unfair offers to signal a preference for fairness. But in small-scale societies such as the Hadza or the Machiguenga, participants are more likely to accept low offers without protest, prioritizing material gain over abstract fairness norms.

In domains such as moral reasoning, self-construal, spatial cognition, and even basic numerical processing, WEIRD samples consistently fall at the extreme end of global distributions. Yet these same samples have formed the empirical backbone of behavioural science for more than half a century. The field's most well-known theories, from heuristics and biases to dual-process models and nudge-based interventions, were built not on global human data, but on narrow, highly specific subpopulations.

This empirical fragility is further compounded by an overreliance on one subgroup within WEIRD societies: university students. Students make up the majority of participants in behavioural experiments, especially those conducted in psychology, behavioural economics, and decision science. Their overrepresentation is often defended on grounds of convenience; students are available, affordable, and logistically easy to access. But this rationale obscures a more serious issue: students differ in systematic ways from the broader populations they are assumed to represent.

In terms of cognition, students tend to show higher levels of abstraction in reasoning, greater emphasis on individual agency, and reduced reliance on contextual or relational cues. In terms of social orientation, they are more likely to value autonomy over interdependence, exhibit looser social networks, and express more liberal attitudes on issues such as diversity and hierarchy.[42–50] Educational exposure has been shown to shape these orientations. When Henrich et al compared less-educated US adults to university students, they found that the former often reasoned in ways more consistent with East Asian collectivist norms than with the assumed American individualism.[50]

Despite this, generalization from student samples has become an unexamined norm. Early foundational studies often reported participant details vaguely, referring to 'subjects'[a] without identifying age, education level, ethnicity, or nationality. In Kahneman and Tversky's Prospect Theory work, for instance, descriptions range from '95 Stanford students' to 'two groups of subjects', with no demographic detail provided.[51] This was not uncommon. Such ambiguity was treated as scientifically acceptable because the default assumption was that these findings described people in general.

By the early 2000s, the dominance of student samples had become near total in some subfields. In social psychology, particularly in studies of prejudice and discrimination, the trend became especially entrenched. A meta-analysis revealed that from 1990 to 2010, the proportion of published studies relying exclusively on student samples increased from 82.7 to 91.6 per cent.[42] Theories about prejudice that are tested almost entirely on 18–22-year-olds enrolled in elite US universities may tell us more about campus culture than about structural inequality, group-based threat, or intergroup dynamics in the broader world.

In behavioural economics, similar issues emerge. Consider the Ultimatum and Dictator Games. Students in US universities often offer around 30 to 35 per cent of the pot, while adults drawn from the general population offer closer to 45 to 50 per cent,[46,49] In one striking study, Missouri adults gave an average of 47 per cent compared with 32 per cent from university freshmen.[52] The difference is not random. Students, particularly undergraduates, tend to be younger, less economically experienced, and more attuned to institutional norms of competition and self-interest.

Across studies, being an undergraduate is one of the few demographic factors that reliably predict behaviour in experimental settings. And yet, for decades, the field treated these findings as generalizable. Rather than being treated as a subgroup whose behaviour might be distinctive, students were framed as a neutral proxy for humanity.

This double distortion, WEIRD and student-heavy, has shaped the way behavioural science defines what counts as 'rational', 'normal', or 'universal'. It has led to theories that appear robust under laboratory conditions but often fail to hold up under real world complexity. More importantly, it has created blind spots. Populations whose behaviour doesn't match student norms are seen as anomalies or as culturally bounded exceptions, rather than as legitimate sources of behavioural insight.

As Samuel Salzer, co-founder of the Behavioral AI Institute and founder of Habit Weekly, has argued, the field is still in a 'wild-west era' when it comes to generalizability. Without a serious reckoning with its sampling practices, behavioural science 'can never achieve the best of what our field could become'. That future depends not just on technical refinement, but on conceptual humility; a recognition that foundational theories must be rebuilt on a more diverse and inclusive base.

In the following section, just how much these biased samples matter when applied outside the lab is examined. When student-based findings shape public health recommendations or social policy, the implications are no longer theoretical. They become ethical and potentially dangerous.

Evidence without reach: the risk of misapplied findings

By itself, the overreliance on WEIRD student samples might seem like an academic concern; a limitation to be noted in the fine print of journal articles. But the implications are far more serious. Findings derived from narrow populations are routinely used to inform public policy, development programmes, and global interventions. And when those findings are treated as universally valid, the consequences can extend well beyond the lab.

A striking case came during the early stages of the COVID-19 pandemic, which, as mentioned in Chapter 3, wasn't exactly a glorious period for behavioural science to begin with. As governments worldwide sought guidance on how to influence public behaviour: mask wearing, distancing, compliance with lockdowns; behavioural scientists were called on to provide answers. One of the most widely cited resources was a 2020 paper titled 'Using social and behavioural science to support COVID-19 pandemic response.'[53] Published in *Nature Human Behaviour*, this paper aimed to synthesize decades of behavioural research into actionable insights for policy makers.

This paper was clear, accessible, and comprehensive. It reviewed a range of topics. From social identity and communication to stress and mental health, and offered practical suggestions for shaping pandemic-related behaviours. But as a group of researchers led by Hans Rocha IJzerman later argued in their three-part article series, the underlying evidence base raised serious concerns. In a series of methodological critiques[54–56], they pointed out that many of the studies cited in the paper relied heavily on WEIRD student samples, often from elite US institutions such as Stanford, New York University (NYU), and Cornell. The pandemic, however, wasn't an exclusively WEIRD problem. It was very much global.

For instance, the recommendation that policy makers could leverage 'stress mindsets' to improve public resilience drew on a series of studies conducted with American undergraduates.[57,58] Similarly, claims about how fear shapes perceived threat imminence were based on tightly controlled lab experiments with small, demographically narrow samples.[59] These findings may have internal validity within their original contexts, but their relevance to populations in Lagos, São Paulo, or Mumbai is far from clear.

To their credit, Van Bavel et al acknowledged that the literature they drew from was preliminary and uneven.[53] As they wrote: 'Research on these topics is ongoing and, in many cases, far from settled … Insights and implications for policy should be interpreted with caution … The quality of the evidence cited varies substantially.'

Yet what went unmentioned, and what IJzerman et al found most troubling, was any explicit recognition that the sample base for much of this research was fundamentally limited.[54] The question of who participated in the original studies was effectively invisible, even though that information is essential for assessing how applicable the findings are to broader contexts.

This omission isn't rare. In much of behavioural science, the limitations of the participant pool are often downplayed or bracketed as methodological caveats, acknowledged in footnotes, if at all. But in moments of crisis, when research is being rapidly mobilized to guide public behaviour, those caveats matter more than ever. As IJzerman et al warn, the failure to foreground sample generalizability 'can lead to misguided conclusions when findings are applied outside the narrow context in which they were derived'.[54]

The issue is not that any one study is flawed. It is that huge parts of the literature, such as the parts on stress, compliance, fairness, and risk perception, have largely been built on evidence from the same kinds of people, and then scaled to inform policies affecting everyone else.

By privileging general theories derived from Western academic settings, behavioural science risks projecting its assumptions onto populations whose lives and circumstances differ in meaningful ways. What's presented as a behavioural 'insight' can quickly become a behavioural prescription: one that fails to account for lived experience, structural constraints, or alternative interpretations of risk and responsibility.

These blind spots have practical consequences. As discussed in Chapter 3, even seemingly benign nudges can backfire when transplanted into unfamiliar contexts. An intervention that increases vaccination uptake in one setting may have no effect, or even reduce trust, in another. Social norms messaging that works well on an American college campus might spark defensiveness or alienation in collectivist cultures. Without context-sensitive testing, even the best-intentioned interventions risk causing more harm than good.

This is especially true in the Global South, where behavioural insights are increasingly used in development, education, and public health programmes. Yet many of the tools being deployed, such as decision aids, default effects, stress reappraisals, have never been tested among the populations they are meant to serve. As Dilip Soman puts it: 'We need to consistently test, using diverse methods, not just RCTs, in the situation in which we want to apply the result.'

And even when interventions fail, the burden of explanation often falls on the recipients, not the model. In development contexts, it is not uncommon for failed behavioural trials to be interpreted as evidence of irrationality, lack of comprehension, or local resistance, rather than as signs that the original evidence base was insufficiently inclusive. This framing absolves the theory while pathologizing the population.

These dynamics are not inevitable. They are the result of a field that has grown rapidly in influence but has not yet reckoned with the full implications of its sampling bias. When a narrow slice of humanity continues to serve as the default subject of study, and when that bias is obscured rather than confronted, the risk is not just poor policy. It is a form of epistemic injustice.

The problem is not simply methodological, it is epistemological. Who gets to define behaviour? Whose cognitive models count as rational? And whose lives are treated as legitimate sources of data?

Whose behaviour counts: lessons from global interventions

Behavioural science doesn't just study behaviour, it prescribes it. It defines which decisions are seen as rational, which emotions count as healthy, and which outcomes signify success. These judgements often emerge from theories and tools built in WEIRD contexts and tested on student populations. But exported globally without adaptation, they can misfire, misdiagnose, or even harm.

When methods don't translate

This chapter started with the TSST. Designed to trigger stress responses in participants by combining public speaking with social evaluation, it reliably elevates cortisol levels in Western laboratory settings. But as it turns out, what triggers anxiety in the German men of Trier does not necessarily apply elsewhere.

This kind of cultural misfit is not uncommon. IQ tests such as the Wechsler Intelligence Scale for Children have long been used as universal benchmarks of cognitive ability. Yet in South American Indigenous communities, children performed poorly not because of inherent cognitive deficits, but because the format, assumptions, and language of the test were unfamiliar. A 1997 meta-analysis found that Western IQ tests yielded significantly lower scores for non-WEIRD groups, especially in nonliterate populations. Qualitative follow-ups in sub-Saharan Africa supported this: Indigenous children often demonstrated complex ecological reasoning and problem-solving skills that IQ tests failed to capture.[60]

The issue here is not simply cultural insensitivity. It is an epistemological one. As Hans Rocha IJzerman, CEO of Entrelacs and founder of the Annecy Behavioral Science Lab, warns:

> Humans are diverse, and we experience things like loneliness and social connection differently depending on our age, culture, or even where we live. I believe our measurement tools need to reflect this diversity … By developing more nuanced and adaptable tools, we can better understand these differences, leading to more accurate data.

Tools that fail to reflect this diversity risk not only inaccuracy, but active exclusion.

The education sector offers another cautionary tale. The concept of 'grit', defined as perseverance and passion for long-term goals, gained popularity in the US and was widely adopted globally. But in South Asian classrooms, perseverance was more closely linked to family loyalty than to individual aspiration.[61] Even within the US, one study found that grit correlated with adaptation only among East Asian students, not South Asian students.[62] When applied uncritically, the concept led to confused expectations and mismatched interventions.

When context is the missing variable

Behavioural interventions fail not only when the tools are wrong, but when the entire context is ignored. In East Timor, for example, a maternal health initiative backed by the United Nations Population Fund (UNFPA) provided clinics, ambulances, and trained midwives to rural communities. Yet expectant mothers often refused to use them. From an office in Australia, their behaviour seemed irrational. But as Swee-Hoon Chuah, Professor of Behavioural Economics and Director of the Behavioural Lab at the University of Tasmania, explained, 'If you're not comfortable challenging your current mindset and challenging the assumptions that you currently hold … this is not the field for you. Because you won't be able to understand the reasons for why behaviours exist.' Chuah's fieldwork revealed that the 'ambulance' was a bare truck without any medical equipment, often driven for hours over unpaved roads to a clinic with no running water and a single midwife serving 15 villages. Traditional birth attendants, despite lacking formal training, were trusted and embedded in the community. What appeared to be 'non-compliance' was, in fact, a rational response to system failure.

This disjunction between model and reality appears in other domains too. A systematic review by Dowswell et al (2010) evaluated antenatal care models across seven RCTs involving over 60,000 women.[63] The World Health Organization's (WHO) standard eight-visit protocol was compared with reduced-visit alternatives used in resource-limited settings. While health outcomes were similar, women in low- and middle-income countries reported greater satisfaction with fewer visits due to lower costs and logistical burdens. Adaptation to context, not rigid adherence to global standards, proved more meaningful.

Diet interventions offer another set of lessons. Western dietary guidelines, such as those from the American Heart Association, are often adopted in low- and middle-income countries without modification. In the Arctic and South Pacific, this has led to a 30 per cent increase in obesity and diabetes due to conflicts with traditional high-fat diets.[64] In contrast, community-tailored programmes have worked. In Alaska, Sharma et al (2010) collaborated with Native communities to promote traditional foods like fish and berries.[65] The intervention led to increased omega-3 intake, lower saturated fat consumption, and improved heart health. A culturally adapted version of the Diabetes Prevention Program (DPP) in American Indian communities reduced type 2 diabetes incidence by 58 per cent.[66] And in Iran, adapting the Mediterranean diet to include familiar herbs and cooking methods improved weight and lipid profiles.[67]

As Dilip Soman Canada Research Chair in Behavioural Science and Economics at the Rotman School of Management, puts it, 'We need to better acknowledge the limited portability of our results … and to make it easier for users of our science to understand when things will work and when it might not.'

Autonomy, agency, and the danger of misfit

In the sphere of economic empowerment, exporting behavioural models without context can backfire just as well. In Bangladesh, microfinance programmes encouraged women to become entrepreneurs. But 63 per cent of women reported that male relatives controlled how loans were used.[68] Instead of promoting independence, the programmes exacerbated household tensions. The problem wasn't the intent; it was the model's assumption that individual agency operated similarly across cultures, especially where gender roles were concerned.

Programmes that respect local values have fared better. The MicroLoan Foundation in Southern Africa combines financial services with business mentoring and group-based structures.[69] This communal model builds trust and reinforces shared responsibility. Other programmes now integrate microfinance with healthcare, climate resilience, and education,[70] or channel resources towards collective goal,[71] reflecting a deeper alignment with local norms.

This theme, assumptions about the individual versus the collective, emerges again in global mental health. Western frameworks often dominate the diagnosis and treatment of trauma. But Post-Traumatic

Stress Disorder (PTSD), as defined by the Diagnostic and Statistical Manual of Mental Disorders (DSM), may not map neatly onto non-Western experiences. In Rwanda, post-genocide trauma interventions based on Western talk therapy saw limited uptake.[72] Community mourning rituals, shared, public, and often spiritual, were more aligned with the culture's healing processes.[73]

Research confirms the limits of imposed diagnostic categories. Across countries like Bosnia and Rwanda, Western PTSD scales often failed to identify distress accurately.[73] In Afghanistan, a study of 300 adults showed that culturally adapted PTSD measures predicted functional impairment significantly better than standard models.[74]

Tools such as the Harvard Trauma Questionnaire (HTQ) have since been updated to incorporate culturally specific symptoms.[75] Adaptations used in Nepal cut PTSD symptoms by 48 per cent over 12 weeks.[76] Among Rohingya refugees, similar changes yielded a statistically significant drop in distress.[77] The Afghan Symptom Checklist (ASC), combined with the Self-Reporting Questionnaire-20 (SRQ-20),[b] a mental health screening tool developed by the WHO, has proven especially effective at capturing local expressions of dysphoria and aggression.[78] Group-based Cognitive Behavioural Therapy (CBT) informed by these tools reduced depression symptoms and improved daily functioning.[79]

These cases show the power of integrating local knowledge into scientific tools. As IJzerman notes, 'Without including diverse populations, we're missing out on important insights about human behaviour.' The consequence isn't just missed nuance, it's flawed science.

The politics of problem selection

When tools and models travel badly, the blame often lands on the people, not the science. But the deeper issue is structural: whose priorities define the behavioural science agenda? As Patrick Forscher, Senior Behavioral Scientist at Busara and former Director of its meta-research group, CREME, observes, 'The field is dominated by researchers from Western countries … and as a result, the issues studied often reflect the concerns and interests of those regions.' This misalignment doesn't just exclude topics like land rights or informal economies; it risks making behavioural science irrelevant in large parts of the world.

Brockington and Igoe's (2006) review of over 250 conservation projects found that many displaced Indigenous communities in the name of environmental protection.[80] These efforts were rooted in Western environmental priorities, often leading to loss of livelihood and community conflict. Participatory models work better. Costa Rica's Payments for Ecosystem Services (PES) programme, funded by a fossil fuel tax, cut deforestation by 10 per cent by compensating the landowners.[81] Brazil's participatory mapping helped Indigenous communities protect the land they felt actual ownership over, reducing deforestation by 60 per cent.[82] In Nepal, Community Forest User Groups increased forest cover by 21 per cent over a decade, by having the profits of sustainable timber to be reinvested in the land itself.[83] Kenya's community ranger model and Botswana's community-based tourism efforts both showed that local ownership improved conservation outcomes and livelihoods.[84,85]

Philipe Bujold, who was previously Senior Behavioural Scientist at Rare, described his work at the NGO focused on behaviour-centred conservation. 'From co-designing intervention strategies with local teams to visiting farmers and fishers and hearing firsthand how these programs have improved their lives and the ecosystems they depend on, it's those moments that make the work feel truly meaningful.'

These initiatives didn't just inform communities, they restructured power. Where top-down interventions imposed outside priorities, participatory models embedded community perspectives into design, implementation, and evaluation. They showed that when behavioural science aligns with local governance and values, it doesn't need to convince people to change behaviour; it can support the behaviours already working.

Still, a critical question lingers: what happens when the research agenda itself is misaligned with local needs?

Most behavioural science research continues to reflect the priorities of the institutions that fund and conduct it, primarily located in the US, UK, and Europe. This centralization skews the field towards topics familiar to Western policy makers: retirement savings, tax compliance, climate action, and digital misinformation. All important issues, but not the only issues.

Umar Taj, Associate Professor of Behavioural Science at Warwick Business School and founder of Nudgeathon, offers a pointed reflection on the consequences:

> I feel that behavioural scientists aren't really tackling wicked problems. I do a fair bit of work on preventing violent extremism. I hardly come across behavioural scientists who are doing this … I think this is a consequence of most behavioural scientists being exposed to a very similar kind of environment (from and based in WEIRD countries) and that's also the environment they're working in. But if you just think globally, there's a lot bigger problems than tax compliance and pension savings.

When researchers work in environments that shield them from the most severe global challenges, those challenges don't enter the research pipeline. The result, Taj notes, is a narrow intellectual ecosystem. Violent extremism, corruption, land displacement, food insecurity, these are urgent behavioural issues, yet relatively few behavioural scientists engage with them. Why? Because the field's centre of gravity is not just intellectual; it is geographical.

Taj continues:

> I'm disappointed that I'm not seeing more breadth in the domains that behavioural scientists are working on. To solve for this, I think we need to encourage young behavioural science students who come from diverse backgrounds, and when I say diverse backgrounds, I mean from different regions in the world, and I think this problem will slowly start to solve itself. They'll learn behavioural science wherever they can, and take that information back to a context where it matters. At least I hope so.

That hope is critical. But structural barriers make it difficult for researchers from non-WEIRD contexts to shape the field. According to the United Nations Educational, Scientific and Cultural Organization (UNESCO), no African country currently spends even

1 per cent of their gross domestic product (GDP) on research.[86] In India, research funding is often tied to short-term political aims, leaving behavioural science, particularly psychology, under-resourced and institutionally marginalized.[87] Without funding, foundational studies don't happen. And without foundational research, behavioural insights remain shallow or inapplicable.

As Forscher et al point out, when behavioural science is absent, economics tends to fill the gap.[56] In India, for example, economists, not behavioural scientists, have led research on public health, caste-based discrimination, gender quotas and monetary policy. Behavioural science is missing from policy conversations where it could offer unique contributions; precisely because it hasn't been embedded into these ecosystems.

This absence perpetuates a cycle: a lack of presence limits impact, which weakens the case for funding, which in turn restricts the scope and location of future research. As Sakshi Ghai, Assistant Professor in the Department of Psychological and Behavioural Science at the London School of Economics (LSE), puts it:

> Another major challenge is funding. It's one of those issues that people know exists but isn't often openly discussed. The reality is that research agendas tend to be dominated by wealthier countries that have the resources and funding capabilities. This creates a sort of feedback loop ... The structure of funding right now is such that it supports the existing power structures, which is problematic when trying to foster genuine diversity.

If behavioural science continues to revolve around WEIRD institutions and researchers, it risks shrinking its purpose, optimizing Western systems rather than advancing a global understanding of human behaviour.

Who gets to do the research

Taj's vision of a bottom-up transformation, where young scholars from underrepresented regions build behavioural science knowledge from the ground up, is a powerful one. But it is also nothing but idealistic without institutional support. A field that continues to concentrate funding, authorship, and editorial power in the Global North cannot claim to speak for the world. Patrick Forscher echoes this ambition:

> I also hope we see an evolution in the kinds of problems the field addresses. Behavioral science has been too focused on Western-centric issues, driven by researchers from the US and Europe. Over the next decade, I'd like to see a broader representation of voices from under-represented regions like Africa and Latin America. This would not only diversify the topics we study … but also make the field more globally relevant.

Yet despite growing awareness of this imbalance, the structure of the field continues to exclude. US-based researchers dominate authorship, editorship, and awards in international psychology journals.[54] One audit found that less than 1 per cent of first authors and study samples in top psychology journals came from Africa.[87] Across the Psychological Science Accelerator, a consortium explicitly built to diversify research, 65 per cent of members are from the US, Canada, and Europe, while less than 1 per cent represent South Asia, Latin America, the Caribbean, or sub-Saharan Africa.[88] The Society for the Improvement of Psychological Science shows a similar pattern, with 53 per cent of members from the US and Canada.[89]

This isn't just a matter of demographics; it shapes the science itself. When submissions from the Global South do make it to leading journals, they are accepted at lower rates.[55] In top developmental psychology journals, less than 3 per cent of authors from 2006 to 2010 were from Central/South America, Africa, Asia, or the Middle East.[90] In international development, a field where behavioural science is increasingly applied, only 16 per cent of papers in the top 20 journals (1990–2019) came from the Global South.[91]

Why does this happen? The reasons are structural. Wealthier countries fund more research and house more institutions. Publishing in English advantages native speakers. Hiring, grant-making, and peer review often favour familiar networks.

This feedback loop, as Ghai has called it, is especially harmful when research is conducted in low- and middle-income countries, but led entirely from afar. So-called parachute research remains common: Western scholars secure grants, design studies, and publish findings, while local researchers are brought in late to translate instruments, recruit participants, or liaise with communities. Despite this critical labour, they are frequently excluded from authorship or decision-making.

Even when local researchers are involved, institutional disincentives persist. Early-career scholars are warned against listing unfamiliar or unprestigious collaborators, as this can dilute their perceived contribution in competitive hiring or grant evaluations. Meanwhile, funders typically prioritize research that demonstrates domestic impact, limiting resources for capacity building abroad or for fostering equitable international partnerships.

The result? Behavioural science gains access to non-WEIRD populations, but does little to build research ecosystems within them. Without long-term investment in training, infrastructure, and mentorship, most local researchers remain confined to data collection roles. They are rarely given space to shape the research agenda, question the assumptions baked into imported theories, or develop locally grounded alternatives.

These dynamics create a troubling paradox. Behavioural science claims to be expanding its reach; working in villages in Kenya, slums in India, refugee camps in Jordan. But the intellectual authorship of that work remains overwhelmingly Western. As long as Global South researchers are relegated to secondary roles, the field will reproduce a colonial logic: data extracted from the margins to serve the centres. As Sarah Osman, founder of Osman Advisory Services and a behavioural science consultant with over two decades of experience in global development, reflects: 'I would love to create an encyclopaedia of what behavioural scientists in the Global South are doing … there might be different social psychology theories that are out there that we don't know enough about.'

Equity requires more than invitations to collaborate. It requires redistributing power. That means funding infrastructure in low-income regions, not just one-off fieldwork. It means supporting long-term, locally led research programmes. It means recognizing qualitative methods and Indigenous psychologies as legitimate forms of knowledge, even if they don't follow dominant norms.

Currently, many promising research traditions remain marginalized. Indigenous psychologies, built in Asia, Africa, and Latin America, often rely on methods the mainstream devalues: ethnography, oral history, community participatory research. These approaches offer insight into relational selves, collective trauma, and moral worldviews that don't map neatly onto Western taxonomies. Yet they remain under-cited, underfunded, and under-published.

Some funders, such as the Wellcome Trust and the Global Challenges Research Fund, have started investing in local capacity and infrastructure.[55] But within behavioural science, such efforts remain rare. Many multi-country projects still operate as top-down partnerships, with little accountability to local priorities. Instead of training researchers who can shape theory from their contexts, the field continues to extract data for theories developed elsewhere.

The cost of this is not just ethical; it is epistemic. When behavioural science sidelines the perspectives of those most familiar with the social, political, and cultural nuances of their communities, it limits its own capacity to understand behaviour. The goal should not be to simply 'include' Global South researchers in a Western project. It should be to rebuild the project itself, so that behavioural science emerges as a truly collaborative, global discipline.

Towards an inclusive behavioural science

If the discipline of behavioural science aspires to be global in relevance and reach, it must first confront the structural exclusions that have long shaped who participate in knowledge production, whose lives are studied, and which ways of knowing are valued. As Ghai puts it, 'We're all aware that this is an issue ... there's more awareness than ever about the lack of diversity, especially around the WEIRD bias.' Yet awareness alone is insufficient. 'Behavioural science', she continues, 'like so many other fields, suffers from the classic "intention-action gap," where we have good intentions, but the actions to bridge that gap aren't always there or easy to achieve'.

This gap is not just a product of individual inertia, but of institutional logics that continue to reward familiarity over innovation, and expediency over equity. Calls to 'diversify' the field often risk being co-opted into vague gestures of inclusion that leave underlying hierarchies intact. To move beyond this impasse, behavioural science must engage in a more radical reckoning, with its participants, its practitioners, and its practices. Meaningful change is not only possible; it is essential. But it will require nothing less than a structural transformation of the systems that shape how behavioural knowledge is created, circulated, and applied.

Step 1. Reform incentives to reward representative research

Efforts to diversify behavioural science often stall not because researchers are unaware of the problem, but because the system they work within disincentivizes doing anything about it. Publishing quickly, frequently, and in high-impact journals is the currency of career progression. These journals overwhelmingly favour research that uses easy-to-access, Western student samples, employs familiar methodologies, and avoids the logistical complexity of working in diverse or under-resourced contexts. Under current norms, taking the time to collect representative data, build local partnerships, or adapt measures to new populations often means professional penalties.

To change this, journals and funders need to start valuing the work they currently overlook. At a minimum, all publications should require detailed demographic reporting, not just age and gender, but region, language, ethnicity, and socioeconomic indicators. Journals should explicitly encourage research with underrepresented populations through submission fee waivers, fast-tracked review for context-specific studies, and special issues tied to Global South themes.

More aggressively, there should be limits on the volume of convenience-sample research accepted. If a study relies entirely on undergraduates from elite institutions, authors should be required to justify its external validity. The burden of proof must shift; it's no longer enough to assume generalizability from WEIRD samples by default.

Critically, hiring and promotion committees should factor representativeness and social relevance into their assessment criteria. Without institutional reform, inclusive research will remain the exception. The current incentive structure rewards familiarity, not impact. Fix that, and everything else becomes easier. As Sam Salzer, co-founder of the Behavioral AI Institute and founder of *Habit Weekly*, puts it: 'Diversity is valuable in all contexts, but especially in a field like ours ... Without diversity we can never achieve the best of what our field could become.'

Practical steps

- Mandate comprehensive demographic reporting: Journals should require detailed participant data (region, language, ethnicity, socioeconomic status (SES) with noncompliant submissions desk-rejected.
- Create publication incentives: Offer fee waivers, fast-tracked review, and themed issues highlighting Global South research.
- Shift the burden of proof: Require authors using WEIRD convenience samples to justify generalizability, not assume it.
- Embed representativeness in hiring criteria: Tenure and promotion committees should explicitly evaluate whether a researcher's work engages diverse contexts.
- Introduce recognition awards: Establish prestigious prizes for studies that exemplify representativeness and societal impact, reinforcing career value.

Reforming incentives will not guarantee global representation, but it will realign the profession's reward structures. When researchers are no longer penalized for inclusive work, systemic inertia gives way to innovation. By making representativeness a career asset rather than a liability, behavioural science can begin to correct its skewed foundations.

Step 2. Democratize the flow of research funding

Efforts to diversify behavioural science often begin with rhetoric but stall at resourcing. Even as research outputs become increasingly global in ambition, the money that enables them continues to flow through a narrow pipeline. This financial asymmetry constrains not just who can do research, but what types of problems are studied, and by whom.

Research conducted in underrepresented contexts is typically more expensive than work with convenience samples. It requires local knowledge, culturally adapted tools, extensive piloting, and often higher participant compensation. And yet, funding decisions still favour proposals that mirror established paradigms, in familiar settings, using familiar methods. As a result, the kinds of research that might challenge prevailing theories or surface novel insights from the Global South often never get funded in the first place.

To shift this pattern, grant-making institutions must move beyond lip service to diversity and embed inclusion in their funding mechanisms. That begins with offering targeted calls for research focused on underrepresented populations, accompanied by simplified application processes and realistic timelines. Critically, funding must also prioritize locally grounded priorities, not just Western-led agendas transplanted elsewhere. Ghai captures this frustration clearly:

> Researchers in low- and middle-income countries struggle to secure the same resources, which impacts the diversity of the science itself. This imbalance in funding means that the voices from the Global South and other underrepresented regions are often left out, even if they're working on highly relevant issues. The structure of funding right now is such that it supports the existing power structures, which is problematic when trying to foster genuine diversity.

Examples such as the Adapted HTQ or the ASC show the value of research rooted in context. But these are exceptions, not norms. To change that, funders, including governments, multilaterals, and NGOs, must shift from evaluating projects through the lens of institutional prestige and instead assess their real world relevance and equity of collaboration.

Finally, funding models must actively incentivize capacity building. This includes supporting local PhD programmes, infrastructure, and long-term institutional partnerships, rather than one-off data collection contracts. By redirecting money towards context-specific expertise, we create the conditions under which Global South researchers can lead the work, not just assist with it.

If funding systems don't change, no amount of rhetoric will diversify behavioural science. Redistribution isn't a luxury; it's a prerequisite.

Practical steps

- Create targeted calls for Global South research: Dedicated funding rounds should explicitly support projects led by or centred in underrepresented contexts.

- Simplify application processes: Shorter forms, translated guidance, and extended deadlines reduce barriers for less-resourced institutions.
- Prioritize local agendas: Require proposals to demonstrate alignment with locally identified needs, not just Western priorities transplanted abroad.
- Fund capacity building directly: Allocate part of each grant to local PhD programmes, infrastructure, and training.
- Balance funding criteria: Assess applications based on contextual relevance and collaboration equity, not just institutional prestige.

Redistributing resources is not charity but necessity. Without structural changes to funding, diversity in behavioural science will remain rhetorical. By shifting where the money flows and whose priorities it reflects, the field can broaden its intellectual base and make space for genuinely global contributions.

Step 3. Reform the publication pipeline to dismantle structural bias

For researchers in the Global South, the hurdles do not end at funding. Even when projects are designed with contextual nuance and data is painstakingly collected in difficult settings, the gatekeeping mechanisms of behavioural science often render such work invisible. One review of developmental psychology journals found that less than 3 per cent of authors between 2006 and 2010 came from Central or South America, Africa, Asia, or the Middle East,[90] an indictment of whose voices are allowed to shape global theory.

A central culprit is the persistence of implicit bias throughout the publication pipeline, from researchers to reviewers to editors. While direct evidence of discrimination against Global South studies is limited, several analyses suggest a consistent pattern of bias in favour of Global North research, with disproportionately higher rejection rates for studies conducted elsewhere.[87]

One particularly revealing study found that US-based researchers were significantly more likely to recommend an identical abstract for peer review when the author was listed as being from the UK rather than Malawi.[92] This finding underlines how credibility in behavioural science can be shaped more by geography and institutional affiliation than by the actual quality of research.

Addressing these disparities requires more than good intentions. It requires structural reform. Journals must adopt double-blind peer review as standard, concealing both author identity and institutional affiliation. Research has shown that such systems reduce favouritism towards prestigious institutions, offering a fairer platform for underrepresented scholars to gain recognition.

In parallel, journals must begin to systematically track and report the demographic and geographic composition of their author pool and accepted papers. These metrics should not sit in the footnotes of annual reports but be used to drive policy changes, such as regional support initiatives, editorial targets, or reviewer training.

The goal is not merely to eliminate bias. It is to break down a system that has consistently rewarded proximity to prestige and power. Until the publication process is rebuilt to recognize excellence across context, language, and geography, behavioural science cannot credibly claim to be a global discipline.

Practical steps

- Adopt double-blind peer review as default: Conceal both author names and institutions to reduce geographic and prestige bias.
- Track author demographics transparently: Journals should publish annual reports on the geographic and institutional diversity of submissions and acceptances.
- Invest in reviewer training: Provide mandatory sessions on recognizing implicit bias in peer review, tailored to global equity.
- Create regional editorial boards: Appoint editors from underrepresented regions with decision-making authority, not token consultation.
- Support translation and editing services: Fund low-cost language assistance for scholars publishing in English to level the playing field.

Fixing the publication pipeline is essential if behavioural science is to move from rhetoric to reality on diversity. By making double-blind review and demographic accountability standard, journals can transform themselves from gatekeepers of exclusion to engines of equity.

Step 4. Replace extractive research with equitable collaboration

Calls to diversify behavioural science often overlook a more entrenched problem: that the same structures claiming to elevate global voices continue to marginalize them through extractive research models. Too often, Global North institutions conduct studies in the Global South without meaningful local involvement: collecting data, publishing in high-impact journals, and monopolizing recognition. Local researchers, even when instrumental in fieldwork, translation, and community access, are frequently left out of authorship, funding decisions, and theoretical framing.

This 'parachute' approach is not merely a failure of etiquette; it reflects and reinforces global inequities in knowledge production. To move beyond this, equitable collaboration must be institutionalized, not improvised. Journals and funders must require formal partnerships that include Global South researchers as co-designers and co-authors from project inception to publication. Authorship criteria should explicitly recognize community engagement, cultural adaptation, and linguistic translation as intellectual contributions. Funding structures should allocate a ring-fenced proportion to training, infrastructure, and leadership development for local institutions.

However, collaboration is not only a matter of recognition, but also a matter of access. Even when partnerships exist in principle, researchers in the Global South face concrete barriers to participation. As IJzerman has noted, 'Political instability and lack of resources in many parts of the world also pose challenges for expanding representation in research.' These include visa restrictions that prevent attendance at international conferences, publication fees that price out contributors, and persistent internet instability that excludes scholars from virtual events.[54] Despite the rise of online formats, access remains uneven and precarious.

Meaningful reform will require dedicated funds to address these logistical challenges; funds that are rarely prioritized in current grant structures. If left unaddressed, they risk undermining even well-intentioned partnerships. Equitable behavioural science cannot be built on relationships that rely on one-sided access to power, infrastructure, and visibility. Levelling the playing field requires dismantling not just ideological hierarchies, but also practical ones.

Practical steps

- Mandate co-authorship for local collaborators: Require Global South partners who contribute data, translation, or engagement to be included as co-authors.
- Redefine authorship criteria: Recognize community engagement and adaptation work as intellectual, not auxiliary, contributions.
- Allocate ring-fenced funding: Require grants to include dedicated portions for local training and infrastructure.
- Remove access barriers: Fund visas, conference fees, and internet support so Global South researchers can fully participate.
- Audit partnership equity: Funders and journals should require disclosure of collaboration terms and ensure fairness in authorship, leadership, and recognition.

Equitable collaboration is not optional; it is the difference between global science and scientific extraction. By ensuring fair recognition, access, and resourcing, behavioural science can transform Global South researchers from silent contributors into equal partners.

Step 5. Build mutual capacity through long-term exchange

Capacity building, however, must be bidirectional. Yet many Global North led projects still operate under the implicit assumption that capacity building is a unidirectional process, from 'experts' to 'recipients', from well-funded institutions to the under-resourced periphery. This framing both underestimates Global South researchers and impedes the mutual learning that effective interventions require.

IJzerman cautions that even the best-designed partnerships often fall short because 'Global North researchers are frequently unprepared for the unique challenges in Global South settings.' Such challenges, be they linguistic, political, or institutional, are not minor technicalities, but fundamental features of the research landscape. When misunderstood or ignored, they compromise the validity and relevance of behavioural science itself.

Models for mutual exchange already exist. The University of Missouri and University of the Western Cape partnership (UMSAEP), for instance, was established to build long-term institutional ties through joint teaching, co-authorship, and mentorship, rather than short-term field placements. Similarly, the collaboration between Florida International University and Pontificia Universidad Javeriana focuses on Amazonian conservation, explicitly emphasizing reciprocal knowledge creation. These models prioritize humility over hierarchy and process over product.

To replicate such models at scale, funders must support institutional relationships, not just individual collaborations. Exchange programmes should be built around extended residencies, co-designed curricula, and shared infrastructure. Critically, they must account for the different starting points of partner institutions: financial parity is not enough if one side lacks grant-writing experience, administrative support, or even reliable internet access.

In other words, capacity building must be mutual, institutionalized, and long-term. Otherwise, we risk replacing one set of extractive relationships with another: more collaborative in form, but no less unequal in substance.

Practical steps

- Fund institutional partnerships, not one-offs: Support multi-year agreements between universities and research centres rather than short-term placements.
- Develop reciprocal exchange programmes: Facilitate Global North researchers spending extended time in Global South institutions, and vice versa.
- Co-design curricula and training: Jointly build graduate and professional training programmes that reflect shared priorities.
- Level the institutional playing field: Provide grant-writing support, administrative resources, and infrastructure for under-resourced partners.
- Document and share mutual learning: Publish case studies of reciprocal benefits, not just outputs from Global South 'sites'.

Capacity building will only matter if it is reciprocal. Long-term, institutionalized exchanges make knowledge-sharing a two-way street and shift behavioural science away from colonial patterns. By embedding mutuality, the field enriches itself as much as it empowers others.

Step 6. Diversify methods to reflect diverse realities

Efforts to decolonize behavioural science often begin with who we study and who conducts the research, but they must also extend to how we study. For too long, methodological gatekeeping has privileged a narrow set of tools: randomized controlled trials, psychometric surveys, and laboratory experiments designed in Global North contexts. These tools are not inherently flawed, but they carry embedded assumptions about what counts as valid knowledge, who gets to generate it, and how it should be expressed.

As IJzerman argues, 'a one-size-fits-all approach isn't effective', particularly when measurement tools are calibrated to WEIRD populations. Research rooted in lived experience demands methodological flexibility. Yet qualitative methods, ethnography, narrative interviews, and participatory action research, remain undervalued. Critics cite concerns about replicability and bias, but such critiques often mask a deeper discomfort: these methods threaten the supposed universality of behavioural science by insisting that context matters.

That discomfort is no small issue. Quantitative dominance has real consequences. Tools such as the HTQ or common depression scales may misrepresent or overlook psychological distress in cultures where symptoms are expressed somatically, relationally, or spiritually. In such settings, adapted instruments, such as the ASC or culturally developed scales from Zimbabwe and Uganda, offer a more accurate reflection of mental health realities. But they are rarely cited, let alone standardized, in global literature.

The path forward is not to abandon quantitative rigour, but to expand what rigour means. Journals and funders must support pluralism in method, including longer timelines and different forms of evidence. Interdisciplinary partnerships, with anthropologists, community organizers, and local experts, should be actively encouraged.

As Sam Salzer puts it, behavioural science must 'embrace the diversity and complexity of human behaviour' and 'provide users with more control and autonomy'. To do that, the field must finally take method seriously; not as a neutral toolkit, but as a political and epistemological choice.

Practical steps

- Legitimize qualitative and participatory methods: Journals and funders must treat ethnography, narrative inquiry, and action research as credible forms of evidence.
- Support adaptation of instruments: Allocate resources for adapting and validating measurement tools for new cultural contexts.
- Promote interdisciplinary collaboration: Encourage partnerships with anthropologists, sociologists, and local practitioners who bring methodological breadth.
- Redefine rigour beyond RCTs: Require justification of method choice in terms of context, not hierarchy of methods.
- Incentivize mixed-methods research: Offer grants and publication routes that explicitly reward the integration of qualitative and quantitative approaches.

Diversifying methods is not dilution but enrichment. By broadening its epistemological toolkit, behavioural science becomes capable of capturing the complexity of human behaviour across cultures. Only then can it credibly claim universality.

Conclusion

At the start of this book, Colin Strong reflected that behavioural science is at a 'tricky' point; a point at which researchers are demanding the field confront its assumptions about power, representation, and relevance. This chapter has shown just how deeply this issue runs through questions of inclusion. For too long, behavioural science has been shaped by WEIRD populations, producing insights that are often exported globally but rarely adapted meaningfully. Neela Saldanha, Executive Director of the Yale Research Initiative on Innovation & Scale (Y-RISE), whose career has spanned over a decade of work in non-WEIRD contexts, already noted in 2019, that she hopes 'to see more research in non-WEIRD contexts', and that sentiment has been echoed by many others. But recognition of the problem is no longer enough. The challenge now is redesign.

What lies ahead is not simply a more diverse behavioural science, but a better one. The reforms proposed here, rebalancing incentives, funding research beyond the Global North, reforming peer review, and investing in reciprocal partnerships, seek to shift the structural defaults of the field. These are not peripheral concerns. They define whose knowledge counts, who gets published, and who is allowed to set the research agenda.

Yet inclusion is not only about who we study or who does the studying. It is also about how we do the science. That is why this chapter ends with a call to diversify methods. A field constrained to experimental designs and standardized measures, developed in and for WEIRD settings, cannot produce insights that resonate globally. As Chaning Jang asked, 'Could we do something similar in the developing country context in non-WEIRD settings? Can we even start spreading that idea?'

This is the work of the next chapter: to explore how method, and the assumptions embedded within it, shapes what behavioural science sees and what it misses. Because if the field is truly to become global, inclusive, and impactful, its tools must evolve alongside its vision.

5

Behavioural Science Will Be More Than Experiments

> The general success of behavioral economics, in my historical accounting, came from importing basic concepts and methods from psychology and putting them in the right place, going from compelling thought experiments (Thaler's great skill, among others) to careful experimental demonstrations, to simple models and structural model applications to field data.
>
> Colin Camerer (2020)

Introduction

Behavioural science has been built on a powerful methodological promise: if we can isolate causes cleanly, we can change behaviour responsibly. As Robert Kirby Professor of Behavioral Economics at Caltech, Colin Camerer argues, the field's success came from importing psychological insight and moving from thought experiments to careful experimental demonstrations and structural models applied to field data. In practice, that promise has often meant privileging a narrow slice of methods, especially laboratory and field experiments, and above all: the RCT. RCTs brought credibility and clarity; they also trained us to ask certain kinds of questions (what works? for how much?) while too often muting another (why?). As Scott Rick, Associate Professor of Marketing at the University of Michigan's Ross School of Business, puts it, 'elegant lab experiments will only take us so far', particularly when human decisions are embedded in messy, real world contexts.

This chapter argues for methodological breadth without sacrificing rigour. It traces how our experimental backbone formed, why its dominance persists, and where it breaks: when simplified tasks underplay stakes and motivation, when samples are narrow, and when design environments diverge from lived ones. As Henry Stott, co-founder and Managing Director at Decision Technology and Head of Research at Agio Ratings, notes, many studies 'don't replicate the actual decision environment, and the decision environment is nearly everything'. That critique isn't an anti-experiment stance; it's a call to align method with mechanism.

Two consequences follow. First, external validity problems: findings that travel poorly beyond their test bed. Second, explanatory gaps: estimates of what without enough why. Both are amplified by who we study (disproportionately WEIRD populations), which limits claims to universality and obscures variation across settings and identities.

The path forward is methodological pluralism with discipline: integrating qualitative approaches (ethnography, interviews, and narrative analysis, to name a few) to surface mechanisms and meanings; using analytics, data science, and adaptive designs to personalize and scale; and reserving RCTs for the questions they're best at answering. The goal isn't to replace one orthodoxy with another, but to build a mixed methods toolkit that is cumulative, portable, and honest about its limits. Only then can we claim to study behaviour as it is lived, not just as it is measured.

A concise history of how we got here

Chris Starmer, Professor of Economics at the University of Nottingham, once reflected that, as an undergraduate, he 'had no idea that economists could employ experiments as useful research tools', since the 'conventional wisdom of the time … was that economics is a non-experimental science'. Yet, because he was drawn to methodology, the chance to engage in something 'novel, or even slightly taboo, was irresistible'. His story captures the wider shift in psychology and economics: from entrenched traditions to the acceptance of experimentation.

In psychology, this began with Wilhelm Wundt's laboratory in 1879, offering controlled environments to isolate variables and test causality.[93] By the mid-20th century, landmark studies by Asch, Bandura, and Milgram had made the lab central to behavioural research. Economics was slower to embrace experimentation, but Vernon Smith's pioneering work challenged resistance, showing that market behaviour could be tested empirically.[94] Kahneman and Tversky's work on cognitive biases and Prospect Theory then helped bring psychology and economics into closer dialogue, while games such as the Ultimatum, Dictator, Trust, and Beauty Contest became disciplinary staples.

The lab's dominance, however, was never uncontested. Concerns over external validity have pushed researchers into the field, seeking data that reflects real world complexity. As Scott Rick has observed, 'Publishing norms still seem to incentivize lower-risk, easier-to-conduct research', but 'elegant lab experiments will only take us so far'. To address 'big, urgent problems', behavioural scientists must spend more time 'testing our ideas in messy, real-world settings'. A sentiment echoed by many scientists.

Laboratory studies offer control, precision, and causal inference, but their artificiality can be limiting. Generosity in dictator games, for example, is typically around 28 per cent of the endowment,[95] far higher than real world donations. In 2021, the average American contribution was $574, a fraction of income;[96] in Australia, $886.75 or just 0.40 per cent of taxable income.[97] Real giving occurs amid competing demands and constraints absent in labs.

The same pattern appears in financial decision-making. Germann and Merkle (2023) found that when fees were equal, 56 per cent of participants chose a robo-adviser, rising above 80 per cent when it was cheaper, with 63 per cent still favouring it by the final round.[98] The implication: price drives uptake. Yet in 2024, robo-advisers in the US were expected to manage $1.46 trillion,[99] only 3 per cent of total assets.[100] In Germany, this number was $18.99 billion, a mere 0.22 per cent. Outside the lab, trust, familiarity, and inertia appear more decisive than cost alone.

Stott has cautioned that even strong experiments can miss real decision environments. In the robo-adviser study, four differences stand out: simplicity (short, repetitive rounds with feedback versus protracted real investing); stakes (earnings of €4–€30 versus significant sums associated with real word investments); sample (young, female students versus typical investors); and motivation (investors seek reassurance and guidance as much as cost savings, benefits Vanguard estimates as an 'Adviser's Alpha' of 3 per cent annually[101]).

Such divergences underline the central challenge: experiments clarify by controlling context, but in doing so risk losing relevance. The question is not whether to abandon the laboratory, but how best to balance its strengths with approaches that capture the complexity of the world beyond it.

Moving towards field experiments

John List, the Kenneth C. Griffin Distinguished Service Professor of Economics at the University of Chicago and Chief Economist at Walmart, has argued that much of the early evidence in behavioural and experimental economics came from laboratory settings 'too far removed from more natural settings', the very contexts researchers sought to understand. For him, the key challenge is 'how to move from theory into formal testing in the field to a much larger extent'. Field experiments, he believes, will 'take behavioural economics to another level … I think they have already. But … that interplay will continue.' His point captures a broader shift: laboratories offer control, but field experiments promise realism, albeit with added methodological and practical complexity.

Behavioural scientists increasingly test interventions in environments shaped by real social norms, constraints, and distractions. The UK's BIT showed the potential of this approach through its tax compliance trials with His Majesty's Revenue and Customs (HMRC).[102] By varying reminder letters, using social norms, personalization, simplification, and deterrence, the team found that telling recipients 'most people pay on time' increased compliance by five percentage points, yielding millions in revenue.

The Busara Centre in Kenya addressed low savings among low-income individuals.[103] Testing four short message service (SMS) reminder strategies with 1,800 participants, they found simple reminders increased savings by 5.9 per cent, goal-based by 12.5 per cent, commitment messages by 28.4 per cent, and combining goals with commitments by 36.3 per cent. The pattern highlighted the power of personalization and goal commitment in shaping financial behaviour.

Other domains reveal similar promise. The Dutch Ministry of Social Affairs improved job application completions by simplifying processes (15 per cent), using personalized deadline reminders (10 per cent), and peer comparison messages (6 per cent).[104] In the energy sector, Opower's large-scale conservation trial used household reports with peer comparisons and smiley-face feedback to reduce usage by 2 to 3 per cent.[105] In charitable giving, Karlan and List showed that matching donations, emotional framing, and public recognition could each significantly boost contributions.[106]

Together, these examples demonstrate the strength of field experiments: not only showing that behavioural interventions work, but revealing where, for whom, and at what scale.

Drawbacks of field experiments

Field experiments are often celebrated as behavioural science's greatest strength. They bring theories into contact with lived reality, showing not just whether interventions can work but how they fare in messy, unpredictable conditions. Yet the power of field trials is frequently overstated. Beneath their allure lie formidable obstacles: high costs, long timelines, political sensitivities, and cultural resistance to experimentation itself. These frictions have prompted behavioural scientists to reconsider their toolkit, increasingly turning to data analytics, data science, and AI as ways to preserve empiricism while avoiding some of its most intractable barriers.

The hidden costs of field experiments

The promise of field experiments lies in external validity, but that promise comes at a steep price. Unlike laboratory studies, which can run with dozens of participants in weeks, or online studies, which can run thousands of participants per week, field trials often require thousands of subjects, tracked across long horizons, embedded in real organisational systems. Designing such studies demands not just statistical power but institutional commitment, infrastructure, delivery mechanisms, and careful monitoring.

Government-led studies are especially demanding. In Australia, improving organ donation registration has involved multi-year programmes of trials, surveys, consultations, and policy development before implementation.[107] Businesses face different but equally significant hurdles. The much-cited robo-adviser study, while compelling in the lab, was never tested in the field first because building a compliant financial advisory system required millions in software, data science, and user experience investment, costs prohibitive for a trial.

Even successful trials are vulnerable to shocks. Banerjee et al's microfinance studies collided with the Global Financial Crisis, complicating inference and dampening effects.[108] Replication introduces another difficulty: Opower's peer comparison energy letters produced strong effects in the US, weaker ones in the UK (0.5 to 1 per cent),[109] and mixed or negative results in Germany, where low-energy users paradoxically increased consumption.[110] These discrepancies reflect cultural and contextual variation, underlining that success in one place does not guarantee success elsewhere.

In short, field experiments generate insight at scale, but they do so at great expense and under constant threat from noise and contextual variation.

Resistance to experimentation

Even when buy-in and resources are secured, another barrier looms: human resistance to being experimented upon. Nick Chater, Professor of Behavioural Science at the Warwick Business School and Director of Decision Technology, put it starkly: 'my biggest frustration is that human nature makes us resistant to systematic experimentation, even when the evidence could guide us towards better decisions'. RCTs remain behavioural science's methodological cornerstone, but the idea of random allocation often clashes with political and ethical realities. Policy makers balk at withholding interventions from control groups, fearing accusations of unfairness. Firms hesitate to risk customer relationships by exposing them to inferior treatments. Duflo and Banerjee write candidly about persuading poor communities to accept trials where some households receive aid while others wait (because they're in a different treatment or in the control group).[111]

And research seemed to support these concerns. Meyer and colleagues documented 'experiment aversion' across 16 studies and nearly 6,000 participants: people preferred universal but untested policies to careful trials, motivated by distrust or the belief that policy makers and other experts 'should already know' the right answer.[112] For governments, this scepticism is toxic: even when evidence could reduce uncertainty, the optics of experimentation threaten reputational damage.

However, this evidence is less robust than it initially appears. In a direct reply, Mislavsky et al demonstrated that the reported effects were largely driven by a statistical artefact, and that opposition is likely to emerge in almost any comparison, because people 'do not dislike a corporate experiment more than they dislike its worst condition'.[113] Building on this, research by Mažar et al using variations in scenario wording, recruitment platforms, and countries in a sample of more than 5,200 participants, found no evidence that experiment aversion generalized across contexts.[114]

Taken together, these findings suggest that while field experiments promise clarity, their reception is often clouded by assumptions rather than evidence. In practice, resistance may be driven less by public hostility than by the beliefs of those responsible for authorizing experiments, who fear, without strong empirical grounding, that experimentation itself could damage public or customer perceptions.

Adapting the 'gold standard'

Ian Fannon, Managing Director at Claremont a strategic communications agency focused on behaviour change communications for social good, has observed that 'the tendency among some purists [is] to believe that anything short of a RCT isn't good enough evidence to base decisions on'. Yet, he adds, in the real world 'most of our clients have neither the time or the budget for RCTs when weighing up how to tackle a social issue – and so we have to do the best we can within those limitations'.

Researchers have responded with pragmatic adaptations. Stepped-wedge designs phase in interventions gradually so all participants eventually benefit; the UK's BIT used this in the UK's National Health Service (NHS) to test text-message appointment reminders.[115]

Adaptive trials evolve as data arrives: BIT's fine-payment trial tested multiple reminder messages simultaneously, then focused on the most effective mid-stream.[116] In the private sector, RCTs have been reframed as A/B testing. Google's famous 2009 trial of 41 shades of blue may seem frivolous, but it generated $200 million in advertising revenue by identifying the most effective colour.[117]

These innovations preserve rigour while softening resistance. Yet they do not eliminate the core difficulties of cost, complexity, and political risk. The deeper question remains: if field trials are so fraught, where should behavioural science turn next?

From trials to data

One answer lies in the data exhaust of digital life. As Carolyn Freeman, Applied CyberPsychology Consultant at Cybercology, argues, 'adding the technology dimension may tweak and enhance this understanding and help us to be much better informed behavioural scientists. It's a very, very exciting time to be in this field'.

Unlike RCTs, data analytics does not require randomization or new infrastructure. Every digital platform already collects behavioural traces: log-ins, clicks, transactions, and shares. These data streams enable scientists to evaluate interventions retrospectively, uncover heterogeneity, and detect unintended effects.

For example, Levi and Benartzi's 'Mind the App' study used transaction data to show how mobile banking apps altered discretionary spending, particularly among lower-income users.[118] Shah et al analyzed retirement saving, revealing that appeals framed as 'family security' increased contributions, but only among older participants.[30]

The advantage is scale. Whereas field experiments can take years, analytics can interrogate millions of data points in weeks, providing insight without the political baggage of randomization.

The rise of data science and AI

Data science builds on analytics with predictive modelling. Rather than merely describing behaviour, it forecasts it, adapting dynamically to new inputs. As Ganna Pogrebna, David Trimble Chair in Leadership and Organisational Transformation at Queen's University Belfast, and formerly Executive Director of the AI and Cyber Futures Institute and Lead for Behavioural Data Science at the Alan Turing Institute, puts it: 'Behavioural Data Science and Behavioural AI is the future.'

One influential example is the Behavioral Ensemble Algorithm for Sequential Tasks Gradient Boosting (BEAST-GB), a model that integrates Prospect Theory into Gradient Boosting[a] methods to predict decision-making under risk.[119] Rather than treating human choices as noise within a statistical system, BEAST-GB incorporates behavioural biases, such as loss aversion, probability weighting, and framing effects, into its core structure. The result is a model that is not only more accurate but also more interpretable to behavioural scientists.

Zurich Insurance's deployment of Gradient Boosting Machines illustrates the practical stakes: by personalizing risk predictions, the firm improved accuracy to 91 per cent, dramatically reducing mispriced risk and enhancing customer targeting.[120]

AI pushes further. Beyond prediction, it can simulate behaviour. As Sameer Munshi, Head of Behavioral Science & Simulation at EY, notes, 'there's a whole synthetic data world out there where you might not even need real consumers to run experiments'. Generative models trained on survey and transaction data have produced 'synthetic participants' whose decision patterns mirror human responses in most scenarios.[121]

This opens the possibility of pre-testing interventions in silico. Governments could trial savings schemes on synthetic populations before real world rollout. Product teams could stress test pricing virtually before exposing live customers.

Still, new challenges arise. Patrick Fagan, co-founder and CSO at Capuchin Behavioural Science and Head of Behavioural Science at KUBIK, warns about quality over all else:

> data quality will likely take a hit with AI bots sneaking into datasets. It's getting harder to tell who is a real respondent and who isn't … you can program AI to act like different personality types … it's cool, but it's also a bit shaky since you're relying on something artificial to mimic actual human behaviour.

His concern points to an ironic twist: while AI promises efficiency, it also risks compounding the problem of artificiality.

Additional challenges remain. Black box algorithms may predict without explaining why, undermining theory-driven science. Biases in training data risk reproducing inequalities in credit or employment.[122] And if synthetic participants substitute for humans, their cultural validity must be scrutinized, especially as data isn't equally available for all humans.

At this point, Shane Timmons, Senior Research Officer in the Behavioural Research Unit at the Economic and Social Research Institute, offers another caution worth taking seriously. He sees huge opportunities for AI, especially for scaling interventions and accelerating analysis, but he is wary of overreliance in areas such as research questions and experimental design. Behavioural science advances when someone tackles a problem in a genuinely creative way, and his concern is that AI will tend to produce increasingly bland designs; technically competent, but conceptually homogeneous. If we let AI set the frame, we may end up optimizing the familiar rather than discovering the unexpected.

Still, the trajectory is clear. AI compresses timelines, reduces cost, and expands scope. As Etinosa Agbonlahor, CEO of Decision Alpha, observes: 'no more lists of biases. It's going to be figuring out how we test and measure, because context matters a lot and will change things'. For her, it is unthinkable that future behavioural scientists will lack data science fluency.

A shifting landscape

The history of behavioural science has often been written as the triumph of the RCT. Yet, its future may be defined less by randomization than by adaptation. Field experiments will remain important, but they will be joined, and sometimes eclipsed, by analytics, data science, and AI.

This chapter is not dedicated to a full exploration of AI's role in behavioural science; such a treatment would require a volume of its own. But the development is too important to ignore. Just as randomized trials transformed the field in the late twentieth century, the interplay of behavioural insight, big data, and AI promises to reshape it again. The real challenge, as many of the interviewees insist, is not to be dazzled by novelty but to remain clear-eyed about what these tools can and cannot achieve.

The consequences of an overemphasis on quantitative methods

As Ian Fannon noted previously, most organisations grappling with challenges that could benefit from behavioural research lack the time or budget for a full-blown RCTs, and must instead rely on 'secondary research, qualitative primary research and iterative development ... through co-design with well-chosen representatives of the end audience', which he argues can be 'a perfectly adequate (and much quicker and cheaper) solution'. This captures the dilemma: privileging quantitative rigour, while valuable in isolating causal claims, often sidelines other approaches that provide equal, if not greater, insight into the complexity of lived experience.

The academic preference for RCTs is understandable. They enable causal inference, meet the evidentiary bar for publication, and seem to offer definitive answers to policy makers. Yet their dominance has created a culture of research that privileges the what over the why. Numbers show whether something changed, but not the deeper story of how, why, or for whom.

Heather Mann, who after almost 8 years of Behavioural Science consulting transitioned to Elementary education, has voiced this critique clearly: 'behavioural science as practiced today tends not to emphasize the broader social, cultural, and political systems within which humans operate'. She argues that the field risks impoverishing its understanding of behaviour by leaning so heavily on quantitative evidence: 'I sometimes feel that we are missing out on fertile insights that can be gained from qualitative research. Over the next 10 years, I would love to see the field expand to incorporate more qualitative methods.' This echoes concerns from sociology and anthropology, which long recognized that outcomes devoid of context obscure meaning, identity, and power.

The limits of counting outcomes

Quantitative studies excel at telling us what happened. Uptake increased by 7 per cent. Savings rose by 12 per cent. Gym attendance improved by 5 per cent. Such numbers are precise and persuasive, yet they leave unexplored the dynamics beneath them. Why did uptake rise? Which subgroups responded most strongly? Was the effect temporary or sustained? What unintended consequences followed?

Behavioural science has often treated these questions as secondary. When interventions fail, explanations are thin: perhaps the sample was 'different', the method flawed, or the context unsuitable. Such accounts rarely draw on deeper engagement with participants or the environments in which interventions unfold.

As Lasana Harris, Professor of Social Neuroscience and Vice Dean for Global Engagement at UCL's Faculty of Brain Sciences, has warned, 'the biggest challenge to behavioural science is the lack of truly globally representative samples in experiments'. Heavy reliance on WEIRD samples (Chapter 4), compounded by lab-based or online methods, generates findings that generalize poorly. The result is a self-reinforcing cycle: researchers study those easiest to reach, with tools best suited to wealthy and technocratic contexts, and then treat these findings as universal.

Context, diversity, and the false promise of universality

Replication failures across cultures illustrate the danger. As discussed in Chapter 4, interventions that may have boosted behaviours in the UK and US produced far smaller effects in countries where the 'nudger' is less trusted or the norms surrounding the behaviour differ. Without qualitative inquiry into local perceptions or cultural values, such discrepancies remain opaque.

Even within a single setting, averages conceal complexity. As Sasha Tregebov, former Director of BIT Canada and now Managing Director at BIT Americas notes, 'we still rely a lot on average treatment effects across really diverse populations', meaning we miss important heterogeneity. 'We could generate so much more impact by getting more targeted and nuanced.' Yet statistical techniques, no matter how sophisticated, flatten divergent experiences. A financial incentive to lose weight may energize some but alienate others. Only qualitative tools, such as interviews, ethnography, co-design, can surface such divergence.

Failures, silences, and blind spots

The emphasis on outcomes also fuels systematic silences. Null results often languish unpublished, trapped in psychology's 'file drawer problem'.[123] Yet knowing why an intervention failed is as valuable as its success. Did participants find the message manipulative? Were structural barriers overwhelming behavioural tweaks? Without qualitative follow-ups, 'no effect' offers little guidance.

Self-reports fare no better.[124] People misremember or present themselves in socially desirable ways. Studies of giving often show a gulf between stated generosity and actual donations,[125] a gap clearer to ethnographers observing donation contexts than to statisticians analyzing survey scales.[126]

The rise of AI and big data creates further risks. Algorithms can identify patterns at scale, but remain mute on meaning. They may predict who responds to a nudge, but cannot explain why it resonates or backfires. Policy makers may see an SMS reminder succeed in one group but fail in another, without understanding whether trust, prior experiences, or cultural framing drives the difference.

Beyond metrics: towards integration

The consequences of overreliance on quantitative evidence are significant. It encourages overestimation of universality, neglects context, and reduces behaviour to measurable outputs while ignoring the systems that shape it.

This is not an argument against numbers but for integration. Quantitative methods provide clarity; qualitative methods provide depth. The challenge is not merely to document what patterns exist but to interrogate the why; the structures and norms that sustain them. The same principle applies here: behavioural science must resist methodological purity and embrace pluralism.

Only by moving beyond the what to the why can the field hope to meet the demands of practice; understanding not just whether interventions work, but how, for whom, and in what context.

Introducing: qualitative approaches

David Grosse, Founder and Lead Consultant for BehavOR, focused on applying behavioural science to the financial services, remarked:

> Use hammers to hit nails, saws to cut wood and Allen keys to build Swedish furniture (that said even the use

> of basic metaphor is troubling, insofar as it implies simple and linear solutions to clearly defined problems, and that is rarely the case with messy reality of human behaviour). There needs to be room for ethnography and big data, for small scale experiments and wider trials, for organizational psychology and neuroscience.

His warning is clear: methods are not interchangeable tools. Behavioural science must draw on a wide repertoire, but without falling into the trap of assuming that human behaviour can be neatly fixed with a single methodological device.

Quantitative approaches, from big data analytics to laboratory and field experiments, are powerful in isolating variables and identifying causal effects. But they often fail to explain the why: the meaning, context, and texture of lived experience. Qualitative methods, such as ethnography, interviews, focus groups, and narrative analysis, fill this gap. They uncover the dynamics of belief, identity, and culture that structure behaviour, and they often generate insights essential for designing interventions that resonate in the real world.

Ethnography

Ethnography immerses researchers in participants' everyday contexts, capturing behaviour as it unfolds within cultural and institutional systems rather than under artificial constraints.

Classic work such as Bourgois' *In Search of Respect* documented how Puerto Rican drug dealers in East Harlem negotiated systemic racism, limited job opportunities, and persistent exclusion, showing violence as a survival strategy rather than pathology.[127] On Wall Street, ethnographies revealed cultures of risk-taking and insecurity, where norms of elitism and short-term profit trumped long-term sustainability.[128] Both studies challenged stereotypes and pointed policy makers toward structural reforms, from labour markets to financial regulation.

More recently, *The Financial Diaries* followed 235 low- and middle-income families for a year, finding that income volatility, not absolute income, was the central financial challenge.[129] Families relied on informal savings groups, payday loans, and kinship networks, while conventional financial products amplified stress. Such work reframed debates about poverty and credit, highlighting the need for products tailored to irregular earnings. In this sense, ethnography generates not only empathy but policy-relevant knowledge.

Interviews and focus groups

Interviews and focus groups uncover beliefs, motivations, and emotions that numbers miss. Luo et al (2023) used a Virtual Reality (VR) interview simulator to examine how candidates react under pressure, showing that behavioural questions induce more anxiety than situational ones, and supportive interviewers improve performance.[130] The findings suggest applications in job training and interviewer development.

Erle et al (2023) ran focus groups on human–robot interaction, showing that responses to robots are shaped by culture, anthropomorphism, and prior exposure.[131] Such insights inform the design of social robots that mitigate bias and enhance trust in public spaces.

These methods are also central to user-centred design. In usability testing, interviews help refine mechanics of digital products, while concept testing validates ideas before costly development.[132] Facebook's research into content related to eating disorders combined interviews with product testing to explore interventions that redirected attention and fostered empathy.[133] Such work illustrates how qualitative techniques directly shape interventions with public health significance.

Narrative analysis

Narrative analysis explores how individuals construct meaning through stories, focusing not only on content but also on structure and social context. Frank's *The Wounded Storyteller* categorized illness narratives into restitution, chaos, and quest forms, offering frameworks for patients to reclaim agency and for clinicians to improve communication.[134]

Beyond health, narrative research on adolescent identity has shown how young men construct masculinity through contrast and exclusion, suggesting interventions to disrupt harmful scripts.[135] Studies of managerial narratives reveal how leaders frame their own careers and workplaces, shaping organisational culture and performance.[136]

At scale, narrative analysis can extend into financial markets. Tuckett et al (2014) developed computational tools to trace evolving investor narratives, showing how 'phantastic objects', compelling stories of limitless opportunity, fuelled speculative bubbles.[137] These findings echo the aforementioned ethnographic accounts of Wall Street culture, demonstrating how collective stories drive behaviour even in ostensibly rational markets.

Why they matter

Together, these approaches demonstrate the richness qualitative methods bring. Ethnography uncovers structural and cultural constraints; interviews and focus groups reveal individual motivations; narrative analysis explains how meaning is constructed and spread. Where experiments show what happens, qualitative approaches help us understand why; and why it matters in context.

Yet despite their value, such methods remain underused in behavioural science. Part of the reason is disciplinary inertia: journals and funders often prioritize experimental precision over contextual depth. Another is methodological discomfort: qualitative research requires different standards of validity, emphasizing depth and interpretation over replicable control. But without such tools, behavioural science risks designing interventions that fail outside the laboratory. As Grosse cautions, there is no universal tool for human behaviour, only the careful alignment of method to problem.

Scientists against qualitative methods

As Patrick Forscher, Senior Behavioral Scientist at Busara and former Director of its meta-research group, CREME, reflected, 'many people in corporate behavioural science are hostile to qualitative methods because they see numbers as more objective. But if you're studying human behaviour, you're dealing with subjective experiences. Psychological processes are inherently subjective and putting numbers on them does not make them objective.' His comment highlights a persistent tension: the privileging of numerical evidence as inherently neutral, and the corresponding suspicion that qualitative work is soft, biased, or even unscientific.

This suspicion has taken several familiar forms. First, qualitative methods are often criticized as overly dependent on researcher interpretation. Interviews, for instance, can be vulnerable to unconscious leading questions or selective attention to certain themes, introducing potential bias and undermining replicability.[138]

A second concern is reliability: methodologies can vary across studies, and as such, thematic analyses of the same data might generate divergent findings.[139]

Third, qualitative samples tend to be small and specific. The cultural situatedness of case studies means that conclusions drawn from one group may not easily transfer to another.[140]

Added to these are practical objections. Such as the concern that transcription and analysis are resource-intensive, often requiring months of labour and teams of researchers[141] and other concerns highlight the analytic difficulties of coding unstructured data without a clear framework.[142]

On the surface, then, qualitative methods appear subjective, inconsistent, narrow, costly, and difficult to manage. But as Forscher suggested, the charge of subjectivity is not unique to qualitative research. Numbers do not eliminate interpretation; they merely cloak it.

Responding to the critiques

Liam Delaney, Professor and Head of the Department of Psychological and Behavioural Science at the LSE and founder of the LSE FORGOOD initiative, reflecting on his experience training students, advised them to 'develop a strong mixed methods toolkit', noting that while quantitative designs dominate, 'you're going to see a lot more people with specialisations in ethnography and qualitative designs increasingly using the terminology of behavioural science'. His point underlines a central flaw in the caricature of qualitative work: it is not the unstructured, unreliable enterprise its detractors assume.

Far from lacking rigour, qualitative researchers actively build it in. Reflexivity, an explicit recognition of the researcher's own assumptions, serves as a safeguard against hidden bias. Systematic frameworks such as Grounded Theory,[143] a qualitative research methodology aimed at developing theories directly from data systematically gathered and analyzed during the research process, rather than testing existing hypotheses, provide step-by-step procedures for data collection and analysis. Meanwhile, software such as NVivo, Dovetail and ATLAS.ti, among many others, allow coded datasets and frameworks to be archived and shared, enhancing transparency and replicability. Indeed, qualitative research has been strengthened, not weakened, by the open science movement, where methodological detail can be scrutinized by others.

Moreover, critics who dismiss qualitative research as 'subjective' rarely acknowledge that quantitative work has been shaken by its own replication crisis. If failed replications undermine the reliability of survey and experimental evidence, then the objectivity of numbers is hardly assured.

The question of generalizability

A second charge, that qualitative research lacks generalizability, misunderstands its purpose. Unlike large-scale quantitative studies, which prioritize breadth, qualitative research values depth and context. Its contribution lies in explaining not just what happens but why and how. For behavioural scientists, this matters: interventions designed on the basis of generalizable averages often fail when applied in different social settings, as discussed in Chapter 4.

Here, too, qualitative researchers have developed strategies to address concerns. Instead of generalization, they emphasize transferability: providing detailed contextual descriptions so that others can judge whether findings apply elsewhere. This is no less cautious than quantitative work, where effects derived from WEIRD populations often collapse in new environments. Yet the critique of generalizability is disproportionately aimed at qualitative work, reflecting not a methodological weakness but an asymmetry in how standards of evidence are applied.

Resources, data, and value

Qualitative research is undeniably labour-intensive. Collecting interviews, transcribing conversations, and coding unstructured data requires substantial time and resources. But dismissing it on these grounds overlooks the richness of the insights it generates. Ethnographic studies, narrative analyses, and in-depth interviews can reveal social dynamics, motivations, and lived experiences that are invisible in large-scale surveys. These insights often justify the costs, particularly when used to inform policy design or organisational practice.

Moreover, advances in technology are transforming the efficiency of qualitative analysis. NVivo, Dovetail and ATLAS.ti now incorporate AI-driven tools for theme detection, reducing time burdens and increasing analytic consistency.

AI as a game-changer

Although this chapter won't address the many things AI can do to improve quantitative approaches to behavioural research, we'd be amiss to not highlight how the recent developments in AI are shifting the landscape further for qualitative methods. Large language models (LLMs) have been shown to be able to automate coding, cutting analysis times dramatically while maintaining strong alignment with human coders.[144] Similarly, Zhang et al (2024) introduced QualiGPT, designed to assist researchers in coding and theme detection, which demonstrated high levels of agreement with human interpretations.[145] AI, then, is beginning to address the very criticisms: scale, efficiency, replicability, that have long been levelled at qualitative research.

Research has also begun experimenting with AI as interviewer, using platforms capable of conducting thousands of conversations in hours.[147] Their findings suggest that participants respond positively, and experts judged the quality of interviews to be comparable with those conducted by humans. If developed responsibly, such tools could democratize qualitative research, making large-scale, diverse data collection feasible for the first time.[146] Yet human expertise remains central. As Cornet and Le Duc (2024) emphasize, AI systems depend on careful human training, annotation, and oversight to ensure accuracy and ethical integrity.[148]

Oliver Hauser, Professor of Economics and Deputy Director of the AI Institute at the University of Exeter and Senior Adviser to the UK Cabinet Office, reflected on the rapid corporate adoption of generative AI, and urged caution:

> people are quick to jump to the conclusion that there will only be upsides to this new technology rather than think about the distributional effects … behavioural scientists have a role to play in designing effective systems … in which we can foster the strengths of new technology while minimising its risks.

Hauser's intervention reminds us that adopting AI is not just a technical matter but a deeply behavioural one, requiring the same systematic scrutiny that we apply to any intervention.

Closing note on criticisms

The debate over qualitative methods is therefore less about inherent flaws than about disciplinary hierarchies. As Patrick Forscher suggested, numbers do not make subjectivity vanish. As Liam Delaney advised his students, behavioural scientists need 'a strong mixed methods toolkit', one that acknowledges the limitations of both numbers and narratives. And as the rise of AI shows, the boundary between scalability and depth is shifting in ways that open new possibilities.

Qualitative research is not a weak cousin to quantitative analysis. It is an indispensable partner, bringing texture, meaning, and context to the study of human behaviour. Far from being undermined by technological change, its future may be strengthened; if researchers retain a critical, reflexive stance, and if behavioural science values rigour in all its forms.

Towards methodological pluralism

Behavioural science stands at a crossroads. For much of its history, the field has been dominated by quantitative methods such as RCTs, survey experiments, and, more recently, big data analytics. These tools have offered breadth, allowing researchers to establish causality and measure the relative effectiveness of interventions across large populations. Yet while powerful, they often fall short of capturing the deeper 'why' that underpins human behaviour: the lived experiences, contexts, and motivations that give meaning to data. For these reasons, qualitative methods, ranging from ethnography and interviews to narrative analysis and participatory workshops, have begun to reassert their value. As Ximena Garcia-Rada, Assistant Professor of Marketing at Texas A&M University, specializing in mixed methods, observes, 'more people will use a mixed methods approach combining lab studies, field experiments, analysis of archival and text data, in-depth interviews, observational studies, etc. to understand important questions in a more holistic manner'. By combining quantitative breadth with qualitative depth, mixed methods approaches open new possibilities for a more holistic behavioural science.

Critics of qualitative research have traditionally dismissed it as subjective, inconsistent, or lacking scalability. These critiques, however, increasingly appear outdated. Rigorous frameworks such as Grounded Theory, analytical tools such as NVivo, and open platforms including the Open Science Framework have strengthened the consistency and replicability of qualitative studies. Meanwhile, the rise of AI is transforming this space. Natural language processing (NLP) now automates transcription, coding, and sentiment analysis, while machine learning systems support the detection of patterns across vast datasets of interviews, focus groups, or open-ended surveys. Far from being unwieldy, qualitative research is becoming more efficient and scalable than ever before.

Hans Rocha IJzerman, CEO of Entrelacs and founder of the Annecy Behavioral Science Lab, captures this shift well:

> The way we measure things isn't effective. I hope we'll see an increased use of ethnographies and qualitative research methods to better understand how different populations experience the same concepts. This requires moving away from a reliance on standard measures developed in Global North populations and toward more inclusive and culturally sensitive methodologies. Another major area for development is the integration of technology, particularly AI and large language models ... the future of behavioural science should be focused on making our measurements more personalized, our methods more inclusive, and our use of technology smarter.

His words highlight both the ethical and practical imperative: the field can no longer afford to rely on measures developed for WEIRD populations while claiming universality. To build a science that resonates globally, behavioural researchers must embrace inclusivity, cultural sensitivity, and technological innovation.

Examples of this shift are already visible. A mobile health (mHealth) app designed to encourage adolescents to self-report substance use used quantitative metrics such as engagement and reporting rates alongside qualitative insights from interviews and usability testing.[149] The combination revealed not only whether the app 'worked' but why users engaged, or disengaged, from it. Similarly, eHealth interventions for improving adolescent health habits have combined body mass index (BMI) measures with focus group discussions to assess the perceived usefulness of digital platforms.[150] In another case, researchers experimenting with humorous chatbots found that step counts and exercise duration (quantitative outcomes) told only half the story: qualitative feedback revealed that humour increased satisfaction and engagement, factors critical for sustained behaviour change.[151] Finally, Costa's study of educational outcomes demonstrated how qualitative insights could refine quantitative datasets. In-depth interviews uncovered contextual variables invisible in large-scale assessments, and once incorporated into the quantitative analysis, these variables transformed the interpretation of existing results.[152]

These examples show how mixed methods research is not a luxury but a necessity for behavioural science, especially as the field extends into complex domains such as health, climate, or inequality. Exploratory sequential designs, where qualitative methods precede and inform quantitative measures, allow researchers to ensure that interventions resonate with lived experiences before large resources are committed. Explanatory sequential designs, where qualitative insights follow quantitative results, help clarify and interpret findings that otherwise remain opaque. The key is methodological inclusivity: recognizing that no single method can capture the full complexity of human behaviour, but together they provide a more complete picture.

As Philipe Bujold, Research Scientist at CSIRO, previously at Rare operating on the intersection of behavioural science and conservation notes, 'If the field is going to move beyond the lab and low-hanging fruit into addressing complex systems like climate change or pandemics, we need to get better at understanding when and why interventions work – and when and why they don't.' In that spirit, the following six practical steps offer a roadmap for building a more methodologically diverse and future-proof behavioural science.

Step 1. Use AI to augment, not replace

AI has already transformed many domains, and behavioural science is no exception. Ali Fenwick, Professor of Organizational Behavior and Innovation at Hult International Business School and Founder of the Dr Fenwick Lab for Human Behavior & Technology, predicted that the field would see 'heterogeneous sampling techniques to develop automated and tailored nudges' as one of the booming areas of investigation. Susan Michie, Professor of Health Psychology and Director of the Centre for Behaviour Change at UCL, similarly noted that 'harnessing the power of machine learning and artificial intelligence has the potential to make much more progress and be much more efficient and productive in terms of the ratio of input to output'. The promise of AI lies not in replacing human judgement, but in amplifying behavioural scientists' ability to scale insight.

When used well, AI can automate the labour-intensive aspects of qualitative research. NLP can analyze thousands of open-ended survey responses to identify emergent themes. Generative agents can simulate responses in structured decision tasks, allowing teams to refine designs before incurring costly field trials. Yet these tools must remain subordinate to human-centred principles. As Jez Groom, one of the co-founders of Ogilvy Change and the founder and CEO of Cowry Consulting, cautions, behavioural science must be 'holistically integrated into the building of these systems from inception' to ensure ethical and meaningful outcomes.

Practical steps, include training behavioural scientists in AI literacy, integrating large language models into workflows for thematic coding and user persona generation, and embedding ethical reviews into projects that use synthetic data. Universities and funders should support pilot projects where AI augments qualitative fieldwork in under-resourced contexts. The goal is to treat AI as a methodological partner: one that accelerates curiosity and discovery while leaving interpretation and lived experience firmly in human hands.

Practical steps

- Embed AI literacy in training: Universities and professional courses should include AI fundamentals, so behavioural scientists understand how to use NLP, LLMs, and generative simulations responsibly.
- Pilot AI-supported qualitative analysis: Run projects where AI codes large volumes of text data (for example, surveys and interviews) and compare against human-coded results, building trust in blended workflows.
- Develop ethical guardrails for synthetic data: Institutional review boards (IRBs) and funders should require explicit protocols when using simulated data to ensure it supplements, not substitutes, lived experience.
- Integrate AI into prototyping phases: Use generative agents to stress test intervention designs before costly rollouts, but pair outputs with stakeholder workshops to validate assumptions.
- Fund AI-for-inclusion pilots: Governments and NGOs should support projects where AI helps analyze under-resourced, multilingual, or hard-to-reach datasets, widening participation.

AI will not replace behavioural science; it will magnify its reach if used well. By embedding AI into discovery and analysis while keeping interpretation grounded in human experience, the field can harness scale without losing sensitivity.

Step 2. Build mixed methods in from day one

Sam Moore, Senior Behavioural Scientist at Evidn, highlighted a persistent challenge: 'How do we move beyond RCTs and nudge-based interventions and take the broader psychosocial system of influences into account?' Behavioural science risks narrowing its scope when it treats qualitative insight as optional. Instead, qualitative discovery must be embedded into the research process from the very beginning.

This means structuring projects so that fieldwork, interviews, or ethnographies inform the framing of interventions, not merely their evaluation. For instance, before launching SMS-based savings nudges in Kenya, researchers might first run focus groups exploring local conceptions of risk, savings, and gender roles. Similarly, climate adaptation projects should begin with community workshops to understand local narratives before testing messaging interventions. As Emily Daniels, Senior Behavioural Researcher at Bupa observes, 'Too often, behavioural science projects falter because the problem hasn't been clearly defined.' Qualitative scoping helps prevent misdiagnosis, ensuring interventions address the real drivers of behaviour.

Funders and review boards can accelerate this shift by requiring a qualitative discovery phase for any field trial conducted in unfamiliar contexts. Universities should train students in structuring qualitative protocols and integrating them into quantitative designs. Even a handful of interviews can dramatically improve the design of an intervention. Building mixed methods into projects from day one is less about perfection and more about humility: recognizing that the people behavioural science seeks to help often know best where problems truly lie.

Practical steps

- Require qualitative scoping before trials: Funders and ethics boards should mandate interviews, focus groups, or ethnographies as precursors to quantitative interventions.
- Train mixed methods fluency: Curricula should prepare students to design qualitative protocols, analyze open-ended data, and integrate findings into experimental designs.
- Develop project templates: Create practical toolkits showing how to embed discovery workshops, interviews, or cultural mapping into each project phase.
- Showcase success stories: Journals and conferences should highlight case studies where qualitative inputs significantly improved intervention outcomes.
- Budget for discovery: Funders must earmark a percentage of grants specifically for scoping and participatory methods, preventing their omission due to cost.

Mixed methods design is not an optional luxury; it is the foundation for interventions that resonate. Embedding qualitative work from the start ensures projects ask the right questions before chasing answers.

Step 3. Create lightweight testing pipelines

Not every project can afford large-scale RCTs. Helena Rubinstein, Head of Strategic Services and Behavioural Scientist at Innovia Technology, warns that 'until we are able to get more systematic evidence for what works and what doesn't, organisations will become cynical about the value of behavioural science'. To maintain credibility while addressing resource constraints, behavioural science needs lightweight testing pipelines.

These pipelines involve rapid, low-cost experimental designs such as A/B tests, adaptive rollouts, or small-sample pre–post comparisons. For example, a municipality exploring new tax letters could test variations in a few districts, collecting directional insights within weeks rather than years. Consultancies and academic labs can create 'minimal viable evaluation' playbooks; templates for running cheap, fast tests using readily available tools such as Google Forms, WhatsApp, or Twilio.

Crucially, AI can also support these efforts by standardizing experimental templates, managing data quality, and helping interpret small datasets. The key is to lower the barriers to experimentation so that organisations remain open to behavioural methods, building a pathway to more rigorous trials later.

Practical steps

- Standardize rapid testing playbooks: Develop clear guidelines for A/B tests, small pilots, and pre–post studies that can be deployed quickly with minimal cost.
- Leverage digital tools for scale: Use platforms such as WhatsApp, Twilio, or SMS systems, for fast feedback loops in resource-limited settings.
- Use AI to streamline analysis: Apply machine learning for quality checks and preliminary interpretations of small datasets, reducing bottlenecks.
- Encourage iterative rollouts: Structure interventions in stages (for example, pilot, adapt, and expand) so evidence accumulates before large investments.

- Normalize 'minimal viable evaluation': Promote acceptance of directional insights as stepping stones to rigorous trials, countering the idea that only large RCTs 'count'.

Lightweight pipelines will not replace gold standard trials; however, they prevent paralysis by perfection. By lowering the entry barrier to testing, behavioural science can remain credible while expanding its reach.

Step 4. Integrate behavioural science into data and product teams

Torben Emmerling, Founder and Managing Partner of Affective Advisory and Founder and Board Member of the Global Association for Applied Behavioural Scientists (GAABS), argued that behavioural science must move beyond implementation to become central to strategic processes in organisations. To do so, behavioural scientists must work within the very teams that design products, manage data, and shape customer experiences.

This integration allows behavioural hypotheses to be embedded directly into product experimentation platforms, whether in fintech apps, government digital services, or healthcare portals. Rather than waiting for stand-alone evaluations, behavioural scientists can test nudges, prompts, or design changes through the same systems that already manage A/B testing for user experience. Susan Michie adds that working alongside practitioners and communities ensures interventions are co-created rather than imposed.

Universities can encourage this integration by offering joint certificates in behavioural science and data analytics, while recruiters can prioritize hybrid skill sets. Governments can second behavioural scientists into adjacent departments to spread methods across institutional silos. The closer behavioural scientists are to operational decision-making, the more their insights will shape outcomes that matter.

Practical steps

- Co-locate behavioural scientists: Place them within data, product, or design teams to ensure behavioural hypotheses are tested alongside user experience changes.

- Embed behavioural insights in experimentation platforms: Align nudge-testing with the same A/B infrastructure already used in tech and product development.
- Create hybrid career paths: Universities should offer joint degrees in behavioural science and analytics, while recruiters prioritize applicants with blended skillsets.
- Facilitate secondments: Governments and large firms should rotate behavioural scientists across departments, spreading methods across silos.
- Encourage co-creation with communities: Behavioural scientists should work directly with practitioners and users during product development, ensuring interventions are both ethical and effective.

Integration into data and product teams ensures behavioural science is no longer a bolt-on. Instead, it becomes embedded in the infrastructure of decision-making, shaping outcomes at scale.

Step 5. Build and share context libraries

A perennial problem in behavioural science is the failure of interventions to replicate across contexts. Dan Bennet, Senior Partner and Head of Behavioural Science at Ogilvy Consulting, foresaw a role for AI in helping 'hold and work with big databases of digital interventions ... to better inform psychological theory'. The need for context libraries: open, annotated databases of what has worked, where, and why, has never been greater.

These libraries would record not only outcomes but also contextual details: sample characteristics, cultural factors, implementation challenges, and stakeholder perceptions. They would allow researchers to avoid reinventing the wheel and help practitioners identify which interventions are likely to transfer successfully.

Institutional support is essential. Organisations like the Organisation for Economic Co-operation and Development (OECD), World Bank, or the Abdul Latif Jameel Poverty Action Lab (J-PAL) could fund their development, while academic journals could require submissions to include contextual applicability statements. Consulting firms could contribute anonymized case notes, and universities could incentivize students to add to the collective record. Such libraries would support both replication and innovation, making behavioural science a cumulative enterprise rather than one that perpetually starts from scratch.

Practical steps

- Develop open-access repositories: International organisations should create global platforms cataloguing behavioural interventions with metadata on context and outcomes.
- Mandate contextual statements: Journals could require submissions to include information on setting, population, and transferability as part of publication.
- Encourage practitioner contributions: Consulting firms and NGOs should contribute anonymized case studies to enrich the collective evidence base.
- Support student participation: Universities can integrate context library contributions into thesis requirements, training students in systematic documentation.
- Fund annotation and maintenance: Governments and multilaterals should support the upkeep of these libraries, ensuring they remain living resources rather than static archives.

Context libraries turn behavioural science from a fragmented toolkit into a cumulative discipline. By recording not just what works but where and why, the field can build durable knowledge.

Step 6. Train behavioural scientists to be context-ready

As Robin Schimmelpfennig, a postdoctoral researcher at the Max Planck Institute for Human Development and United Nations Behavioural Science & AI Fellow, whose work explores the societal and psychological implications of human–AI interaction, observes that too much of the field still focuses on past success stories rather than building methodological adaptability. For behavioural science to thrive globally, practitioners must be 'context-ready': able to adapt tools, test assumptions, and work ethically across diverse settings.

This requires a shift in training. Academic programmes should mandate field placements, intercultural modules, and case-based learning. Students should learn to adapt interventions to new populations and interpret unintended effects. Professional development should likewise prioritize adaptability. Philipe Bujold summarizes the ethos well: 'Being a behavioural scientist means tackling tasks you never really prepared for. Some of my biggest successes started with me thinking, "I have no idea how to do this, but I can learn."'

Governments, NGOs, and businesses can build capacity by creating peer-exchange networks across countries and sectors, ensuring practitioners gain exposure to varied contexts. Toolkits must extend beyond statistical design to include localization, stakeholder engagement, and ethical reflexivity. Above all, practitioners should be judged not solely on significance levels but on their ability to listen, adapt, and ensure interventions resonate with the populations they serve.

Practical steps

- Mandate field placements: Academic programmes should require immersive experiences in diverse contexts to teach adaptability firsthand.
- Teach localization as a skill: Courses should cover how to adapt interventions, measures, and communications to cultural and linguistic realities.
- Normalize failure as learning: Evaluation frameworks should reward practitioners for documenting unintended effects, not just successful outcomes.
- Build peer-learning networks: Governments and NGOs can sponsor exchanges across countries and sectors, exposing practitioners to varied contexts.
- Broaden evaluation metrics: Judge success not just on statistical significance, but on community trust, adaptability, and long-term resonance.

To be context-ready is to accept that uncertainty is the norm. The most effective behavioural scientists will not be those with the most elegant interventions, but those who can adapt, listen, and learn across settings.

Conclusion

Behavioural science has always been at its best when it lets method follow the question, not the other way around. This chapter argued for that stance explicitly: a plural toolkit where experiments earn their keep, qualitative inquiry surfaces the 'why', analytics and data science provide scale, and AI accelerates discovery without displacing judgement. How the field's experimental backbone delivered credibility was traced, and how overreliance on a narrow slice of methods created predictable blind spots: WEIRD sampling, thin mechanisms, designs divorced from lived decision environments, and interventions that travel poorly beyond their test beds.

The corrective is not to dethrone experiments but to right-size them. Field trials remain powerful, yet they are costly, politically sensitive, and fragile to context. Mixed methods design, scoping with ethnography, co-design with communities, explanatory interviews after trials, turns results into understanding. Data analytics and AI can widen aperture and speed iteration, provided we keep transparency, consent, and cultural validity front and centre. And the practical reforms set out; embedding discovery from day one, creating lightweight testing pipelines, integrating behavioural scientists into product and data teams, building context libraries, and training practitioners to be context-ready, move the field from one-off cleverness to cumulative capability.

Methodological pluralism is not only about better answers; it is about better claims. When breadth and depth are combined, the temptation to overgeneralize from elegant but brittle effects is reduced. When context is documented as carefully as outcomes, it is easier for others to learn, adapt, and, crucially, fail productively. And when AI is treated as an amplifier rather than an oracle, people, interpretation, and ethics remain in the loop.

All of which leads directly to the concern of the next chapter: replication. The replication crisis is often framed as a statistical problem: underpowered studies, p-hacking, selective reporting. It is that, but it is also a methodological and organisational problem. Effects that depend on narrow samples or contrived settings are less likely to hold when conditions change. Projects that skip qualitative scoping misdiagnose problems and then 'fail to replicate' because they never targeted the right mechanism. Interventions that are tested once, briefly, and reported without context are difficult to reproduce by design. In short: how we study behaviour shapes whether our findings endure.

Together, these chapters form a single arc. This chapter asked us to broaden how we know; the next insists we strengthen how we show. Plural methods without reproducible practice risk becoming anecdote; rigorous replication without methodological breadth risks becoming sterile. The future of behavioural science lies in the combination: cumulative, context-aware, and honest about its limits. If influence can be paired with accountability, methodological and ethical, we can move beyond the era of clever nudges into one where our claims are both useful and reliable. The promise is not that every effect will travel, but that our science will.

6

Behavioural Science Will Replicate

> Replicability is the cornerstone of science and without it we would be left with mystical woo-woo like astrology, horoscopes and the Myers Briggs test.
>
> David Grosse (2022)

Introduction

In 1998, a set of studies introduced the idea that self-control works like a muscle; use it too much, and it tires out. The concept, known as 'ego depletion', quickly became a textbook staple and a cultural touchstone.[153] It seemed to explain everything from failed diets to workplace fatigue, and for years was cited as one of psychology's most reliable insights. But when two dozen laboratories later attempted to replicate the finding across thousands of participants worldwide, the effect simply disappeared.[154]

Ego depletion is just one example, but it illustrates a larger reckoning. Over the last decade, many of behavioural science's most high-profile results, from priming studies[155] to power posing,[156] have struggled to survive replication attempts. For some, these failures are treated as isolated embarrassments. For others, they strike at the heart of the discipline's credibility.

The damage has not been confined to academia. As Emily Daniels, Senior Behavioural Researcher at Bupa, observed, the replication problem has made it 'quite easy for sceptics to dismiss behavioural science as a collection of biases and flashy nudges, rather than a rigorous scientific discipline'. That perception stings because it reflects more than outside scepticism; it reflects real vulnerabilities in how knowledge has been produced and rewarded.

Replication is more than a methodological hurdle; it is the test of whether behavioural science can sustain itself as a cumulative field. Without it, theories rest on fragile ground, interventions risk being built on sand, and public trust erodes quickly. And yet, calling this only a crisis risks missing its generative role. Replication clarifies as much as it destabilizes. It cuts away what is weak, sharpens what is strong, and points the way toward practices that can make the science more durable.

This chapter examines how the replication problem emerged, what it has cost behavioural science, and how facing it directly might become the very foundation for the field's future.

The replication crisis: a historical explanation

Patrick Fagan, co-founder and CSO at Capuchin Behavioural Science and Head of Behavioural Science at KUBIK, captured the unease many feel about the fragility of behavioural science:

> I think it's an issue across social sciences, but behavioural science has a lot of shaky ground – half the time, facts don't last. In seven years, research findings are often debunked or updated, and that's problematic. How can we base an entire field on findings that don't hold up over time?

His frustration points to a deeper truth: the replication crisis was not a sudden rupture, but the culmination of long-standing structural incentives.

As described in Chapter 1, psychology's experimental boom in the 1960s and 1970s produced iconic studies, but often with small samples and fragile methods. Instead of maturing into more rigorous practice, the field became increasingly driven by academic incentives that valued novelty and statistical significance above replication or robustness. By the late 20th century, publication had become the currency of success, and what counted as publishable was rarely what was most reliable. The result was what has been referred to as the 'four horsemen' of fragile science: *experimenter bias*, *p-hacking*, *HARKing*, and *publication bias*.

This culture set the stage for collapse. As David Grosse, Founder and Lead Consultant for BehavOR, warned, 'Pride comes before a fall, and as behavioural scientists we should all be mindful of the replication crisis and the importance of context, context and context'. That fall came most visibly in the 2010s, when systematic replication projects began to test foundational claims. The Open Science Collaboration (2015) found that only 39 per cent of 100 psychology studies replicated successfully.[155] The Many Labs projects, which tested classic effects, such as anchoring and framing, across thousands of participants, revealed the same pattern: some findings held, but effect sizes were far smaller than originally reported and varied across settings.[157,158]

The crisis also came into sharp focus through high-profile failures. One of the most famous was 'power posing'. The original research suggested that standing in expansive postures increased testosterone, lowered cortisol, and encouraged risk-taking.[159] The finding was irresistible to media and management trainers alike. But a large-scale, preregistered replication found no hormonal or behavioural effects, only a slight boost in self-reported feelings of power.[156] Meta-analyses later confirmed the effect was inconsistent at best, yet by then power posing had already become one of the most widely cited, and widely questioned, exports of behavioural science.

Priming offered another cautionary tale. Early studies suggested that subtle cues could unconsciously shape behaviour, like the 'age priming' experiment, where exposure to words such as 'grey' or 'retired' supposedly slowed walking speed.[160] But replications that introduced more rigorous measurement found no such effect.[161] Other celebrated findings, from 'cleanliness priming'[162] to 'money priming',[163] also crumbled under replication attempts, revealing how methodological weaknesses and experimenter expectations had produced results that looked more robust than they really were.

As Scott Rick, Associate Professor of Marketing at the University of Michigan's Ross School of Business, observed, the persistence of these fragile effects reflects how 'publishing norms still seem to incentivize lower-risk, easier-to-conduct research over more ambitious and adventurous projects'. In other words, the problem was not individual misconduct but systemic misaligned incentives: research was rewarded for being clever, not cumulative. The replication crisis made those incentives impossible to ignore.

Scientific reasons for non-replication

Bob Sugden, Professor in the School of Economics at the University of East Anglia, cautioned against exaggerating the 'replication crisis', noting that journals should be seen as 'repositories of certified reports of specific experiments', not as permanent statements of universal truth. In this light, failed replications are not always signs of malpractice, but can reflect the self-correcting nature of science. In the following section, some scientifically valid reasons why results may not replicate are explored.

Changes in sample

As Serene Koh, Director of the BIT in Singapore, argued, many researchers overgeneralize their results: 'Human beings are complex and the world is a diverse place. If behavioural science is to have true universal impact, then behavioural scientists need to be more open to studying how an intervention's results are related to its context.' Replication failures across cultures or socioeconomic groups often highlight limited generalizability rather than outright error. The real concern is when an effect disappears simply by increasing sample size.

Peter Wakker, Professor of Behavioral Economics at the Erasmus School of Economics and research fellow at the Tinbergen Institute, pointed to statistics as a common culprit: 'Part of the problem lies in the unsound statistical techniques commonly used, which make it unavoidable that some things go wrong'. Small samples inflate effect sizes and increase Type I errors. Many interventions produce small real effects (Cohen's $d < 0.2$), yet are tested as if effects were more likely to be medium or large. Underpowered studies are therefore set up to mislead. While larger, preregistered samples improve accuracy, they also frequently reveal that celebrated effects were far weaker than initially advertised.

Changes in methods

Replication attempts often falter because the original methods were poorly described. Even small details, such as stimulus type, timing, or instructions, can alter outcomes. Roy Baumeister, Emeritus Professor at the School of Psychology at Queensland University, warned that the 'cure' of overcorrection has been worse than the disease: 'Much of social psychology has abandoned the lab methods that made the field an important center of ideas, replacing them with Mechanical Turk online surveys ... when it becomes the sole or dominant method in a large field of study, that field is in trouble.' His point is that shifts in methodology can change what is being tested, not just how.

Scott Rick similarly emphasized the need for real world testing: 'Humanity has some pretty big, urgent problems to address, and elegant lab experiments will only take us so far.' Here, failures of replication may reflect not dishonesty but the gap between tightly controlled labs and messy real world contexts.

Changes in measurement and analytics

Max Mawby, Managing Director of Applied Behavioural Science at Thinks Insight & Strategy, whose career spans leadership roles at the BIT, Plum Fintech, and Kantar Public, argued that the replication debate is really a call for greater rigour: 'Wherever you're doing experiments, making sure that you are recording and sharing your analysis plan and your data ... it adds rigour and means your work is just that much more likely to stand the test of time.' Advances in measurement and analytics mean that older findings sometimes fail simply because today's tools are more precise.

For example, wearable devices, eye-tracking, and neuroimaging now provide richer, more objective data than older self-reports.[164–167] Interventions tested with VR or AI personalization often generate stronger effects than static text-based studies.[168] Analytical techniques such as machine learning and Bayesian re-randomization uncover subgroup effects and causal structures that earlier methods could not.[169] A study that once looked robust may fail replication, not because it was fraudulent, but because new tools show the underlying mechanism was weaker or different than assumed.

Changes in context

Replication also depends on timing. As Ian Bright, previously Managing Director of Group Research at ING, pointed out, focusing narrowly on behavioural interventions can miss wider economic realities: 'I find it insufficient to emphasise behavioural approaches to helping people save when a key element for many is that they simply do not have enough income.' Social and economic shifts alter whether interventions still work.

Interventions can also lose potency as people adapt. Calorie labelling, for instance, initially reduced consumption[170] but quickly wore off as consumers grew accustomed to it.[171] Similar 'familiarity effects' have been observed in financial nudges[172, 173] and COVID-19 measures.[174] Technological change has the same effect: early studies on 'algorithm aversion' found people distrust AI forecasts,[175] but as AI has become more widespread, trust has increased in some domains while remaining absent in others.[176]

Testing boundary conditions

Finally, some replication failures highlight the boundaries of theories. As Ryan Hamilton, Associate Professor of Marketing at Emory University, explained, 'There's no theory of behavioural science that applies to everyone all the time ... some replication problems suggest dishonesty or error, but others reflect that we've crossed into a different population, time, or method.'

Rather than undermining behavioural science, these boundary conditions clarify its limits. Failed replications often show us not that the original result was meaningless, but that it was more context-dependent than first assumed. Mapping those limits is part of maturing into a more robust discipline.

Summary

Replication failures are not always signs of weakness. Many stem from differences in samples, methods, measurement, or context. Recognizing these scientifically valid reasons prevents us from overreacting to every failure as scandal, while still pushing the field to tighten its standards. Replication, then, is not just about catching errors; it is about refining our theories and practices so behavioural science becomes more resilient and credible over time.

Non-scientific reasons for non-replication: the four horsemen

Samantha Lamas, Senior Behavioral Researcher at Morningstar, reflected on how the crisis reshaped the field: 'In the past, behavioral science has kind of been about these cute little stories that get everyone's attention … and I think we're stepping away from that for good reason. The whole replication crisis kind of scared us all.' Her comment captures the shift from catchy 'party tricks' to a demand for rigour. But to understand why this change was necessary, we need to confront the four horsemen of the replication crisis: experimenter bias, p-hacking, HARKing, and publication bias.

Experimenter bias

One of the earliest concerns about replicability was the unconscious influence of experimenters themselves. In the 'elderly priming' study, participants allegedly walked more slowly after being exposed to words related to old age.[160] Replications later suggested that this effect may have been due to experimenter expectations rather than genuine behavioural change. Doyen et al (2012) demonstrated that when experimenters were blind to conditions, the priming effect disappeared, showing how subtle cues like tone or body language could bias outcomes.[161]

Empirical reviews confirm the point. *Forbes* (2013) concluded that blinding reduces bias in both clinical and behavioural trials,[177] while Holman et al (2015) found that non-blinded studies in life sciences reported significantly inflated effect sizes.[178] Today, blinding participants and experimenters has become best practice in behavioural labs, reducing this first horseman of replication failure.

P-hacking and fraud

Zsófia Belovai, Associate Director of Behavioral Science at Novartis and previously Behavioral Science Lead at MoreThanNow, warned that the challenge is not just methodological but ethical: 'The replication crisis has been a big issue for a while … the greatest challenge for us is to establish frameworks that help prevent the need to use fraudulent practices.' Her concern echoes what Simmons, Nelson, and Simonsohn (2011) demonstrated: that undisclosed researcher degrees of freedom, or p-hacking, can make almost anything statistically significant.[179]

The most notorious cases of misconduct went far beyond p-hacking. Diederik Stapel admitted in 2011 to fabricating data across at least 55 papers, many of them in top journals.[180] Investigations revealed systematic invention of entire datasets, shaking confidence in the publication process. Around the same time, Brian Wansink's 'food psychology' lab came under scrutiny. In a now-infamous blog post, Wansink described how his team 'tortured' data until it produced publishable results.[181] Scholars quickly uncovered more than 150 errors across his publications.[182] Cornell University opened an investigation, and in 2018, the *Journal of the American Medical Association* (JAMA) and other journals retracted multiple papers.[183]

Steve Wendel, co-founder and Head of Methodology of sistemaFutura, previously at Busara and Morningstar, was blunt about the need for consequences: 'We're slowly getting our house in order. That includes people being fired, which is necessary and healthy.' His comment reflects the mood following the Ariely and Gino controversies. In 2012, the paper 'Signing at the beginning makes ethics salient' claimed that signing honesty declarations reduced dishonesty.[184] In 2021, the Data Colada blog identified anomalies in the dataset, including duplicate records and fabricated observations.[185] Ariely denied responsibility, attributing the data to an insurance company that later publicly disputed his claim.

More recently, Harvard professor Francesca Gino has become the most prominent face of misconduct in behavioural science. In 2023, Data Colada presented evidence of manipulated data in four of her studies,[186–189] Harvard placed her on leave while investigations proceeded. Gino retaliated with a $25 million lawsuit against Harvard and the Data Colada authors, but in September 2024, a judge dismissed her defamation claims while allowing breach-of-contract allegations to proceed.[190] By May 2025, the university took the extraordinary step of revoking her tenure, the first such decision in over 80 years, and formally terminated her employment, citing multiple instances of misconduct.[191,192] In July 2025, a federal court declined to force her to pay Data Colada's legal fees, while earlier in the year her original legal team partially withdrew, leaving her represented by a smaller firm.[193] The saga has since escalated further: in September 2025, Harvard countersued Gino for defamation, alleging she had doctored and backdated a spreadsheet on her laptop to make it appear she had received falsified data from another researcher rather than altering it herself. As of mid-2026, both suits remain unresolved and headed toward a joint trial tentatively scheduled for December 2026, with recent forensic filings adding further detail to Harvard's fabrication claims.[194]

These scandals, although rare, have outsized effects. Fraud erodes trust not only in the individuals involved but in behavioural science as a whole, reinforcing scepticism that the field rewards 'cute stories' rather than cumulative science. As Belovai and Wendel suggest, the only path forward is a systemic one: open data, preregistration, and publication norms that reward rigour, not manipulation.

HARKing

Jason Collins, Senior Lecturer at the University of Technology Sydney, who previously led behavioural economics and data science teams at the Australian Securities and Investments Commission (ASIC) and PwC Australia, was direct: 'I try to approach behavioural science with rigour … treating it as science rather than storytelling. Behavioural science is often presented as a list of 'party tricks'. His critique speaks to the third horseman: HARKing, which was a term coined by Kerr in 1998 to describe when researchers retroactively adjust their hypotheses to match results.[195]

Empirical evidence shows the practice is widespread. A survey of psychologists found that many admitted to reframing hypotheses post hoc.[196] Academic research has similarly documented high rates of 'questionable research practices', including selective reporting and HARKing.[197] The effect is to mislead both academic and applied audiences, giving the impression of theoretical confirmation where none exists.

The consequences extend well beyond academia. When policy makers use evidence tainted by HARKing, they may commit resources to ineffective or harmful interventions. As such, post hoc storytelling systematically inflates false positives and distorts cumulative science.[198]

Publication bias

The fourth horseman is publication bias, or what Rosenthal (1979) termed the 'file drawer problem'.[123] Felicity Algate, Economics Director at Ofcom and former Director at the BIT and the UK's Competition and Markets Authority, underscored the danger: '[Publication bias] means that the body of research ... may be biased in favour of research which shows surprising or interesting results.' This structural issue ensures that null results remain unpublished, skewing the evidence base.

The effects are well documented. Ioannidis (2005) argued that most published research findings are false, partly because of selective reporting.[199] Similarly, it's been shown that over 60 per cent of null results in political science experiments remained unpublished.[200] This means that, when unpublished studies are included, meta-analytic effect sizes dropped substantially.[201]

The nudge literature illustrates this vividly. As mentioned in Chapter 3, the 2022 meta-analysis of nudge interventions reported a moderate effect size (Cohen's d = 0.43).[4] But a reanalysis using Robust Bayesian Meta-Analysis found the true effect size to be much smaller (d = 0.09).[5] Elisabeth Convery, Principal Adviser and Head of Research (APAC) at the BIT, described the cultural barrier underlying this distortion: 'There's still this undercurrent in academia where publishing null results feels like career suicide.' Unless that culture shifts, publication bias will continue to erode the reliability of evidence syntheses.

Summary

The four horsemen: experimenter bias, p-hacking, HARKing, and publication bias, represent the non-scientific drivers of replication failure. They have fuelled scandal, mistrust, and wasted resources. But they also point to solutions: preregistration, open data, valuing null results, and shifting incentives away from novelty toward rigour. Only then can behavioural science shed its reliance on 'cute little stories' and build a more durable foundation.

Impact of the replication crisis

Swee-Hoon Chuah, Professor of Behavioural Economics and Director of the Behavioural Lab at the University of Tasmania, put the reputational stakes plainly:

> With the replication crisis and the cases of questionable research ethics being in the news lately, our reputation

> is being damaged. Haters use just one or two examples to discredit our entire body of work. The majority of behavioural scientists are ethical, and do rigorous work, good work, and we're making impactful contributions.

Her warning highlights how a handful of scandals and failed replications can overshadow the vast majority of rigorous, ethical research.

Reputation and application

Koen Smets, Head of Change Management at PSM Consulting and Adjunct Assistant Professor at Saint Louis University, noted that 'low-credibility findings, whether due to sloppy design, small sample size, or lack of representativity, give rise to two consequences. One is that the reputation of the field is being damaged; the other is that some of that low-quality research is being adopted uncritically, and predictably leading to poor results.' His point underscores how weak evidence harms both the academic reputation of behavioural science and its applied credibility.

One striking example is the policy debate around defaults in organ donation. Johnson and Goldstein's celebrated paper showed that opt-out systems dramatically increased donation rates.[202] The finding was hailed as behavioural science's calling card and became widely cited in policy circles. Yet replications across different institutional contexts revealed mixed outcomes: in countries with weaker healthcare systems, defaults alone had little effect.[23, 203] Critics seized on these results to question whether behavioural science was overselling its reach. Similar dynamics have played out in interventions such as calorie labelling, which initially showed promise in reducing consumption, but whose effects diminished as consumers habituated.

The visibility of fraud magnifies these doubts. The misconduct cases mentioned previously dominated headlines and became shorthand for the supposed unreliability of the entire field. In reality, fraud remains rare. But perception matters. Policy makers and private organisations, wary of being burned, now treat behavioural interventions with suspicion. Governments demand multiple replications before scaling policies, while businesses often retreat to conventional economic or marketing tools. Practitioners find themselves in a defensive crouch, spending more time justifying behavioural science than advancing it.

Academic consequences

Within academia, the replication crisis has reshaped standards. Sasha Tregebov reflected: 'The "replication crisis" is a meaningful concern and has brought quite a few formerly accepted results into question, so it would be great to continue seeing fundamental theories being tested and refined using the most robust available methods.' The reforms he describes, preregistration, open data, and large-scale replications, are now becoming standard expectations.

The Many Labs projects illustrate this cultural shift. The first, in 2014, replicated 13 classic psychology findings across 36 independent samples, finding that some effects held while others were weaker or vanished entirely.[157] Many Labs 2 expanded this to 28 studies across 125 samples, showing that context: culture, language, and even timing, significantly shaped outcomes.[158] These projects built trust in the effects that replicated, but they also showed how fragile many 'classic' results were.

While these reforms strengthen the field, they impose costs. Publications take longer; review is stricter; null results, though more valued, are still harder to publish. Early-career researchers (ECRs) bear the brunt. Their careers depend on producing publications quickly, but replications are resource-intensive and under-rewarded. The irony is striking: senior scholars, whose careers were built under looser standards, retain their prestige, while ECRs are held to higher bars in a less forgiving environment.

Theoretical consequences

Paradoxically, the replication crisis has barely altered the field's theoretical foundations. As Adam Mastroianni (2023) noted in *I'm So Sorry for Psychology's Loss, Whatever It Is*,[a] even high-profile retractions have had little impact on core theory.[204] Stapel's fabricated studies accumulated over 10,000 citations, but when retracted, no major models collapsed. Ariely's work on honesty interventions and Gino's studies on behavioural ethics were influential but peripheral. Their removal did not force revisions to central theories.

This raises a deeper concern: why did misconduct not matter more? The answer lies in the incentive system. Flashy, media-friendly findings, 'cute little stories', as Samantha Lamas put it, propel careers but rarely build cumulative theory. Longitudinal research, field RCTs, and careful methodological refinement do more to strengthen theory but are harder to publish and less rewarded. The replication crisis exposed not just unreliable findings, but a system that consistently elevates results that never carried theoretical weight.

Human consequences

If theory has endured, people have not. Brian Nosek, co-founder and Executive Director of the Center for Open Science and Professor at the University of Virginia, diagnosed the structural incentives: 'Researchers know how to succeed under the current system – get published in high-impact journals, get citations, get tenure. Trying something new is risky if no one else is doing it.' This environment punishes risk-taking and rewards questionable shortcuts.

For ECRs, the fallout has been devastating. Students who built dissertations on priming or power posing found themselves stranded in intellectual dead zones once replication failures mounted.[205] Replication attempts that revealed null results were undervalued by journals, leaving ECRs with little to show for years of labour.[206] Others were tainted by association with senior figures implicated in fraud, even when they had no role in misconduct.

The psychological toll has been equally significant. Researchers describe disillusionment and burnout after chasing effects that proved irreproducible.[207] Some left academia entirely, a haemorrhage of precisely the talent most invested in reforming the system.[208] As Inzlicht and Friese (2019) argued in reviewing the ego depletion saga, the field's tendency to overpromise and underdeliver leaves young researchers especially vulnerable to career and emotional collapse.[209]

Not unique to behavioural science

Felicity Algate reminds us that the replication crisis is not confined to behavioural science: 'There is a significant amount of work being devoted to trying to reduce publication bias (for example, pre-registration) but there still seems to be a significant problem.' Other fields face the same structural incentives, publish-or-perish, novelty bias, and selective reporting, but often without the same visibility.

Medicine provides some of the starkest parallels. Turner et al (2008) found that 94 per cent of positive antidepressant trials were published, compared with just 31 per cent of null results.[210] Begley and Ellis (2012) reported that only six of 53 landmark preclinical cancer studies replicated, attributing the failures to selective reporting and underpowered designs.[211–213] In economics, Reinhart and Rogoff's (2010) paper on public debt and growth[214] shaped global austerity policy before a graduate student revealed a spreadsheet error undermining its conclusions.[215] Climate science has weathered politicized attacks on Michael Mann's 'hockey stick' graph,[216] validated by the US National Research Council[217] but tarnished by accusations of opacity.[218] Even physics, often seen as the gold standard of rigour, has endured major fraud cases, from Jan Hendrik Schön's falsified semiconductor results[219] to Victor Ninov's fabricated evidence for element 118.[220]

As Emily Daniels put it: 'The replication crisis, combined with a lack of transparency outside academia, has really damaged trust in the field.' Her point is crucial. The crisis is not uniquely behavioural science's problem, but behavioural science, by virtue of its policy relevance and media appeal, has become its most visible case study.

Towards a credible and replicable science

The replication crisis shook the foundations of behavioural science. It showed us that fragile methods were only part of the problem: deeper structural issues, perverse incentives, weak infrastructure, over-reliance on narrow samples, and poor communication, which meant that even well-intentioned research often failed to deliver lasting insights. Yet if the crisis exposed our vulnerabilities, it also opened a path forward. Replication is not simply a technical challenge. It is a cultural, institutional, and practical imperative that must be woven into every layer of the discipline, from theory and training to practice and communication.

The question, then, is not whether behavioural science can survive the replication crisis, because it will, but what kind of field it will become as a result. The following six strategies offer a roadmap: aligning incentives, building infrastructure, grounding replication in the real world, training for transparency, making replication global, and communicating rigour with compelling stories.

Step 1. Align incentives with better science

For Hans Rocha IJzerman, CEO of Entrelacs and founder of the Annecy Behavioral Science Lab, the issue could not be clearer:

> Who gets jobs, promotions, or grants still often depends on the number of papers published, not on the quality of the research or the robustness of the methodology … We've been aware of the issues with replication, open science, and data sharing for years, but the field still hasn't fully embraced the necessary changes.

For decades, novelty was the currency of academic success. A researcher who produced a counterintuitive, statistically significant result, say, that thinking of the elderly makes people walk more slowly, could catapult their career forward, even if that finding later collapsed. The incentives were simple: eye-catching results meant high-impact journals, citations, and tenure. Reliability was secondary.

The replication crisis revealed the damage. Findings that could not be reproduced were not just wasted effort; they became the foundation for new studies, policy recommendations, and media narratives. When those crumbled, the credibility of the entire field suffered.

Changing this dynamic means redesigning the incentive system. Universities must reward open science practices in hiring and tenure decisions, not just publication counts. Funding bodies should dedicate grants to replication projects and mandate preregistration and data sharing. Journals must evolve too, adopting registered reports, where research plans are peer-reviewed before results are known. This flips the incentive: what gets rewarded is not a surprising finding but a transparent process.

Brian Nosek, one of the leaders of the open science movement, captured the scale of the challenge: 'Science as a system is very conservative. Peer review today looks like it did in the 1960s, even though everything else in the world has evolved. I want to flip that – so that science is always innovating on how it does its work, not just what questions it asks.'

Incentive reform must also address misconduct. Cases such as Diederik Stapel, Dan Ariely, and Francesca Gino have shown how a few instances of fraud can erode trust across the entire field. Robust governance is needed: independent integrity boards, whistleblower protections, and transparent retraction processes that protect innocent co-authors while holding perpetrators accountable. Aligning incentives is not just about rewarding replication; it is also about reducing the temptation to cut corners.

Practical steps

- Reform hiring and promotion metrics: Universities should move beyond counting publications and instead weigh evidence of open science practices, preregistration, and data sharing in hiring and tenure. Committees can adopt explicit rubrics where replication efforts and transparency carry equal weight to novelty.
- Create targeted replication funding: Research councils should carve out specific funds for replication, particularly of high-impact studies that inform policy. Grants could require public preregistration and the posting of all data, regardless of outcomes.
- Adopt registered reports widely: Journals should incentivize robust design over surprising results by reviewing study plans before results are known, guaranteeing publication if protocols are followed.
- Strengthen research integrity systems: Independent integrity boards should oversee investigations into misconduct, supported by whistleblower protections. Transparent retraction policies should safeguard innocent co-authors while ensuring accountability for fraud.
- Celebrate transparency: Professional societies should introduce awards for replication and open data, signalling that careers can advance through credibility as much as innovation.

Aligning incentives is the foundation of reform. Without it, open science will remain a niche practice and replication an afterthought. But if universities, funders, and journals reward transparency as much as novelty, the field can shift from fragile flashes of insight to durable progress. Replication will no longer be seen as career suicide, but as a hallmark of scientific excellence.

Step 2. Build shared infrastructure for replication

Incentives alone are not enough. Even motivated researchers cannot do rigorous replication work without the right infrastructure. At present, behavioural science is patchy: some labs use the Open Science Framework (OSF) or AsPredicted to preregister studies, while others still rely on internal spreadsheets. Applied teams may produce high-quality reports, but these often remain hidden behind paywalls or confidentiality agreements.

Shane Timmons, Senior Research Officer in the Behavioural Research Unit at the ESRI and Adjunct Professor of Psychology at Trinity College Dublin, frames this as a collective action problem. The field benefits when organisations share what they tested, including what failed, because it prevents duplication and accelerates cumulative learning. But individual teams often face the opposite incentives: disclosing null findings can feel reputationally risky, commercially sensitive, or simply unrewarded. The result is predictable: knowledge accumulates locally, but not collectively. Replication becomes harder not because people don't care about rigour, but because the system makes openness optional.

This fragmentation wastes resources. If one team quietly fails to replicate an effect, others may unknowingly repeat the same experiment, only to reach the same null conclusion years later. Without shared repositories, we cannot learn collectively.

What's needed is coordinated infrastructure:

- Centralized databases of interventions coded by population, context, and outcome. Imagine if every nudge, replication, and null result were logged into a living, searchable system.
- Standardized reporting templates for replication studies, so that multi-site collaborations are easier to coordinate and compare.
- Open repositories where both academic and applied teams can upload findings, reducing the secrecy that currently hampers learning.

Oliver Hauser, Professor of Economics and Deputy Director of AI Institute at the University of Exeter and Senior Adviser to the UK Cabinet Office, has shown the power of coordination. In one international replication, his team's original study held up across multiple labs and contexts: 'When other researchers were asked to predict which studies would replicate, our study was predicted as the most likely to be replicable.' That level of confidence only comes from building replication into the design itself.

Shared infrastructure ensures replication is not occasional or ad hoc. It becomes a natural part of how behavioural science operates.

Practical steps

- Create a central replication registry. A global body such as the OECD, American Psychological Association (APA), or OSF could host a searchable registry where all behavioural interventions, successes and failures alike are logged with contextual details.
- Standardize reporting templates. Common formats for replication studies would allow results from different labs to be compared directly. Templates should capture sample, setting, measures, and deviations from protocols.
- Break down silos. Applied teams in governments and companies should be encouraged and funded to share anonymized results in open repositories. Confidentiality concerns can be managed through secure access tiers.
- Develop metadata standards. Interventions should be tagged with information about population, delivery mode, and outcome type; therefore, patterns can be detected across contexts.
- Sustain infrastructure. Funder consortia should support not just building platforms but maintaining them, with dedicated teams to curate entries and ensure usability.

Shared infrastructure transforms replication from an occasional act into a cumulative enterprise. When failures and successes are openly recorded, others can build instead of repeating mistakes. A culture of openness supported by collective tools makes replication not just easier but inevitable.

Step 3. Bring replication into the real world

Replication is hardest outside the lab. Controlled settings strip away noise, but applied interventions unfold in the messiness of real life. As Renos Vakis, Head of eMBeD at the World Bank, observed, 'We now have over 600 behavioural science teams in the public sector alone ... some are incredibly rigorous, while others are much more superficial.' The rapid expansion of applied behavioural science has created wide variation in quality.

Patrick Forscher, Senior Behavioral Scientist at Busara and former Director of its meta-research group, CREME, was even sharper: 'Many applied behavioural science practices, especially in corporate and policy sectors, lack the rigorous standards that should define scientific inquiry.' When practitioners adopt behavioural interventions without preregistration, open data, or replication, the result may be more consultancy than science. Shane Timmons makes a related distinction: the real contribution of behavioural science is not the popularity of its concepts, but the disciplined application of the scientific method to behavioural problems. Applying well-known findings without testing or evaluation may be pragmatic, but without measurement and scrutiny, it is not behavioural science in the full sense.

This is not just a methodological problem; it is a reputational one. Helena Rubinstein, Head of Strategic Services and Behavioural Scientist at Innovia Technology, warned:

> Until we are able to get more systematic evidence for what works and what doesn't and also how long the effects last, we will find it difficult to design effective interventions or make strong recommendations. If the behavioural solutions we recommend are partially effective, or worse, non-effective, organisations will become cynical about the value of behavioural science.

The consequences are already visible. Interventions that once looked promising: calorie labelling on menus, or default options in pensions, now face scepticism when results fade over time. In finance, robo-advisers once hailed as the future of behavioural applications have failed to gain widespread trust, despite supportive lab evidence. After COVID-19, public willingness to follow behavioural interventions such as social distancing nudges declined sharply as fatigue set in.

The lesson is simple: replication in applied settings cannot be an afterthought. It requires systematic reform:

- Preregistration should be standard practice, even if repositories are private, to protect sensitive data.

- Multi-site replications should precede major policy rollouts.
- Publication of null results must be mandatory for government-funded projects, preventing wasted effort.
- Open white papers and industry reports should document interventions, not just peer-reviewed articles.

As Linnea Gandhi, Lecturer at the Wharton School and Adjunct Assistant Professor of Behavioral Science at the University of Chicago Booth School of Business, put it, behavioural science must stop producing one-off 'stories' and start producing 'structured products': living, cumulative evidence bases.

Practical steps

- Make preregistration the norm in applied settings. Even when confidentiality is necessary, preregistrations can be kept in restricted repositories with release after publication. This signals rigour while protecting sensitive data.
- Require multi-site replications before major policy rollouts. Governments should avoid scaling interventions based on one-off trials. Independent teams in different contexts can test whether effects hold before costly investments are made.
- Mandate reporting of null results in public projects. Funders should insist that evaluations, whether successful or not, be published in accessible formats to prevent wasteful duplication.
- Encourage white papers alongside academic articles. Industry reports, when transparent, can fill the gap between consultancy deliverables and peer-reviewed publications, offering practical insights to others.
- Develop applied science benchmarks. Professional associations can create checklists for applied teams: covering preregistration, data transparency, and replication, that distinguish rigorous science from superficial consultancy.

Applied replication protects credibility. Without it, behavioural science risks being dismissed as consultancy dressed up as science. By embedding rigour into fieldwork and insisting on transparency, the discipline can show that its insights work not only in theory but in practice.

Step 4. Train for transparency

Cultural change begins in training. For Eric Singler, Senior Adviser at Ipsos BVA, founder of BVA Nudge Consulting, as well as co-founder and President of NudgeFrance, humility is the first lesson: 'Context is so important … universal learnings can often be questioned. We still have a lot to learn.'

That humility must be built into behavioural science education. Students need to learn not only how to design clever interventions but how to preregister hypotheses, share reproducible code, interpret null results, and collaborate with rivals. These are the skills that will make replication a default, not an exception.

James Healy, founder of The Behaviour Boutique and former Principal for Human Capital Consulting at Deloitte, stressed the personal side of this training: 'You're constantly testing approaches, constantly realising that things you previously thought aren't true, and constantly being reminded of your own shortcomings' For Joseph Devlin, Professor of Cognitive Neuroscience at UCL and co-founder of Applied Consumer Neuroscience, the message was practical: 'Even if you plan to go the full academic route, having experience using behavioural science outside the lab is invaluable. The complexity of the real world often means that our best laid plans can go awry in unforeseen, but often interesting, ways.'

In practice, this means embedding replication into curricula: adversarial collaborations as class projects, fieldwork that shows how messy real interventions can be, and exposure to failed replications as learning opportunities. Mentors must model these values, rewarding transparency and integrity rather than flashy results.

Training is where culture shifts begin. Without it, reforms will remain fragile.

Practical steps

- Embed replication skills in education. Curricula should require students to preregister projects, share reproducible code, and analyze failed replications. Training should make transparency second nature.
- Use adversarial collaborations as teaching tools. Students should work in teams with differing hypotheses, designing experiments

that can adjudicate fairly between them, learning humility and openness.

- Incorporate case studies of failure. Classes should analyze famous failed replications and fraud cases, teaching not only statistics but ethics and responsibility.
- Reward open practice in hiring. Institutions can require applicants to provide open datasets, preregistrations, or replication work as part of job applications.
- Train supervisors and mentors. Senior academics must model the behaviours they want in trainees, publishing their own code and data to set the standard.

Transparency is not just a skill; it is a culture. Training the next generation to value openness over flashiness is the only way to ensure reforms last. If students see transparency as integral to good science, replication will become a habit, not an exception.

Step 5. Make replication global and inclusive

The replication crisis is not just about methodology; it is also about who gets studied. Behavioural science has been overwhelmingly WEIRD (Chapter 4). Replication across cultures is essential if we are to claim universal insights.

Serene Koh, Director of the BIT in Singapore, put it plainly: 'If we do not frame our work as being universal insofar as it is adaptable to different contexts, then … large populations of the world … will not benefit from the good that behavioural scientists can do.'

Replication that ignores diversity risks reproducing inequities. For example, default enrolment in pensions works well in high-income countries with established financial systems, but has little relevance in low-income settings where access to pensions is rare. Similarly, nudges that assume literacy or digital access may fail in populations without those resources.

Funders must therefore prioritize global replication, investing in labs in the Global South and supporting international collaborations. Journals should mandate demographic transparency and encourage submissions that test interventions across cultures. Inclusivity is not an optional add-on; it is central to replication. Only by mapping boundary conditions globally can we distinguish genuine universals from local effects.

Practical steps

- Prioritize Global South research capacity. Funders should invest in local labs, infrastructure, and training to enable replications outside WEIRD contexts.
- Mandate demographic transparency. Journals should require full reporting of participant demographics, including socioeconomic status, ethnicity, and region, so that limitations are visible.
- Build international replication consortia. Global collaborations testing the same intervention across multiple countries can reveal true boundary conditions.
- Train for cultural adaptation. Courses should teach researchers how to adapt measures, interventions, and consent processes to local contexts.
- Reward boundary-mapping. Journals and funders should explicitly reward research that defines where an effect works and where it does not, instead of penalizing complexity.

Replication that ignores diversity is replication in name only. A global science must test its claims globally, mapping boundaries and respecting cultural variation. Only then can behavioural science claim universality without arrogance.

Step 6. Communicate rigour with storytelling

Replication has an image problem. Prince Ghuman, Head of Marketing at Nurp and former Head of Marketing at Turbine Capital and Pop Neuro, lamented that 'the communication of research behind behavioural science was not calibrated to the public at large.' Too often, we communicate in one of two extremes: dense academic jargon or overhyped TED-style soundbites. Neither builds trust.

Jason Collins, Senior Lecturer at the University of Technology Sydney, who previously led behavioural economics and data science teams at ASIC and PwC Australia, warned against presenting behavioural science as 'party tricks'. The danger is that if communication remains focused on clever but fragile results, the discipline will forever be seen as consultancy rebranded. Instead, we must learn to tell better stories of process. Shane Timmons reminds us that replication only strengthens science if it is understood.

Findings must be communicated in ways that policy makers can use. Otherwise, transparency remains internal, and sceptics fill the vacuum with simpler stories. Communication, then, is not public relations. It is the final step in making replication matter. Replication can be narrated as detective work: hypotheses tested, preregistrations logged, unexpected setbacks confronted, null results revealed. Fieldwork provides opportunities for compelling human-centred narratives, researchers negotiating with schools, governments, or firms, learning from failures as much as from successes.

As Brian Nosek argued, poor communication prevents valuable findings from influencing practice. To counter this, we must normalize celebrating null results: not as 'failures', but as clarity gained. A null result tells us what doesn't work, saving others from repeating mistakes. If communicated well, this honesty builds credibility.

To make this shift, training must include communication skills: how to visualize workflows, narrate setbacks, and explain technical choices clearly. Journals, conferences, and funders should actively reward transparency in communication, highlighting best-in-class replication reports.

Because here is the hard truth: if we only reward what is exciting, we will keep producing fragile research. But if we celebrate the beauty of good process: rigorous, transparent, cumulative, we will finally build a field that lasts.

Practical steps

- Teach communication skills in training. Graduate programmes should include modules on writing for the public, creating accessible visuals, and narrating research processes.
- Reward transparent storytelling. Journals and conferences should highlight exemplary replication papers that explain setbacks and null results clearly.
- Promote open-access narratives. Applied teams should publish public-facing white papers and blogs that explain replication findings without jargon.
- Celebrate null results. Professional bodies can create awards or showcases for studies that provide clarity by showing what does not work.

- Build media partnerships. Collaborations with science journalists and communicators can help translate rigorous replication into compelling public stories.

Conclusion

The replication crisis has been a painful reckoning, but it has also been clarifying. It showed us that the weaknesses of behavioural science were not limited to fragile studies or statistical missteps. They were embedded in the very structures that shaped the field: an obsession with novelty, incentives that rewarded quantity over quality, and a culture that treated null results as failures rather than as knowledge. For Swee-Hoon Chuah, the reputational consequences of these failures remain severe: critics seize on a few scandals to 'discredit our entire body of work'. Yet, as she stresses, the majority of behavioural scientists are ethical, rigorous, and making important contributions. The task now is ensuring that the systems we operate in reward that rigour, rather than undermining it.

Signs of change are real. Large-scale replication projects, preregistration, and open data practices are no longer fringe concerns but increasingly mainstream. As Hans Rocha IJzerman observed, 'a lot of emphasis is placed on replication, open science, and improving the quality of our research, and I believe that will continue to grow'. ECRs, in particular, are pushing for reform, often at personal cost to their career progression. They are demonstrating, by example, that it is possible to build a more transparent and cumulative science. Multi-lab collaborations now make it much harder for weak effects to slip through, and they help shift our focus from single 'hero studies' to collective evidence.

At the same time, progress remains uneven. Senior academics, who built careers in an era of looser standards, often resist reforms that challenge their authority. Applied behavioural science faces its own constraints: the demand for fast results, client confidentiality, and political pressures can sideline replication and transparency. As Helena Rubinstein warned, without 'systematic evidence for what works and what doesn't and also how long the effects last', organisations will become cynical about behavioural science altogether.

Yet the crisis is best understood not as a collapse but as a crossroads. It forced behavioural science to ask what kind of field it wants to be.

Francesca Pape, Behavioural Economist at the European Commission and previously at the OECD, put it bluntly: 'A lot of behavioural science's credibility depends on being transparent about what works and what doesn't. That means publishing replication failures, even when it's uncomfortable.' Transparency is not just a technical reform; it is the basis of public trust. If we can embrace this ethos, the crisis becomes not an end but a foundation for renewal.

Patrick Forscher captured this vision well: 'In the next 10 years, I hope behavioural science moves beyond being seen as a "trendy" tool and becomes a field known for its rigour, transparency, and global relevance.' That is also my hope. As ultimately, this chapter, well, this entire book, is not about what behavioural science is, but what it could become. Getting our methods right is only part of the story. The next step is to confront an equally urgent challenge: how to make sure the science is not only reliable, but also ethical.

Which brings us to Chapter 7. For a science that claims to influence human behaviour, replicability is not enough. We must also ask whether we are doing so ethically: who benefits, who bears the risks, and what values are embedded in our interventions? Only by combining methodological rigour with ethical responsibility can behavioural science live up to its promise; not as a passing trend, but as a discipline that genuinely serves the societies it studies.

7

Behavioural Science Will Be Ethical

> It's also not always easy to determine what's ethically correct; you really have to push on questions from multiple angles and play out potential future scenarios to come to a position, and I don't think we're used to applying that type of rigor.
>
> Amy Bucher (2020)

Introduction

Behavioural science today stands at a crossroads. As Amy Bucher, Chief Behavioral Officer at Lirio, has noted, the field has been here before:

> [I]mmediately post-World War 2, it was apparent that behavioral scientists needed to get their house in order in light of how the science had been used and mis-used. Much of modern oversight of human subjects research comes from reforms at that time. We're now in a new era where technology has introduced new opportunities to behave ethically or not.

On the one hand, behavioural science is celebrated for its capacity to improve lives, from encouraging healthier choices to boosting retirement savings. On the other hand, it is criticized as manipulative, opaque, and paternalistic. The uncomfortable truth is that it can be both. As Preeti Kothamarthi, Director of Behavioural Science and User Research at Swiggy, put it:

> the other extremely important role a behavioural scientist should take, irrespective of whether they are explicitly asked to or not, is that of a guardian of ethics. Businesses will use whatever it takes to help them reach business goals. It's up to a behavioural scientist to be that person who reminds the company about ethical implications.

This duality frames the purpose of this chapter. Ethics in behavioural science cannot be reduced to a checklist of principles or outsourced to compliance teams. It is about embedding reflection and accountability into everyday practice, recognizing that what counts as 'ethical' is shaped by context. As Natalia le Gal, behavioural science consultant and founder of the consultancy Behava, observed, applied behavioural science 'is often the Wild West. Unlike academia, which has strong ethical frameworks, applied work lacks consistency and accountability. We need better awareness from policy makers and clearer standards, similar to what we've seen in the UK's financial sector when it comes to nudging.' This chapter, therefore, examines how ethics is handled differently in academic versus applied settings, unpacks the frameworks that attempt to guide practitioners, and argues that ethical concerns are ultimately symptoms of a deeper issue: the lack of standardization across the applied field. In doing so, it sets the stage for practical steps towards building a behavioural science that earns not only credibility but also legitimacy in the eyes of the societies it seeks to serve.

The ethical tension

The ethical status of behavioural science is not determined by the tools it uses but by the contexts in which those tools are applied. This is where the tension arises: a field that offers powerful ways of shaping behaviour must also grapple with whether those applications genuinely serve the public good.

Christopher Boyce, Wellbeing Economist at BiGGAR Economics, has described this vividly: 'my main critique of behavioural science stems from what might be called the dark nudge ... the context design that takes place routinely in the private sector to encourage people to go against their better interests'. What he calls the 'dark nudge' is now a well-recognized category of practice, often grouped under the label of 'dark patterns'.[221–224] These are design strategies that use the same insights as public health interventions or retirement nudges, but in ways that exploit people's vulnerabilities rather than protect them.

The most common examples are depressingly familiar. Subscription services that offer free trials but bury the cancel button in layers of menus; checkout pages where hidden costs appear only at the final stage; or opt-out buttons designed to guilt-trip the user into staying 'No thanks, I hate saving money'.[223] These tactics are effective because they exploit well-documented biases such as inertia, salience, and loss aversion. In this sense, they represent behavioural science 'working', but in a way that undermines rather than enhances welfare.

Researchers and regulators have attempted to categorize these practices.[221–224] Some of the most prominent include:

- Roach Motel: easy to join, hard to leave;
- Forced continuity: free trials that quietly become paid subscriptions;
- Confirmshaming: opt-out language designed to shame users ('No thanks, I don't care about the environment');
- Endless scroll and auto-play: interfaces that remove natural stopping points;
- Trick questions: confusingly worded choices that manipulate consent.

Such practices illustrate the field's ethical fault lines. When behavioural insights are deployed without transparency or user benefit in mind, it is difficult to defend them as ethical. And yet, in the absence of agreed standards, these practices continue to proliferate.

Autonomy and paternalism

Beyond dark patterns, behavioural science is also criticized for its paternalistic tendencies. Fabio Tadashi Suzaki, Managing Partner at Nudge.biz and former Chief Research Officer at neoxs, observed: 'I think that we will go through a period of disillusionment and skepticism with respect to biases and nudges. This has already started, and I expect it will continue for some time as practitioners wrestle with the practical and ethical limits of the discipline.'

The critique is straightforward: nudges and other interventions often rest on the assumption that policy makers or businesses know what is best for people, and therefore have the legitimacy to guide decisions in that direction,[225] a concern also tackled in Chapter 3. In particular, automatic enrolments and defaults have come under scrutiny because they remove deliberation about the specific behaviour being promoted.[21,226,227]

Defenders of libertarian paternalism counter that nudges preserve freedom of choice while improving welfare: defaults can always be changed, opt-outs always exist.[228] Cass Sunstein and Richard Thaler's original case for nudges rested on the idea that choice architecture is inevitable; given that environments are always designed in some way, it is better to design them consciously and with human welfare in mind.

But critics argue that the boundary between help and coercion is thinner than this defence admits. As Rebonato (2012) pointed out, even when interventions are reversible, they still steer, and the very need to 'opt-out' can create asymmetries of power.[227] In corporate settings, this tension sharpens further. A cafeteria redesign that nudges children towards fruit over crisps may plausibly be in their interest. A streaming platform that nudges viewers into hours of continuous content is harder to defend.

Transparency and trust

The ethical murkiness of nudging also extends to transparency. Bridgette Collado, Consumer Experience and Transformation Manager at Corewell Health, reminded practitioners: 'you're not really truly doing behavioural science if you're not also considering the ethics of what you're doing, which can sometimes get murky and require thoughtfulness'. One of those murky areas is how much transparency interventions should involve.

Critics argue that nudges exploit cognitive biases covertly, reducing autonomy by making it harder for people to act on reflective preferences. Examples include default privacy settings that encourage people to share more data than they might intend, or loyalty schemes that lock consumers into repeated purchases.[229] In these cases, people may technically have choices, but the way those choices are presented undermines their ability to act freely.

Some practitioners worry that too much transparency would undermine interventions altogether. If people know they are being nudged, won't they resist? Recent evidence challenges this assumption. Studies suggest that disclosure does not reduce effectiveness, and in some cases, interventions are evaluated more positively when they are transparent.[230,231] In other words, people prefer being nudged when they feel respected.

Yet ethical complexity remains. In academic studies, informed consent is typically secured through participant information sheets and ethics review boards. In real world field experiments, disclosure can compromise validity: if participants know they are being studied, they may alter behaviour simply because of that awareness. Research shows that support for an intervention can fall dramatically if it is described as an 'experiment', even when outcomes are beneficial.[112] Although that result has not been found to be generalizable or consistent, [113,114] this paradox, that transparency can reduce both effectiveness and public support, epitomizes the ethical dilemmas behavioural scientists must navigate.

The stakes

Sarah Kneebone, Founder of Skyflower Solutions and former Education Manager at BehaviourWorks Australia, summarized the challenge: 'From an ethical perspective alone, we must be able to check that our intervention has benefitted humanity, and not backfired.' Backfiring is one of the central risks for behavioural science. Even interventions designed with good intentions can unravel when deployed without sensitivity to context. A common response is psychological reactance: people push back against messages about healthy eating or pension saving when they feel patronized or coerced.[232–234] Instead of encouraging better decisions, such interventions can erode trust and reduce the very behaviours they were meant to support.

The challenge is amplified when moving from the lab to the field. Findings that appear robust in controlled conditions often falter when scaled, reinterpreted, or applied to the complexity of everyday life, as discussed in Chapter 6. Equally troubling, what works neatly with a university sample may misfire when applied to more diverse populations, as discussed in Chapter 4. Without careful field testing and adaptation, interventions risk losing efficacy or even producing unintended harms.

A further weakness lies in the absence of long-term evaluation. Too often, interventions are judged on short-term behavioural shifts, with little attention to whether those changes endure. Default enrolment can boost initial pension savings, but long-term engagement and effectiveness, especially during financial hardship, remain uncertain.[232–234] Likewise, 'one-shot' nudges, such as reworded tax letters, may spark temporary compliance; however, they rarely shift entrenched habits once the prompt disappears.[235,236] Without continuous monitoring and iterative refinement, behavioural science risks generating appealing but shallow fixes: interventions that succeed in trials but fail to deliver lasting impact.

As Quique Belenguer Saborit, Behavioural Economics Discipline Leader at BBVA, cautions,

> I think there's still a misunderstanding about what behavioural science actually is. Some people think it's just about persuasion – getting people to do things they wouldn't otherwise do. But it's not about manipulation, it's about understanding how people make decisions and designing better systems around that. We need to keep educating businesses, governments, and the public about what behavioural science really brings to the table. If we don't, we risk being misunderstood or misused.

Without shared standards, these failures aren't isolated accidents; they are predictable outcomes of a field that remains under-defined and under-regulated. Until behavioural science agrees on what counts as ethical practice, it will continue to risk undermining not just its credibility, but also its potential for positive impact.

What counts as ethical behavioural science?

If behavioural science is to claim legitimacy, it must do more than demonstrate that interventions work. It must also define what ethical practice looks like in contexts where influence is unavoidable. But as soon as we try to pin this down, the complexity emerges: an intervention judged ethical in one domain may be condemned in another. Defaults that boost vaccination uptake are celebrated in health, yet defaults that increase credit card debt are criticized in finance. The same behavioural principle takes on different ethical weight depending on who deploys it and toward what end.

Frameworks and principles

In response, scholars and practitioners have proposed frameworks to formalize ethical reflection. One of the most prominent is the FORGOOD framework, which distils seven principles to guide practice: Fairness, Openness, Respect, Goals, Opinions, Options, and Delegation.[22] Each highlights a pressure point where interventions can slide from legitimate to questionable:

- Fairness. Interventions should be equitable, not systematically advantaging one group at the expense of another. Fairness implies actively considering power imbalances, distributional effects, and the potential for interventions to exacerbate existing inequalities.
- Openness. The design, intent, and mechanism of behavioural interventions should be transparent. Stakeholders should be able to understand how and why an intervention works, avoiding secrecy or manipulation.
- Respect. Interventions must preserve individual dignity and autonomy. This means avoiding coercion, manipulation, or exploitation of vulnerabilities, and ensuring that people remain agents in their own choices.
- Goals. The objectives of an intervention must be legitimate and aligned with the welfare of those affected, rather than serving only institutional, political, or commercial interests. Clear articulation of goals is central to accountability.
- Opinions. Interventions should be designed and implemented with sufficient attention to the perspectives, values, and lived experiences of the people it seeks to influence.
- Options. Behavioural insights should expand or clarify choices, not eliminate them. People should feel they retain meaningful alternatives and are not boxed into a single pathway by design.
- Delegation. Those affected by interventions should have some voice in their design or oversight. This principle emphasizes participatory approaches, stakeholder consultation, and democratic legitimacy in applying behavioural science.

These principles provide a language for ethical reflection. Yet, as Natalia le Gal observes, 'There's also the lack of ethical debate in the field. We don't talk enough about whether it's okay to influence people, even for good. We take it for granted.' Principles exist on paper, but in practice, they are applied inconsistently, if at all.

From principles to practice

This inconsistency has consequences. What looks neat in theory often dissolves in the realities of applied work. Frameworks may be cited in presentations or tucked into the appendices of reports, but they rarely govern day-to-day decisions about design or evaluation. When ethical guidelines are treated as optional extras, the results are predictable: variation in standards, uncertainty for practitioners, and confusion for the people affected.

It is here that practitioners sound the alarm themselves. Helena Rubinstein describes applied behavioural science as 'the wild west': some organisations oversimplify methods, others overcomplicate them, leaving clients and users unable to judge quality or ethics. Sarah Osman, founder of Osman Advisory Services and a behavioural science consultant with over two decades of experience in global development, makes a similar point: even within the same organisation, 'it was often unclear what standards they were using or abiding to'. And Patrick Forscher, Senior Behavioral Scientist at Busara and former Director of its meta-research group, CREME, warns that many applied practices 'lack the rigorous standards that should define scientific inquiry'.

Together, these voices point to the same conclusion: without common benchmarks, behavioural science is fragmented. Each organisation, sometimes each team, defines 'ethical practice' on its own terms. And this is not something a framework such as FORGOOD can fix.[22] However, it's a good start.

The push for professionalization

Attempts to close this gap are emerging. GAABS is one of the first organisations to offer accreditation and a code of conduct specific to the field. Its aim is to provide independent oversight and establish a benchmark for methodological and ethical standards. GAABS is still building global maturity, and membership is voluntary, but it signals a recognition that behavioural science requires more than individual conscience to guide practice.

Kelly Peters, Global Behavioural Economics Leader and Partner at Deloitte and former CEO and co-founder of BEworks, has argued for similar forms of professionalization: accreditation systems, shared codes, and ethical oversight bodies that would hold practitioners accountable. Yet progress has been uneven, and many applied teams continue to operate without consistent standards. Eric Singler, Senior Adviser at Ipsos BVA, founder of BVA Nudge Consulting, as well as co-founder and President of NudgeFrance, insists that 'the behavioral science community must be focused on the ethical application of our learnings'. But for now, that responsibility often falls on individual practitioners rather than institutions.

Regulatory patchworks

It is important to acknowledge that behavioural science does not operate in a complete vacuum. Many of the domains where it is applied already have regulatory bodies and compliance boards. In health, research ethics committees and medical regulators oversee patient safety and informed consent. In finance, regulators enforce consumer protection and fairness standards. In technology, frameworks such as the General Data Protection Regulation (GDPR) govern data privacy and consent.

The problem is not the absence of regulation but the lack of integration. Health nudges may pass medical review but fail to consider autonomy. Financial nudges may satisfy regulators on disclosure while still exploiting biases.[a] In technology, data protection boards may guard privacy but remain silent on engagement-maximizing design. This patchwork leaves practitioners navigating inconsistent expectations, with no single standard to unify the field.

Context matters

This fragmentation matters because ethical judgments are not abstract; they are context-dependent. In health, a vaccination reminder default may be seen as proportionate to public benefit. In finance, a default that locks consumers into overdraft fees would be condemned as exploitative. In tech, the same behavioural principle that supports healthy eating nudges in schools is deployed to keep users scrolling past midnight. The ethical valence of an intervention cannot be divorced from the domain in which it is applied.

Beyond compliance

Even where frameworks and boards exist, they often function as compliance checklists rather than living commitments. Filling in forms about fairness or respect is not the same as embedding those values into design. When calorie labelling exacerbates eating disorders, or privacy nudges make opting out unnecessarily difficult, the public sees not ethical principles but ethical failures.

For ethical reflection to become meaningful, it must be integrated into practice from the start. This means asking: Who benefits most from this intervention? What risks might it create for vulnerable groups? Will the effects hold across diverse populations and over time? Would people still support the intervention if they knew how it worked?

Toward coherence

The absence of standardization makes ethical failures predictable. Rubinstein's 'wild west', Osman's fragmented standards, and Forscher's warning about rigour are not just criticisms but reminders of what is at stake. Without common benchmarks, behavioural science risks undermining its credibility as both a science and a practice.

GAABS represents a step towards coherence, as do calls for accreditation and professional codes. But voluntary frameworks are not enough. To be recognized as an ethical field, behavioural science must integrate with existing regulatory structures in health, finance, and technology while also articulating its own shared standards. Only then can it move from patchwork oversight to a coherent professional identity.

When ethical principles aren't protected

Fairness

The principle of Fairness asks whether interventions burden disadvantaged groups. Abdel-Sater and Chevallier (2025) highlight this challenge in the context of green nudges, identifying two mechanisms through which fairness can be compromised.[233] First, many green nudges impose private costs, such as choosing eco-friendly products or offsetting carbon emissions, that weigh more heavily on low-income individuals, despite their smaller contribution to overall pollution. Second, behavioural biases that nudges exploit may operate more strongly among poorer populations, meaning the same intervention can disproportionately shift their behaviour. This creates a regressive effect: those least responsible for environmental harm bear the greatest cost of change. Unless explicitly addressed, such nudges risk deepening rather than reducing inequality.

Similar dynamics emerge in behavioural finance. Automatic enrolment in retirement savings plans has been widely lauded for boosting participation, but it also introduces fairness concerns.[232] Choi et al (2004) demonstrated that while participation rates in US 401(k) plans increased dramatically under default enrolment, many employees stuck with the low default savings rates and conservative investment options for years.[234] For higher-income employees, this inertia posed limited long-term harm because they could rely on other assets. However, for lower-income employees, being anchored to inadequate default risk leaves them with insufficient retirement wealth.[234] Here, a tool designed to increase savings overall ended up distributing its benefits unequally.

Staying in the domain of retirement savings, a 2025 *Forbes* article critically evaluates who is really benefiting from 401(k) employer matches,[235] approaching inadequate defaults not from an anchoring perspective, but from a design perspective. The issue? It's all based on percentages. Nearly half the $200 billion that employers contribute annually accrues to the top 20 per cent of earners, while the bottom 20 per cent receive just 6 per cent.[236] Percentage-based match formulas, such as '50 per cent up to 6 per cent of salary', appear uniform in design but inherently privilege higher earners, who can afford to contribute more. For low-income employees, often living paycheck to paycheck, participation is limited by immediate financial constraints, meaning they contribute less and lose out on the employer match. In addition, a standard match of 50 per cent up to 6 per cent of salary means a worker earning $200,000 could receive $6,000, while someone earning $50,000 might only get $1,500. While the percentage-based system initially appears equitable, in practice, it skews heavily towards higher earners, who are more likely to contribute the maximum and more likely to find the match meaningful. For low-income workers, 6 per cent of a modest salary is often unaffordable; and even when contributed, it remains inadequate for long-term security. Therefore, what appears as a neutral, fair default actually exacerbates inequality, entrenching disparities between those who can save and those who cannot. Some companies, such as Microsoft, have shifted to flat-dollar matches, redistributing benefits more evenly across employees;[235] but such approaches remain rare.

These examples illustrate why fairness cannot be treated as secondary. Behavioural interventions must be evaluated not only on whether they work, but on who they work for, and at what cost. Without explicit safeguards, even well-intentioned interventions can leave the most vulnerable worse off.

Openness

The principle of openness insists that behavioural interventions must be transparent both in their intent and in their implementation. Yet behavioural science has often struggled with this commitment. As Loewenstein et al (2015) argued, nudges are most effective when they operate subtly, but this very subtlety raises concerns about whether individuals truly understand how and why their choices are being steered.[231] When citizens learn they have been nudged without their awareness, the result is often mistrust. Even if the intervention was benign. Openness, then, is not simply a matter of disclosure but of cultivating trust through clarity about mechanisms and goals.

Recent evidence suggests that people do not universally resent nudges when they are transparent.[230] A lot of interventions are quite clear in their approach and the goal they are aiming to achieve. However, just because the end is accepted, it does not mean the means are. The stakes become even clearer when we contrast interventions for good with the aforementioned dark patterns. One of the key differences between a nudge and a dark pattern is openness: how it works and whether its intent is clear. Without this distinction, behavioural science risks being conflated with manipulation, and the legitimacy of the field is undermined.

And this undermining comes with consequences. In Europe, the Cookie Banner Taskforce under the European Data Protection Board has firmly condemned manipulative consent designs. Its 2023 report underscores that cookie banners must include a visible 'reject all' option in the first layer, disallowing opaque interfaces that nudge users towards consent through confusion or frustration.[237] This crackdown signals a clear shift: dark patterns are not merely poor design, they are increasingly treated as unacceptable and enforceable infractions.

Across the Atlantic, the US Federal Trade Commission (FTC) has taken a similarly firm stance on subscription systems riddled with dark patterns. In 2021, the FTC issued a sweeping Enforcement Policy Statement declaring that 'tricking consumers into subscription programs or trapping them when they try to cancel is against the law'. Its 2024 joint review with international consumer protection networks further revealed that 76 per cent of subscription websites/applications deploy one or more dark patterns, often designed to confuse users or obscure key information.[238] This isn't just regulatory rhetoric; it's warning companies that opacity invites both consumer backlash and legal consequences.

Openness, therefore, is not optional. It is a safeguard against backlash, a means of securing legitimacy, and a pathway to interventions that people both accept and support. Without it, even the most well-designed intervention risks undermining the credibility of the field.

Respect

The principle of Respect asks whether behavioural interventions uphold the dignity, autonomy, and self-worth of those they target. This is particularly critical when interventions are designed to shape behaviour not just through information or choice architecture, but through emotional levers such as guilt, shame, or fear. As Sugden (2018) reminds us, individuals should be seen as members of a 'community of advantage', capable of making their own judgments about what serves their interests.[239] Respect, in this sense, is not about shielding people from all influence but about ensuring they are treated as partners in decision-making, not as passive subjects to be nudged into compliance.

Food labelling provides a clear illustration of where respect can be compromised. Nutritional traffic light systems, where red, amber, and green labels signal the healthiness of products, were developed to simplify consumer choices. Yet research shows these systems can evoke unintended emotional consequences; while green signals can encourage healthier purchases through positive emotions, red warning labels can generate guilt and shame.[240] These emotional responses may drive some consumers to change behaviour but can also lead others to disengage, resent being judged, or conceal their choices. In such cases, respect is undermined because the intervention crosses from providing information to moralizing behaviour.

Similarly, climate-friendly labelling experiments reveal that colours associated with moralized cues, such as red or green, can evoke not only pride but also shame and resentment; research found that the colour-coded climate labels designed to encourage sustainable purchases backfired by eliciting negative emotions, particularly among consumers with limited financial means to consistently act on them.[241] Here, a tool meant to empower choice instead risks humiliating those least able to comply, creating a sense of exclusion rather than inclusion.

Finance offers another domain where respect can easily be undermined. Framing messages around savings behaviour through guilt, for instance, highlighting how much an individual has 'failed to save' compared with peers can push people towards greater financial caution. However, Loewenstein et al (2014) warn that such approaches may stigmatize vulnerable groups, particularly those already living paycheck to paycheck.[242] What may look like a benign informational strategy from a policy maker's perspective can feel like moralizing intrusion to the very people it seeks to help.

Public health campaigns have long grappled with similar tensions. Anti-smoking or obesity prevention initiatives frequently use fear-based imagery, designed to shock individuals into compliance. Hastings et al (2004) argue that while such fear appeals may produce short-term behavioural change, they often fail to sustain it and can undermine trust in health authorities.[243] In addition, these campaigns risk alienating or stigmatizing the very groups they target, breeding resentment rather than fostering collaboration. Goldenberg and Arndt (2008) similarly show how fear-based health messages, rooted in mortality salience, may provoke defensive reactions rather than constructive engagement.[244]

From these examples, the central lesson is clear: interventions that rely heavily on shame, guilt, or fear may achieve surface-level compliance, but they do so by compromising respect. They risk turning behavioural science into a tool of control rather than empowerment, eroding the very trust and dignity on which sustainable change depends. Respect demands that we move beyond strategies that humiliate or stigmatize, and towards those that engage people as equal partners, capable of deliberation and deserving of dignity.

Goals

The principle of Goals asks whether an intervention genuinely aligns with the objectives of the people it targets, rather than the objectives of those designing it. Nudges and choice architectures are often justified as helping individuals overcome biases and act in their own long-term interests. Yet interventions can easily drift towards serving institutional, corporate, or political goals instead. When this happens, the integrity of behavioural science is compromised, and the trust of those affected is eroded.

Some of the clearest examples of goal misalignment come from the world of dark patterns in digital design. Brignull (2011) coined the term to describe interface strategies that trick people into choices they would not otherwise make, such as enrolling in subscriptions that are difficult to cancel. Later analyses expanded this critique, showing how dark patterns systematically shift control away from users.[222] These design practices often frame their deception as 'helping' users, but in practice, they privilege corporate profit over consumer welfare.[221] A large-scale audit of 11,000 shopping websites confirmed how widespread these tactics are, from hidden costs to manipulative countdown timers.[224] While sometimes justified as nudges, such practices clearly violate the principle of Goals: they advance organisational objectives while undermining individual ones.

At the extreme are cases of addiction by design. Schüll's (2012) ethnography of machine gambling in Las Vegas showed how slot machines are engineered to create a 'zone' of continuous play, exploiting cognitive and behavioural tendencies to maximize time on a device.[245] While superficially offering entertainment, the system is calibrated to benefit casinos, not players. This represents the far end of goal divergence, where behaviour actively harms the user while enriching the institution.

Misaligned goals also appear in subtler forms of applied behavioural science. Employers promoting wellness apps or financial products may nudge employees towards options that reduce company costs, even if those options do not fully match employees' preferences or financial needs.[221] A striking example is Unlimited Paid Time Off (PTO). Marketed as a hallmark of empowerment, it promises rest and flexibility. However, evidence shows that in toxic work cultures, it primarily benefits corporate balance sheets while leaving employees pressured and burned out.[246] Employees often take fewer days off under unlimited PTO than under capped systems, constrained by unclear norms and fear of being judged.[247] Research further reveals inequities: women are 43 per cent less likely, and non-white workers 19 per cent less likely, to use their full entitlement compared with their counterparts.[248] What appears as a generous benefit becomes a liability: the company avoids accruing vacation pay obligations, while employees, especially from marginalized groups, lose the very rest they need. To genuinely support staff, policy must be paired with culture, with leadership modelling time off and making expectations explicit. Otherwise, unlimited PTO remains a textbook case of goal misalignment, serving accounting strategies rather than employee well-being.

These cases illustrate why behavioural interventions must be tested not only for efficacy but also for alignment. Protecting Goals means asking whose interests are prioritized, anticipating unintended consequences, and involving target populations in design. Without such safeguards, behavioural science risks being seen less as a discipline serving human welfare and more as a toolkit for institutional advantage.

Opinions

The principle of Opinions asks whether an intervention is designed and implemented with sufficient attention to the perspectives, values, and lived experiences of the people it seeks to influence. Too often, policies or nudges that appear technically sound in design fail in practice because they neglect to account for how people feel about being targeted. Interventions are not just behavioural levers; they are social signals. If those signals clash with cultural norms or lived realities, they risk alienating the very groups they aim to support.

Mentioned previously, food policy provides a clear illustration. Nutritional 'traffic light' systems, which mark foods with red, amber, or green labels to indicate healthiness, were introduced to make healthier decisions easier at the point of purchase. Evidence shows such labels can promote self-regulation by evoking positive and negative emotions.[240] Yet they also reveal how opinions matter: some consumers resent the implied moral judgement, interpreting a red label not just as information but as a rebuke. A review of front-of-pack nutrition labels shows that while these interventions often improve understanding of food content, their effects on purchasing behaviour vary widely, shaped by individual attitudes towards authority and autonomy.[249] Similarly, a review by del Valle et al (2022) found that while the policy increased awareness, it also reinforced weight stigma, with unintended negative effects on individuals already facing discrimination.[250] Instead of fostering empowerment, the labels amplified social judgements, particularly in communities where obesity is highly stigmatized. Where people feel patronized, compliance drops, aligning itself with the Respect principle.

Beyond food, the principle of Opinions is increasingly salient in the digital era. Public concern about privacy profoundly shapes responses to information-based nudges. People often report discomfort when they sense that their online behaviours are being monitored or manipulated, even when the intention is to personalize experiences.[251] A recommendation algorithm framed as 'helpful' can just as easily be perceived as intrusive or exploitative, depending on the level of transparency and control afforded to users.

A further dimension of Opinions concerns how people evaluate interventions when they understand their actual effectiveness; a topic under consistent scrutiny in behavioural science (see Chapters 3 and 6). Research conducted by Sunstein has shown that individuals generally prefer System 2 nudges over System 1 nudges, yet this preference is not stable: when participants are informed that a System 1 nudge is significantly more effective than a System 2 alternative, many shift to favouring the former.[252] This demonstrates how opinions can switch from a principled, reflective stance to a pragmatic one, anchored in effectiveness rather than process. One then wonders how this would tie in with the work on the effectiveness of i-frame versus. s-frame solutions, with most of the behavioural interventions operating at the i-frame level, with very debatable (longitudinal) effects.[38]

And when opinions aren't positive, interventions can really backfire. Think of the Yellow Vests (Gilets Jaunes) protests in France in 2018 against the fuel tax, which was framed as a pro-environmental measure to reduce carbon emissions. While economically rational and environmentally defensible, thousands took to the streets, as for many rural and low-income citizens, the policy symbolized elite disregard for their daily struggles. Similarly, there have been protests and issues with compliance during the COVID-19 pandemic as a response to several interventions, especially as trust in science and governments came crashing down.

These examples underscore that the success of behavioural interventions is inseparable from how they are perceived by those affected. If people feel judged, stigmatized, or manipulated, they resist, regardless of the intervention's technical merit. Respecting Opinions means engaging with communities early, testing for unintended emotional reactions, and recognizing that legitimacy derives as much from perception as from outcomes. Without this sensitivity, behavioural science risks not just ineffectiveness, but reputational harm, as people come to view its methods as coercive rather than supportive.

Options

Coming back to the debate on the i-frame/s-frame,[38] the principle of Options asks whether behavioural interventions are truly the best available policy instrument, or whether alternatives, such as regulation, incentives, education, or structural reforms, would be more effective and just. Nudges are often praised for their low cost and ability to preserve autonomy, yet they are only one tool in a much wider policy toolkit.[173,253,254] When nudges become the default response to complex social problems, they risk crowding out more powerful or appropriate interventions.

Consider climate change. Small green nudges, such as labelling or defaulting people into renewable energy tariffs, can encourage pro-environmental choices, but as Hagmann et al (2019) show, reliance on these measures can reduce public support for stronger systemic policies such as carbon taxes.[255] In this case, the nudge not only proves insufficient on its own, but it also diverts political will away from the measures that matter most. Thaler and Sunstein themselves acknowledged that 'the most important step in dealing with environmental problems is getting the prices right', underlining that nudges cannot substitute for broader structural reforms.[256]

And the price, or sometimes better phrased as *cost-effectiveness*, is another important dimension. Benartzi et al (2017) argue that nudges are among the most cost-effective policy tools available, with very high returns per dollar spent.[257] Yet Deaton and Cartwright (2018) caution against relying too heavily on general claims of effectiveness, since the impact of nudges can vary dramatically across contexts and may be modest compared to stronger interventions such as subsidies or mandates,[258] in line with the writing of Chater and Loewenstein.[38] A weak nudge that is politically attractive but ineffective represents a missed opportunity; an ethical failure in the allocation of scarce policy resources.

As discussed in Chapter 3, even if a behavioural intervention is preferred to address a specific problem, nudges are hardly the only tool available. Options as a principle also requires attention to be paid to alternative strategies like boosts, which aim to build skills and competencies rather than bypass biases.[34,35,259] For example, teaching financial literacy may be slower and more costly than auto-enrolment defaults, but in the long run, it equips individuals with tools for many contexts beyond retirement saving. Nudges, by contrast, often improve outcomes only in the narrow decision environment where they are applied, see Chapter 3 for a more detailed review.

Ultimately, the principle of Options requires policy makers to ask: is a behavioural intervention the best available choice, or is it a distraction from more impactful reforms? Often, the best approach will be a policy mix, where nudges complement other tools rather than replacing them. Only by weighing alternatives carefully, on effectiveness, cost, and political trade-offs, can behavioural science avoid becoming a convenient excuse for inaction.

Delegation

The principle of Delegation reminds us that the authority to design nudges is not self-generated; it is entrusted to practitioners through laws, institutional roles, or professional mandates.[260,261] To use this authority responsibly, behavioural policy makers must ask whether their position was conferred legitimately, through transparent and fair processes, or whether it reflects less accountable forces such as lobbying or corporate influence. Delegation also demands vigilance against conflicts of interest: when interventions marketed as promoting public welfare in fact serve institutional or corporate goals, their legitimacy erodes. Crucially, authority must not only be valid but also perceived as such. Communicating why behavioural actors are entitled to shape decisions is essential for trust.

Competence is equally central. Delegation only holds if those entrusted with influence have the skills to design and evaluate interventions responsibly. Yet policy makers, like all humans, are subject to cognitive and institutional biases.[262] Short-termism, political incentives, and overconfidence can lead to poorly designed nudges, and the replication crisis underscores the need for epistemic humility in applying behavioural insights. Competence also involves recognizing institutional limits and securing interdisciplinary expertise when required, rather than overstretching capacity.

The rise of AI-driven behavioural systems introduces a new dimension of delegation. Somewhat ironically, a lot of AI was deployed to get rid of the biases associated with human decision-making. However, this belief fundamentally misunderstands how AI works, or rather, is taught to work. Examples from algorithmic credit scoring reveal how such systems can reinforce existing inequalities, denying loans disproportionately to minority or low-income applicants, even when the models are presented as neutral.[263] Similarly, a review by Raghavan et al (2020) critically examines the claims made by companies developing algorithmic hiring tools, particularly their promises to reduce human bias and increase fairness.[264] Their paper highlights that these tools can perpetuate or even exacerbate existing inequalities if not carefully designed and validated. The authors distinguish between different hiring algorithms, from resume screeners to video interview analyzers, and show how each raises distinct fairness concerns, especially stressing that algorithmic bias is not solved simply by removing sensitive attributes such as race or gender because proxies embedded in other data often reintroduce these biases. Importantly, the authors argue that transparency and rigorous auditing are essential: many hiring systems are black boxes, making it difficult for employers, regulators, or candidates to evaluate their fairness or validity. While algorithmic hiring, among many other AI applications, has the potential to assist in reducing human prejudice, real progress depends on embedding accountability, continuous monitoring, and independent evaluation into the deployment of these systems. And increasingly, these predictive models are raising questions of accountability and legitimacy. If authority is delegated further, from humans to opaque algorithms, who ensures that the system acts in line with ethical norms? Without transparency, human oversight, and mechanisms of redress, the chain of delegation breaks: individuals find themselves subject to interventions whose logic is hidden and whose accountability is diffused.

Delegation, then, requires more than technical competence or good intentions. It is an ongoing responsibility to examine why authority was granted, how it is exercised, and to what extent emerging technologies change the dynamics of influence. Ethical behavioural science is not just about designing interventions for others but about demonstrating that the institutions and systems applying behavioural science are themselves worthy of trust.

Power and responsibility

Behavioural science is not just a set of tools; it is a form of power. To understand its ethical stakes, we must ask not only what interventions achieve but who has the authority to design them, to profit from them, and to be held accountable when they go wrong. Power shapes whether behavioural science is experienced as enabling or manipulative, democratic or technocratic. Responsibility determines whether that power is wielded in service of the public good or private gain. Within the FORGOOD framework,[22] this would sit within the domain of Goals, as well as Delegation, for which we'll now do a slightly deeper dive, as they are incredibly important.

Structural asymmetries

At the heart of behavioural science lies a structural imbalance. Interventions are almost always designed by governments, corporations, or institutions, and applied to individuals or communities who rarely have a say in their design. In public policy, citizens encounter nudges in tax systems, benefits enrolment, or vaccination campaigns, but they seldom influence the assumptions underlying those designs. In the corporate world, consumers face digital interfaces optimized to maximize time, clicks, or purchases, often without awareness of the strategies being used.

This asymmetry matters. Those who design interventions hold disproportionate influence over the choices of those subject to them. Without checks and balances, behavioural science risks amplifying the power of institutions at the expense of the very people it claims to serve.

Responsibility diffusion

In theory, responsibility for ethical practice should rest with organisations: governments and corporations that choose how behavioural insights are deployed. In practice, however, it often falls on individual practitioners.

Preeti Kothamarthi underscores this dynamic: 'Businesses will use whatever it takes to help them reach business goals. It's up to a behavioural scientist to be that person who reminds the company about ethical implications.' That framing reveals the problem and the burden. Individual behavioural scientists are cast as ethical gatekeepers, expected to challenge powerful institutional incentives with little formal support.

Natalia le Gal goes further, warning that behavioural science is already being used 'to influence at scale, often without consent or transparency'. Responsibility cannot remain at the level of individual conscience; systemic accountability is needed. Yet too often, practitioners face a double bind: raise concerns and risk being sidelined, or remain silent and risk contributing to practices they find troubling.

Accountability mechanisms

To address this gap, behavioural science must embed responsibility into its structures, not leave it to personal courage. Several mechanisms are already being explored:

- Internal ethics boards. Modelled on IRBs in academia, these committees could oversee the ethical dimensions of applied interventions within governments or firms. These bodies would provide behavioural scientists with an institutional ally, ensuring ethical reflection is not an individual's burden but an organisational mandate.

- External oversight. Regulators in health, finance, and technology already monitor issues like safety, fairness, and data privacy. Behavioural science must integrate into these existing frameworks rather than operate in their blind spots. For example, a nudge that passes consumer protection law should also be scrutinized for autonomy and transparency.
- Professional accreditation. Initiatives such as the GAABS are building voluntary codes of conduct and accreditation pathways. While still limited in uptake, they point towards a future where practitioners signal their commitment to ethical standards in the same way lawyers or doctors do.
- Transparency practices. Responsibility is not just about internal checks but about external visibility. Publishing reports on the ethical reasoning behind interventions, or creating public registers of applied projects, would allow citizens and peers to hold the field accountable.

The risk of ethics-washing

Of course, accountability mechanisms bring their own risks. When organisations adopt ethical frameworks without meaningful enforcement, they risk slipping into 'ethics-washing', using codes and committees as public relations tools rather than genuine checks on power. The danger is particularly acute in the private sector, where the pressure to demonstrate responsibility can be met with glossy charters and voluntary guidelines that are rarely tested against outcomes.

This is why responsibility must be substantive, not symbolic. Ethical oversight should have teeth: the power to pause or redirect interventions that pose risks, and the authority to demand long-term evaluation rather than short-term gains. Without this, responsibility will remain a slogan rather than a safeguard.

Trust as the ultimate measure

At stake is not only the welfare of individuals but the credibility of behavioural science itself. As Eric Singler argues, 'The bigger our power to influence is, the more we have a strong responsibility to promote a relevant and ethical application of it with concrete recommendations including new laws and regulations.' Trust is not built on promises of good intentions but on demonstrated responsibility.

Public trust in behavioural science will depend less on how persuasive its interventions are and more on whether people believe those interventions are aligned with their interests. If citizens come to see nudges as tools of manipulation, the legitimacy of the entire field could collapse. Concerns that we have seen before during the COVID-19 pandemic.

In contrast, if behavioural science is consistently transparent, participatory, and accountable, it can strengthen trust in itself and in the institutions that use it.

Power with, not power over

The deeper ethical shift, then, is from seeing behavioural science as 'power over' people to seeing it as 'power with' them. Responsibility means designing with communities, not just for them; inviting public debate about goals; and ensuring interventions enhance, rather than diminish, autonomy. Examples of this can be found in Chapter 4, where co-design was the only way to make interventions accepted as well as effective because the researchers needed to better understand the environment in which the interventions were deployed, and how the participants were impacted by them, and would potentially resist them.

Only by redistributing power in this way can behavioural science move from being a technique of influence to an effective practice of democratic problem-solving.

Embedding responsibility

Responsibility in behavioural science cannot be left to lone practitioners or voluntary charters. It must be institutionalized via oversight boards, regulatory integration, accreditation, and transparency. Most importantly, it must be judged by whether interventions maintain public trust.

If behavioural science is to avoid the fate of being dismissed as manipulation science, it must align power with accountability.

Influence is inevitable; responsibility is a choice. The future of the field depends on making it a collective one.

Towards a more ethical science

If behavioural science is to avoid being remembered as either a passing fad or a manipulative toolkit, it must show that it can be effective and ethical. The debates so far, about unintended consequences, the lack of standardization, and the risks of unchecked power, point towards a central truth: good intentions are not enough. The field needs systems and habits that embed ethics into everyday practice.

Frameworks such as FORGOOD help by setting principles, but principles only matter when they are lived. What's needed now is a set of concrete practices that make ethics part of how the field works day-to-day. In this section, six steps are outlined towards that future. They are not exhaustive, but together they offer a roadmap for making behavioural science credible, responsible, and sustainable.

Step 1. Professional standards and ethics training

For behavioural science to be seen as a profession, it needs the same infrastructure that gives fields such as medicine or law their credibility: accreditation, clear standards, and embedded ethics training. Kelly Peters recognized this when she observed that 'efforts are underway to enhance the professionalism of the field with explorations of things like accreditation, standards, and ethics codes. This will provide much needed guidance to the people who want to work in the field and to those who want to hire them.' Without such standards, anyone can claim expertise, leaving clients and the public unable to distinguish between rigorous practice and opportunism.

Accreditation must go beyond technical expertise. Torben Emmerling, Founder and Managing Partner of Affective Advisory and Founder and Board Member of GAABS, argued that 'the field now needs a professional association that sets the right standards for technically and ethically-sound applications of behavioural insights by professionally qualified people'. Those standards must include explicit ethics training. Practitioners should be expected to complete courses on informed consent, unintended consequences, and cultural sensitivity; not as optional extras but as part of the credential itself.

GAABS has started piloting accreditation, but uptake is limited. To be effective, such accreditation must be backed by a broad coalition of academic, public, and industry stakeholders and tied to procurement policies so that accredited professionals are preferred in hiring. Only then will accreditation drive meaningful change.

By embedding ethics training into professional standards, accreditation would do more than certify competence; it would signal a collective commitment to trustworthy, ethical practice.

Practical steps

- Establish a governing body. A broad coalition of academic, public, and industry stakeholders should define accreditation requirements and set binding standards for technically and ethically sound practice.
- Mandate continuing professional development. Accredited practitioners should complete regular CPD credits that include a dedicated ethics component covering informed consent, unintended consequences, and cultural sensitivity.
- Create bridging pathways. Experienced but non-accredited practitioners should have structured routes to gain formal credentials without being required to start from scratch.
- Tie accreditation to procurement and hiring. Public and private sector organisations should require or prefer accredited professionals, ensuring that credentials translate into meaningful career incentives.
- Pilot with GAABS before scaling. Schemes should be tested with GAABS or similar organizations at a manageable scale, with early results used to refine standards before any global rollout.

Accreditation will not resolve every ethical challenge, but it will establish the infrastructure for trust. It would distinguish trained professionals from opportunistic amateurs, and embed ethical competence at the core of behavioural science.

Step 2. Ethics by design

If behavioural science is to avoid being remembered as either a passing fad or a manipulative toolkit, it must show that it can be effective and ethical. The debates so far, about unintended consequences, the lack of standardization, and the risks of unchecked power, point towards a central truth: good intentions are not enough. The field needs systems and habits that embed ethics into everyday practice.

Frameworks such as FORGOOD offer a foundation, but to matter, they must be operationalized. Natalia le Gal warned that 'we need frameworks. We need accountability. Behavioural science is being used to influence at scale, often without consent or transparency.' Embedding ethics into project lifecycles, from scoping and design through evaluation, ensures interventions are scrutinized not only for efficacy but also for fairness, transparency, and respect for participants.

This also means tackling the issue of consent. Many nudges are invisible to participants, fuelling suspicion of manipulation. Ethical design should include clear communication strategies, such as opt-outs, disclosures, or public engagement, that give people agency in the interventions that affect them. Transparency to participants, not just regulators, must become part of professional norms.

Making ethics by design standard practice requires organisational policies that demand compliance reports, staff training, and regular audits. Such as the GDPR for data, it may be unpopular at first, but ultimately raises trust and quality across the field.

Practical steps

- Require an ethical compliance report for every project. Proposals should not proceed without documentation covering fairness, transparency, and respect for participants at scoping stage.
- Provide practical tools for ethical reflection. Organizations should develop templates, checklists, and decision trees that make ethics by design straightforward to apply, not an additional burden.
- Introduce mandatory disclosures and opt-outs. Participants should be given clear communication about interventions that affect them, with genuine agency built into the design rather than added as an afterthought.
- Audit compliance annually and tie it to performance. Adherence to ethical standards should be tracked through regular audits and linked to staff KPIs, giving accountability real teeth.

- Adapt frameworks to each sector. Health, finance, and technology present different risks and contexts; ethics guidelines should be tailored accordingly rather than applied as a one-size-fits-all checklist.

Ethics by design will not eliminate every risk of misuse, but it will normalize ethics as a practical, everyday concern rather than an afterthought. By embedding reflection, consent, and accountability into project lifecycles, the field signals its commitment to influencing responsibly, not covertly.

Step 3. Institutional oversight and long-term accountability

Individual practitioners cannot carry ethical responsibility alone. As Preeti Kothamarthi put it, 'behavioural scientists must be guardians of ethics in their organizations. Businesses will use whatever it takes to help them reach business goals. It's up to a behavioural scientist to be that person who reminds the company about ethical implications.' But this reminder cannot rely on individual courage.

What's needed is structural oversight. Applied behavioural science should have ethics committees, similar to IRBs in academia, embedded in companies, NGOs, and government. These committees should review projects before launch, monitor implementation, and critically, require long-term evaluation of effects. Too many nudges produce short-term compliance but fade or even backfire over time. Committees could mandate follow-ups 6 months or 1 year later, ensuring interventions deliver lasting benefit rather than shallow fixes.

William Mailer, Chief Behavioural Scientist at the Commonwealth Bank of Australia, called for 'more work on setting quality standards and more professionalization of the field, moving towards common ethical principles, coordinated testing programs and shared lessons'. Ethics committees embody this vision by institutionalizing review and embedding accountability at the organisational level.

For smaller organisations, shared committees or partnerships with universities could provide access to oversight without prohibitive costs. Academic IRBs, for instance, can be extended to cover applied projects. In every form, oversight must shift from individuals to institutions, making ethical practice a systemic expectation rather than a personal battle.

Practical steps

- Establish ethics committees at the organizational level. Companies, NGOs, and government bodies should embed internal review structures modelled on academic IRBs, or share committees where costs make standalone oversight impractical.
- Recruit multidisciplinary members. Committees should include ethicists, legal experts, and community representatives, ensuring that review draws on perspectives beyond behavioural science itself.
- Require both pre- and post-intervention review. Projects should be assessed before launch and followed up at 6 and 12 months, ensuring interventions deliver lasting benefit rather than short-term compliance that fades or backfires.
- Publish annual reports on ethical decisions. Organizations should make their oversight activity visible, summarizing the cases reviewed, concerns raised, and actions taken, to build trust and share lessons across the field.
- Partner with academic IRBs where needed. Smaller organizations without the capacity for standalone committees should formalize links with university ethics boards, extending rigorous review to applied projects without prohibitive cost.

Ethics committees cannot guarantee perfect behaviour, but they can make accountability systemic rather than personal. By mandating reviews and long-term follow-ups, they transform ethics from the burden of individuals into a shared institutional responsibility.

Step 4. Transparency and evidence sharing

Transparency is both a safeguard and a signal of maturity. Cale Hubble, Adviser to BETA, emphasized that 'transparency is key, both for building trust in the field and for demonstrating the evidence base behind our work'. Without it, behavioural science risks cherry-picking successes and hiding failures, fuelling scepticism about its reliability.

Public registries and repositories are the solution. Every intervention, successful or not, should be logged with details of design, population, outcomes, and ethical review status. This would deter covert experimentation and support cumulative science. Helena

Rubinstein argued that to professionalize, behavioural science must 'set standards including ethical standards, define best practice approaches, create databases of theories and interventions describing how and why they work'.

Importantly, registries should not only capture immediate results but also long-term outcomes. A pension default that boosts sign-ups but fails to sustain savings behaviour should be flagged as incomplete success. Longitudinal reporting would allow researchers and practitioners to understand persistence and boundary conditions, turning transparency into a tool for genuine learning.

Adoption will require incentives. Governments and funders can mandate registration as a condition of contracts or grants; professional accreditation can tie credentials to registry use. Tiered disclosure can balance transparency with commercial confidentiality.

Practical steps

- Create a global open-access registry for behavioural interventions. Every project, successful or not, should be logged with details of design, target population, outcomes, and ethical review status, deterring covert experimentation and supporting cumulative science.
- Define minimum reporting standards. Submissions should include methodology, outcome measures, and ethics approval as a baseline, giving the field a common language for evaluating and comparing evidence.
- Require long-term updates where applicable. Interventions with time-sensitive outcomes, such as pension defaults or health behaviours, should be followed up to capture whether effects persist, fade, or backfire.
- Link registry compliance to funding and accreditation. Governments and funders should make registration a condition of contracts and grants, while professional credentials should be tied to consistent registry use.
- Protect sensitive commercial details through tiered disclosure. A graduated system can balance the field's need for transparency with legitimate confidentiality concerns, removing the commercial disincentive to participate.

Transparency alone will not make behavioural science ethical, but it will make it credible. Public registries and repositories create accountability by exposing both successes and failures, supporting cumulative science, and ensuring the field learns not just quickly, but honestly.

Step 5. Context-specific safeguards

Ethical risks are not uniform. A nudge in healthcare is not the same as one in finance or education. Quique Belenguer Saborit captured the current confusion: 'we have scattered models – EAST, MINDSPACE, Rubicon, COM-B – but no unified toolkit'. The absence of tailored guidance leaves practitioners improvising, sometimes with harmful consequences.

Sector-specific best practices offer a way forward. In healthcare, guidelines should emphasize informed consent, equity, and patient privacy. In finance, they should protect vulnerable consumers from defaults that may lock them into inappropriate products. In education, parental consent and developmental appropriateness are critical. Swee-Hoon Chuah warned against fragmentation: 'we need to work together, not have these turf wars, to come up with solutions to these massive challenges'. Developing playbooks for each domain would bring clarity where currently there is inconsistency.

The main blockers are coordination and funding. As Natalia le Gal put it bluntly, 'there's no money in ethics. But if we don't start having those conversations, we're doing ourselves a disservice.' Still, highly regulated sectors such as health and finance are well placed to lead, given their existing oversight structures.

By creating sector-specific safeguards, behavioural science can respect the unique risks of different contexts while ensuring consistent standards of professionalism and ethics across the field.

Practical steps

- Convene sector-specific working groups. Practitioners, ethicists, and regulators in healthcare, finance, and education should collaborate to identify the distinct ethical risks in their domains rather than applying generic frameworks that miss context-specific harms.

- Draft playbooks specifying red lines and minimum standards. Each sector should produce clear guidance on what constitutes unacceptable practice – from inappropriate financial defaults to interventions that bypass informed consent in clinical settings.
- Secure endorsement from regulators and professional associations. Playbooks without institutional backing risk being ignored; legitimacy requires sign-off from bodies with the authority to make adoption consequential.
- Incentivize adoption through procurement and insurance requirements. Organizations that follow sector-specific safeguards should be rewarded in commissioning and contracting decisions, creating a practical reason to comply beyond goodwill.
- Pair rollout with training and capacity building. New standards are only effective if practitioners understand how to apply them; guidance documents should be accompanied by workshops, case studies, and accessible decision tools.

Sector-specific best practices will not solve every ethical dilemma, but they recognize that one-size-fits-all guidance is inadequate. Tailored safeguards ensure that behavioural science adapts to the risks and responsibilities of each domain, while reinforcing the field's collective professionalism.

Step 6. Inclusive and multidisciplinary collaboration

No single discipline can foresee all risks. As Antoine Ferrère, co-founder of lumenx.ai and President of the Behavioural AI Institute, explained of his work at Novartis where he was the Global Head of Behavioural Insights, Data Analytics and AI, true impact required bringing together behavioural science, compliance, and organisational psychology to create lasting cultural change: 'This wasn't just about engagement surveys but generating rigorous perception data … Simple tweaks in how managers framed one-on-one meetings significantly boosted psychological safety, encouraging employees to speak up when they noticed unethical behavior.'

Collaboration cannot stop at technical experts. Quique Belenguer Saborit stressed, 'a behavioural science team can't exist in a silo – it needs to be embedded within organizations … The best behavioural science teams work alongside product teams, marketing, HR, cybersecurity – anywhere decisions are being made.' This means embedding practitioners across functions while also ensuring the voices of diverse populations and communities are included. Without attention to diversity, interventions risk being designed for narrow samples and failing when scaled.

Practical collaboration requires structures: innovation labs, joint ethics boards, participatory workshops with affected communities, and formal partnerships with universities or NGOs. These models, already common in public health, ensure interventions are context-sensitive and legitimate.

Cross-disciplinary and inclusive collaboration will demand resources and patience. But without it, behavioural science risks being seen as manipulative or exclusionary. With it, the field can design interventions that are not only effective but fair, representative, and enduring.

Practical steps

- Establish cross-functional teams as standard practice. Behavioural science units should be embedded alongside product, HR, compliance, and ethics functions rather than operating as standalone teams, ensuring decisions are scrutinized from multiple angles.
- Create participatory workshops with affected communities. The people targeted by interventions should have a voice in their design, not just their evaluation, reducing the risk that nudges are built for narrow samples and fail when scaled.
- Formalize partnerships with universities and NGOs. Structured relationships with external research and civil society organizations bring independent scrutiny and methodological rigour that internal teams alone cannot provide.
- Embed diversity checks in project design and evaluation. Every intervention should be assessed for whether it was developed with and tested on representative populations, with gaps flagged before deployment rather than after.
- Allocate dedicated funding for collaboration and inclusion. Cross-disciplinary working and community engagement require time and resources; without ringfenced budget, they are the first things cut when projects face pressure.

Collaboration will not erase the tensions of competing goals or diverse interests, but it broadens the conversation beyond narrow expertise. By embedding diverse voices and disciplines into the process, behavioural science strengthens both its legitimacy and its ability to anticipate harms before they occur.

Conclusion

Behavioural science has been here before. As highlighted by Amy Bucher, after World War 2, the field accepted that its methods could harm as well as help and built guardrails around human subjects. Today's dilemmas are different in their tools, digital platforms, data abundance, automated choice, yet familiar in their stakes: who is influenced, by whom, to what end, and with what accountability. Much of the unease traced through this chapter stems from the way the field has grown: an overreliance on nudging as the signature technique; a WEIRD evidence base that often travels poorly; a methodological tilt toward short-horizon, quantitative wins that reward what is easy to measure; and the replication crisis, which exposed fragility in findings and, with it, a deeper ethical obligation to be transparent about what we know. And what we don't.

These threads are ethical, not merely technical. A narrow diet of nudges invites paternalism and opacity. WEIRD samples are a fairness problem: when evidence is built on unrepresentative populations, scaling it can entrench inequity. A fixation on short-term metrics creates perverse incentives to celebrate immediate movement and ignore persistence, spillovers, and unintended harm. And replication is not just about credibility; it is about the duty of care. People live with the consequences when we are wrong.

This chapter's argument is straightforward: the problems look like 'bad apples', but they are mostly systemic. That is why the solutions proposed are structural as well as practical. Professional standards with explicit ethics training, ethics by design and consent, institutional oversight with long-term evaluation, transparency through registries, sector-specific safeguards, and inclusive, multidisciplinary collaboration. None of these, alone, makes behavioural science ethical. Together, they begin to shift responsibility from individual conscience to shared infrastructure, and from promises to verifiable practice.

The next chapters take up this challenge. Chapter 8 turns to the skills the future behavioural scientist will need to do this work well: not only methodological rigour and data fluency, but also curiosity, creativity, communication, and above all, ethical reflection. These are the foundations for building a practice that avoids past pitfalls while shaping new possibilities.

Chapter 9 then moves from skills to practical advice on how to grow in the field: how to start doing, how to collaborate, how to find your place, and how to stay flexible as behavioural science evolves. If Chapter 7 has shown why ethics matters, Chapters 8 and 9 show how to embody it, through the competencies we cultivate and the choices we make in our careers.

Behavioural science's future will not be secured by insights alone. It will be secured by people prepared to pair influence with responsibility, evidence with humility, and ambition with care. This isn't a book about what behavioural science is. It is about what it could become: credible, cumulative, and worthy of trust because it chooses to bind its influence to accountability.

8

The Skills Behavioural Scientists Will Need

> Behavioural science can add so much value to the world and I hope more people choose it as their professional path.
>
> Silja-Riin Voolma (2020)

Introduction

Behavioural science stands at a critical juncture. In the decades since its rise to prominence, it has earned its place in public policy, business, technology, and beyond. Yet it still carries growing pains: fragmentation between academic and applied wings, a lingering overreliance on WEIRD samples, and a replication crisis that shook confidence in its foundational claims. It's a field that has had big wins, but now faces big questions.

The interviews conducted throughout this book reflect a discipline grappling with its identity. While many celebrate behavioural science's expansion into real world domains, others worry it's being flattened into a 'toolbox', a buzzword-laden menu of nudges and biases stripped of nuance, rigour, and ethics. If it is to mature, the field must evolve beyond its foundational tropes.

That evolution begins with its people. As Silja-Riin Voolma, Strategy and Growth Lead at Newel Health and former Head of Behavioral Science, makes clear in opening this chapter, the future of the field depends on who chooses to build within it. The next generation of behavioural scientists will not succeed simply by mastering Kahneman's greatest hits or mimicking experiments in controlled settings. Instead, they'll need a robust, multidisciplinary skill set, combining methodological depth with creative application, data literacy with stakeholder empathy, and scientific rigour with ethical reflection.

This chapter synthesizes the collective wisdom of over 250 behavioural scientists to map out what those future skills look like, not just in theory, but in the practical demands of doing behavioural science in the world as it is. From curiosity and critical thinking to experimental design, communication, and ethical judgement, the behavioural scientist of the future will need to be more than a technician or an academic; they'll need to be an integrator, translator, and designer of change.

The core mindset

Curiosity

Technical skill is essential, but it isn't where most behavioural scientists start. Across hundreds of interviews, one trait was mentioned more than any other: curiosity. Not just curiosity about data or theories, but about people, patterns, and problems that don't yet have answers.

Kurt Nelson, President and Founder of The Lantern Group and co-founder of the Behavioral Grooves podcast, on which he has interviewed over 200 behavioural scientists, said the one throughline he sees in all of them is a tendency to ask, 'Why did this person respond this way and not a different way?' That instinct, to look at something ordinary and see a mystery, is foundational to the work. His co-host, Tim Houlihan, agrees, but argues that curiosity is more than a mindset; it's a requirement. 'Our world's greatest findings', he says, 'come from researchers whose thirst for understanding is never quenched'. This kind of curiosity isn't passive. It drives behavioural scientists to notice unexpected behaviours, to question accepted wisdom, and to persist when results are unclear or uncomfortable.

Ganna Pogrebna, David Trimble Chair in Leadership and Organizational Transformation at Queen's University Belfast, and formerly Executive Director of the AI and Cyber Futures Institute and Lead for Behavioural Data Science at the Alan Turing Institute, takes it a step further. In her view, curiosity is a stand-in for something bigger: passion, imagination, and the drive to solve problems worth caring about. 'You can always acquire new skills', she told me, but you can never acquire imagination'. She shared the story of a student with no background in statistics or programming who was so committed to solving an urban data problem that she learned Python in 3 months, built collaborations with researchers at UCL and MIT, and now runs a successful AI company. The technical skills came later. What mattered most was that she cared enough to start.

This active form of curiosity often leads behavioural scientists into the field in the first place. Christian Hunt, Founder of Human Risk Limited and former Managing Director of Behavioural Science at UBS, described the phenomenon of the 'accidental behavioural scientist'; people who fall into the discipline by chance but stay because they can't stop asking questions. He encourages early-career professionals to be open to that same kind of discovery: to reach out, follow their interests, and embrace the emerging, uncertain nature of the field.

The advice here is deceptively simple: be relentlessly curious. Not just about the literature, but about the world. About how people think, act, and decide. About what happens when things don't work. And about how to keep learning when there's no single playbook to follow.

Open-mindedness

Alongside curiosity, open-mindedness is one of the most frequently cited traits for anyone working in behavioural science. It's also one of the most difficult to maintain. Studying human behaviour means confronting the limitations of your own perspective, again and again, and resisting the temptation to force the world into neat theories or familiar frameworks.

Lasana Harris, Professor of Social Neuroscience and Vice Dean Global Engagement Faculty of Brain Sciences at UCL, puts it well: 'Studying human behaviour is perhaps the hardest science because we are studying ourselves.' Remaining open to the idea that your assumptions might be wrong isn't just good practice. It's essential for credible research. In this sense, open-mindedness is not about being vague or uncritical; it's about treating your own beliefs as hypotheses to be tested, not truths to be defended.

Ali Fenwick, Professor of Organizational Behavior and Innovation at Hult International Business School and Founder of the Dr Fenwick Lab for Human Behavior & Technology, calls this an 'experimental mindset'. It's about being willing to constantly challenge what you think you know. 'Compared to yesterday, today is already a new world.' He urges behavioural scientists to treat their own thinking like software: always in need of updates.

That openness also extends to methods. Behavioural scientists who rely on a single approach, whether that would be lab experiments, RCTs, or surveys, risk missing the nuance of the problems they're studying. As Sam Salzer, co-founder of the Behavioral AI Institute and founder of Habit Weekly, points out, a behavioural economist, neuroscientist, and evolutionary psychologist will all describe the same behaviour in different ways. 'None of them have the complete answer', he said. The ability to step out of your bucket and into different ones is important.

Ralph Hertwig, Director of the Research Center for Adaptive Rationality at the Max Planck Institute, echoes that point, openness applies not only to ideas, but to people. Engaging across disciplines, perspectives, and lived experiences expands the kinds of questions you ask and the kinds of answers you're able to see.

Open-mindedness, then, isn't just a personality trait. It's a professional discipline. It means being willing to revise your models, adopt unfamiliar methods, work with collaborators who think differently, and remain sceptical of easy conclusions. Especially your own.

Scientific integrity

With the rise of behavioural science in public discourse, there's been a shift in how success is defined. On the academic side, catchy findings often receive more attention than methodological rigour. In applied settings, results are expected to keep pace with business cycles and stakeholder expectations. Both pressures can erode scientific standards, and both require deliberate resistance.

For Graham Loomes, Emeritus Professor at Warwick Business School, the issue isn't just about technical competence. It's about attitude. He emphasizes 'curiosity about people and the heterogeneity of their behaviour', but pairs it with 'scepticism about appeals to what is "natural" or "self-evident"'. Integrity, in his view, means being willing to challenge the assumptions. Even the ones that sell well.

Robin Schimmelpfennig, a postdoctoral researcher at the Max Planck Institute for Human Development and UN Behavioural Science & AI Fellow, argues that popularity has come at a cost. Too much focus is placed on past success stories, often pulled from books or blog posts, while rigorous testing is neglected. She makes a clear case for returning to experimental roots, and stresses the basics: control groups, solid data, and clear analysis.

The replication crisis has made these concerns harder to ignore. Max Mawby, Managing Director of Applied Behavioural Science at Thinks Insight & Strategy, whose career spans leadership roles at the BIT, Plum Fintech, and Kantar Public, described it as a call to raise standards across the board: being transparent about analysis plans, publishing results honestly, and resisting the temptation to bury failure. For him, the lesson is simple: be as rigorous as you can, wherever you're working.

Scientific integrity also means accepting that most ideas won't work, and being willing to say so. Dan Benjamin, Professor of Behavioral Economics and Genoeconomics at the University of California, Los Angeles (UCLA), put it clearly: 'If you're not failing sometimes, then you're probably not pushing yourself.' That acceptance of failure isn't a sign of weak science; it's a sign that the scientific method is being used properly.

The behavioural scientists who earn the most trust in the field aren't just smart. They're transparent, methodical, and clear about what their work can and can't claim. They know that in a field dealing with real world consequences, good intentions aren't enough. Rigour isn't optional. It's the scaffolding that allows the rest of the work to stand.

The technical toolkit

Methods of study

If behavioural science wants to be taken seriously as a science, then its methods must be more than performative. Understanding heuristics and biases might make for engaging presentations; however, real impact comes from how those insights are tested. Whether in the lab, the field, or within an organisation, sound methods are what turn behavioural theory into behavioural evidence.

Joseph Devlin, Professor of Cognitive Neuroscience at UCL, and co-founder of Applied Consumer Neuroscience, was candid about the gap between concept and practice. 'It's great to know all the latest, greatest science, but it's quite another to accurately predict the consequences of implementing an intervention.' For him, the essentials are clear: understand experimental design, know your statistics, and measure the outcomes that matter. Nothing should be taken for granted. Even the best-looking idea needs to be tested properly.

That view is echoed by Adam Ferrier, Founder of Thinkerbell and one of Australia's leading consumer psychologists, who spent years working in marketing and advertising. He described the industry as having relied too long on instinct and unstructured guesswork. 'If you come into this space with a solid background in behavioural sciences or even a research discipline, that's gold', he said. Rigour isn't just a scientific value; it's a commercial advantage.

But methodology isn't about blindly applying experiments. Serene Koh, Director of the BIT in Singapore, makes a key distinction: you start with the problem, not the tool. 'Don't fixate on the lever', she advised. Put the problem at the heart of your endeavour.' This shift in mindset, from solution-first to question-first, demands intellectual restraint and methodological flexibility.

That flexibility includes knowing when not to rely on quantitative methods at all. Emily Daniels, Senior Behavioural Researcher at Bupa, points out that qualitative research remains undervalued in many behavioural science teams, despite its role in uncovering motivation and mental models. Tools such as interviews, user journeys, and even simple card-sorting exercises can yield insights that no A/B test will reveal.

Patrick Forscher, Senior Behavioral Scientist at Busara and former Director of its meta-research group, CREME, supports a more blended approach. He's learned that combining qualitative and quantitative methods doesn't weaken a study; it strengthens it. The point isn't to choose sides. It's to understand when and how each method adds value.

As the field matures, the most capable behavioural scientists won't be defined by their allegiance to a specific technique. They'll be defined by their ability to select the right approach for the right question, and to defend that choice with clarity and care.

Statistics and data interpretation

Behind every well-designed intervention is an equally strong understanding of data. In behavioural science, being able to design experiments is only half the equation. The other half is knowing how to interpret what the data actually says. This requires more than basic numeracy. It demands fluency in statistics, comfort with uncertainty, and an ability to distinguish signal from noise.

Torben Emmerling, Founder and Managing Partner of Affective Advisory and Founder and Board Member of GAABS, believes this combination starts with mindset. He describes the behavioural scientist as someone who must not only be interested in decision-making but also enjoy analyzing data and uncovering causal relationships. It is the curiosity to understand human judgement, paired with the discipline to evaluate it rigorously, that separates intuition from insight.

Many behavioural scientists, especially those with academic training, learn these skills early. But Dan Goldstein, Partner Research Manager at Microsoft Research and former professor at London Business School, warns against treating statistics courses as optional. 'Take all the stats and data science courses you can', he said. 'It is much harder to pick up that stuff once you are out in the world.' The basics may feel dry, but they become crucial when your credibility depends on getting the analysis right.

For those without a strong quantitative background, the gap is not insurmountable. Nick Mishkin, Senior Business Analyst at GA Telesis and former data scientist at Intelichain, advises aspiring behavioural scientists to master at least one statistical software package, whether it be R or Python. He sees real value in combining psychological insights with econometric models. When done well, this integration allows for analysis that is both robust and relevant.

Peter Wakker, Professor of Behavioral Economics at the Erasmus School of Economics and research fellow at the Tinbergen Institute, makes a similar point, warning that poor statistical technique has led to some of the field's more persistent problems. Methodological sloppiness doesn't just affect results; it erodes trust. A commitment to clean, thoughtful analysis is not a technical preference. It is an ethical stance.

Behavioural science is not defined by its tools, but the quality of thinking behind them. Whether analyzing a small pilot or a large-scale field study, the goal remains the same: make sense of the data, avoid overstating the case, and be honest about what can and cannot be concluded.

Data science

As behavioural science continues to intersect with technology, the boundary between data analysis and data science is becoming less distinct. It is no longer enough to be comfortable with survey results and t-tests. Increasingly, behavioural scientists are expected to engage with larger, messier datasets and apply more advanced analytical tools. This shift opens new possibilities, but it also raises the bar.

Christina Gravert, Associate Professor of Economics at the University of Copenhagen and co-founder of Impactually, is clear about the stakes. For her, knowing how to run experiments is essential, but standing out in the field often comes down to something more technical. 'The harder the skills, the less other people will have them', she said. She encourages students to invest in data science early, before the demands of work make upskilling more difficult.

The emerging connection between data science and behavioural science is more than a trend. It reflects a deeper shift in how behavioural problems are framed and solved. Darcie Piechowski, Global Performance Leader at IBM, sees this convergence as inevitable. She believes behavioural science will become increasingly central to how businesses approach human–AI interactions, making it essential for practitioners to be fluent in both fields.

Gaëlle Vallée-Tourangeau, Professor of Behavioural Science at Kingston University, adds that being a good behavioural scientist today also means being a competent data manager. She emphasizes the importance of curating datasets, documenting metadata, and working with behavioural data in ways that preserve meaning and enable reuse. Good science does not stop at analysis. It also involves transparency and stewardship.

However, as the field moves into more complex technical territory, it risks leaving behind those without formal training in data science. Colin Camerer, the Robert Kirby Professor of Behavioral Economics at Caltech, has pointed out that behavioural economics was slow to embrace machine learning, and as a result, many of the most innovative applications are now emerging from adjacent disciplines.

This gap presents both a challenge and an opportunity. Those who can bridge it will help shape what behavioural science becomes.

The message is consistent. You do not need to become a full-time data scientist, but you do need to understand how the tools work, what their outputs mean, and where their limits lie. In a field that increasingly deals with personalized interventions, real time feedback loops, and algorithmic decision-making, behavioural scientists cannot afford to be passive consumers of data. They must know how to build with it.

Bridging theory and practice

Understanding context

Behavioural science does not happen in a vacuum. Interventions may be designed with care, grounded in evidence, and statistically sound, yet still fail in practice. The missing ingredient is often context. Whether working in health, education, finance, or tech, behavioural scientists must understand not only the behaviour they aim to influence, but the systems and constraints that shape it.

Neela Saldanha, Executive Director at Y-RISE, put it plainly. 'Unless you know the domain area well and understand the problem, you will be like a hammer looking for a nail.' In other words, context is not a backdrop. It determines which interventions are feasible, which are meaningful, and which will never take hold. A good behavioural scientist studies the environment as carefully as they study the behaviour itself.

Aline Holzwarth, co-founder and Senior Adviser at Nuance, after having worked as Behavioural Science Lead at companies such as Apple and PatternHealth, cautions against the temptation to cut and paste successful interventions from one setting to another. 'We can't forget that the beauty of behavioural science is in its methods far more than in its findings', she said. An intervention that works in one city, company, or culture may fall flat elsewhere. Understanding the local conditions, social, economic, and institutional, is essential to understanding what the data really mean.

Liz Barker, previous Director of Global Behavioural Intelligence at the Behavioural Architects, encourages a slower, more careful approach. She advises researchers to spend time on the ground, observing behaviours in situ and asking the right questions. What are people doing now, and why? What else might be shaping their actions? She believes behavioural science becomes more accurate, and more ethical, when built on this kind of qualitative insight.

But context is not only about users or citizens. It also includes the organisations and systems behavioural scientists work within. Shane Timmons, Senior Research Officer in the Behavioural Research Unit at the Economic and Social Research Institute, makes the organisational version of 'context' explicit: 'Most behavioural scientists would say, 'Get us in earlier.' If we're involved at the design stage we might be able to anticipate problems rather than fixing them after the fact.' In practice, many behavioural scientists are brought in after core constraints are locked in: product architecture, policy timelines, vendor contracts, risk settings, when the only remaining moves are cosmetic. The skill is not just diagnosing user behaviour, but spotting where decisions are being made upstream and earning a seat there early enough for evidence to shape the system, not just tweak the interface. Scott Young emphasizes the importance of understanding business needs, constraints, and internal dynamics. Success often depends on knowing which solutions are politically feasible, which stakeholders have influence, and what evidence is persuasive in a given environment.

Gareth J. Harvey, Behavioural Scientist at Severn Trent and previously Director of Consumer Psychology at DECIDE, offers a helpful reminder: sometimes, things are designed the way they are for good reasons. A behavioural scientist who rushes to 'fix' a process without first asking why it exists may end up proposing changes that are either irrelevant or impossible. True understanding begins with listening, not assuming.

The skill here is not only analytical. It is relational. It requires behavioural scientists to engage with context at multiple levels: individual, organisational, and cultural, and to adapt their methods accordingly. The goal is not to find the universal intervention, but the right one for the situation at hand.

Creativity and design thinking

Once the problem is well understood, the next challenge is crafting a solution that works. This is where many behavioural scientists stumble. Understanding theory is one thing. Applying it creatively in real world settings is something else entirely. Designing effective interventions requires more than academic precision. It requires imagination, collaboration, and the ability to think in systems rather than silos.

Steven Johnson, former Chief Behavioural Officer and WPP behavioural science leader, described his approach as sitting at the intersection of behavioural insights, data science, and human-centred design. For him, knowing the science is just the starting point. The real skill is in bringing it to life. This mindset is becoming increasingly common among behavioural scientists working in applied roles. It reflects a recognition that knowing what people do is not the same as knowing how to help them do something differently.

Jez Groom, CEO and founder of Cowry Consulting, is even more direct. He believes behavioural science has often lacked the creative tools needed to scale its influence. 'A lot of psychologists and economists I meet are great scientists but don't have the skills to bring their ideas to life', he said. His team at Cowry emphasizes behavioural design specifically because many ideas fail not on scientific grounds, but because they are dull, poorly framed, or impossible to implement.

Creativity, then, is not just about aesthetics. It is about generating options, spotting constraints, and finding workarounds that still preserve the core behavioural goal. Ali Fenwick argues that creative thinking is one of the most undervalued skills in the field. He's run simulations to measure it in organisations, and the results are consistent. Most of us are not as creative as we think we are. But he insists, creativity can be trained, and it should be.

Etinosa Agbonlahor, CEO of Decision Alpha, makes a compelling case for what this training might look like. The most effective behavioural scientists, she argues, are those who pair technical depth with creative range. They know the theories, but they also know how to adapt them. They are fluent in models of decision-making, but also able to guide stakeholders through messy design problems that require iteration and compromise.

Colin Camerer offered a helpful framing: to break the rules, you need to know them. That tension between scientific rigour and creative exploration is not a flaw in behavioural science. It is the space in which some of its most useful work happens.

Design thinking is not a replacement for science. It is what enables science to matter in the real world. And as the field matures, the behavioural scientists who will lead it forward are those who can combine evidence with imagination, and theory with action.

Communication and influence

In behavioural science, generating insights is only half the task. The other half is getting people to understand and use them, something Jez Groom already mentioned, is a struggle for a lot of behavioural scientists. Whether the audience is a policy maker, business executive, or the general public, communication is what determines whether behavioural science stays in a report or drives change in the world.

Amy Bucher, Chief Behavioral Officer at Lirio, made the point clearly: 'The best behavioural scientists are also great communicators', she said. That means being able to distil complex research into clear narratives that speak to different audiences. It also means knowing how to adapt your message depending on who is listening. What resonates with a chief marketing officer will differ from what convinces a government official or a community leader.

Dan Gilbert, the Edgar Pierce Professor of Psychology at Harvard University, was even more direct. 'Learn to write', he said. 'It doesn't matter how smart you are if you can't get other people to understand it and feel excited by it.' Scientific precision is important, but behavioural science cannot have an impact if the insights are buried in technical language or impenetrable charts.[a]

Sarah Newcomb, previously the Director of Financial Psychology at Morningstar and now driving behavioural research at Edward Jones, highlighted a challenge many academics face. The rigour that defines good research is often impractical in commercial settings. Simplifying without distorting is difficult. But learning how to do so adds value. It allows behavioural scientists to function as translators, bridging the gap between evidence and execution.

April Vellacott, Behavioural Science Lead previously at Cowry Consulting, spoke about the importance of bringing people along for the ride. She described the 'aha moment' as a key part of any behavioural scientist's toolkit. When others begin to see what you see, the process of buy-in becomes much easier. Teaching, storytelling, and shared problem-solving all help build this connection.

David Perrott, founder of Circles in Time and former founding partner of Gravy Ideas, working at the intersection of behavioural science and community development, expanded this point by naming the skills explicitly: storytelling, public speaking, persuasive writing, and communication. These skills not being bonuses, but core competencies of a good behavioural scientist. Without them, even the strongest behavioural ideas can stall. And without stakeholder engagement, even the best-designed intervention may never get off the ground.

Communication is not just about clarity. It is also about influence. Sameer Munshi, Head of Behavioral Science & Simulation at EY, compared it to sales. If behavioural scientists cannot convince others of the value of their work, projects will not move forward. Competing priorities, organisational inertia, and risk aversion are all part of the landscape. Knowing how to frame behavioural insights so that they feel relevant, timely, and aligned with broader goals is essential.

This does not mean compromising scientific standards. It means learning how to express those standards in ways that others can act on. The goal is not just to inform. It is to persuade, engage, and equip others to make better decisions.

Ethics as a skillset

Behavioural science shapes how people make decisions. That influence comes with responsibility. Whether working in policy, product design, or communications, behavioural scientists are often in a position to guide behaviour in subtle but powerful ways. This is where ethics stops being a theoretical concern and becomes a practical skill.

Preeti Kothamarthi, Director of Behavioural Science and User Research at Swiggy, sees ethics as a core part of the role. In her view, behavioural scientists must be more than advisers. They must be safeguards. 'Businesses will use whatever it takes to help them reach business goals', she said. 'It's up to a behavioural scientist to be that person who reminds the company about ethical implications'.

Sarah Kneebone, Founder of Skyflower Solutions and previously Education Manager at BehaviourWorks Australia, highlighted one way to do this: evaluation. Measuring the outcomes of an intervention is not just about impact. It is about accountability. Without careful assessment, it is impossible to know whether an intervention caused harm, helped only a few, or produced unintended consequences. Ethical work starts with evidence.

David Perrott underscored the complexity of this task. He described ethics as the ability to anticipate not only first-order effects but also second- and third-order ones. Changing behaviour in one area can create ripple effects in others. Understanding those potential trade-offs is part of doing responsible science.

Bridgette Collado, Consumer Experience and Transformation Manager at Corewell Health, added that ethical reflection cannot be separated from the research process. She recommends building it into every stage of a project, from design to evaluation. Even if you are not the person leading the ethics review, she said, you should be the one asking ethical questions. If you are designing for behaviour change, you are responsible for the change it creates.

Darcie Piechowski, Global Performance Leader at IBM, pointed to a common risk: manipulation. Sometimes it is deliberate, as in the case of exploitative marketing. Sometimes it is accidental, driven by well-meaning interventions that backfire. Either way, the line between persuasion and coercion is not always clear. That makes transparency, reflection, and humility critical.

This is especially important in applied contexts where the definition of a 'successful' outcome may differ depending on who is asked. Steven Johnson warned that a focus on behaviour change alone can miss the bigger picture. Interventions that appear effective in the short term may create dependency, exclude certain groups, or shift power in ways that were never intended.

Kelly Peters, Global Behavioural Economics Leader and Partner at Deloitte, having also been CEO and co-founder of BEworks for over a decade, pointed out that the field is still catching up. Conversations about accreditation, standards, and ethical codes are underway, but behavioural science does not yet have a shared framework. That puts even more pressure on individuals to act with integrity.

Ethical skill, in this context, is not about having all the answers. It is about being willing to ask the right questions, involve the right people, and reflect honestly on the implications of your work. It is a practice grounded in transparency, long-term thinking, and the humility to admit when something should not be done, even if it could be.

Conclusion

The future of behavioural science will not be defined by its theories alone, but by the people who shape and apply them. As the field grows in reach and complexity, the expectations placed on behavioural scientists will grow with it. The skills outlined in this chapter: curiosity, open-mindedness, methodological rigour, creative problem-solving, clear communication, and ethical reflection, are not simply ideal qualities. They are necessary tools for navigating a discipline that sits at the intersection of science, society, and real world decision-making.

That said, not every behavioural science role requires every skill at the same depth. Someone working in policy may lean more heavily on stakeholder engagement and ethics, while a product researcher might focus on experimental design and UX collaboration. A data scientist in the field will need strong statistical fluency, while a strategist may excel in framing and influence. No one is expected to do it all. What matters is understanding the demands of your context and developing the tools to meet them.

However, it is clear that the behavioural scientists of tomorrow will need to do more than identify biases or run experiments. They will need to understand systems, work across disciplines, and act as both analysts and designers. They will be asked to explain the value of their work to people who do not speak their language, and to adapt their methods to problems that do not fit neatly into any textbook. They will face competing priorities, organisational politics, and ethical trade-offs. And they will need to make thoughtful choices, often without a clear guide.

However, they will also have the opportunity to shape a field that is still young, still flexible, and still being defined. That opportunity brings responsibility, but also hope. The challenge now is not to scale behavioural science for its own sake, but to deepen its foundations. To build a discipline that values curiosity as much as competence, ethics as much as evidence, and progress as something that is not only possible, but intentional.

In the next chapter, we turn from skills to advice; direct guidance from those already working in the field about how to find your place within it. The message is clear. You do not need to master everything at once. But you do need to begin.

9

How to Make a Career in Behavioural Science

> When you're starting out, look for opportunities that have three things: where you can develop a skill, where you can test out a career you're interested in, and where you can work with people who are willing to mentor you.
>
> Evan Nesterak (2022)

Introduction

Chapter 8 looked at the kinds of skills that will matter most for the future of behavioural science, from technical fluency and research design to collaboration, communication, and ethical awareness. But understanding what skills are needed is only part of the picture. The harder question is: how do you actually start building them?

As co-founder and Editor-in-Chief of *the Behavioral Scientist*, Evan Nesterak has seen firsthand how early career choices compound and how mentorship and experimentation shape long-term trajectories. That's what this chapter is about. Not abstract encouragement, but practical advice. What follows draws directly from conversations with behavioural scientists across sectors, disciplines, and career stages. Some have entered the field via academia. Others came through policy, design, consulting, or international development. All have found different ways to make behavioural science part of their work. And their work is part of the field.

This chapter is organized around five central themes: starting by doing, building relationships, finding your place in the field, working collaboratively, and staying flexible as the field continues to evolve. Together, these offer a way to think strategically and realistically about growing in the profession; whether you're just entering the field, looking to make a shift, or simply deepening your practice.

Start by doing

There's no single route into behavioural science. Some people arrive via formal study and internships. Others come later, after years in adjacent fields, such as policy, consulting, UX, marketing, and international development. This variety is part of what makes the field vibrant. But for anyone trying to break in, it can also make things unclear. With so many pathways, where do you start?

Elisabeth Costa, Global Chief of Innovation and Partnerships at the BIT, offers a simple answer: begin with doing. 'There's no substitute for doing', she says. Whether it's qualitative research, field trials, or practical problem-solving, the point is to get as close to the work as possible. That might mean finding a formal internship. But it could also mean bringing a behavioural lens to a project you're already working on.

You don't need permission to begin. Peter Slattery, Research Scientist at MIT FutureTech and a member of the OECD.AI Expert Group on AI Incidents, stresses that waiting for the ideal opportunity can slow you down. 'The best way to develop any skills in behavioural science, and as a result hopefully a career, is by doing it', he says. Internships help, but they're not always available. Instead, he encourages people to design interventions, write insights, or run experiments, no matter how small. The best way to learn is to practise.

These projects don't have to be high-stakes. Analyzing user journeys at your current job, setting up a basic A/B test, or reflecting publicly on what you're learning can all help you build credibility and confidence. The key is to treat each small act as a chance to get better.

Nina Mažar, Professor of Marketing at the Boston University Questrom School of Business, reinforces the value of this kind of real world exposure. Her advice is to 'get your hands dirty as soon as possible', and seek out environments where you'll encounter practical obstacles. That's where the deepest learning happens, not in theory, but in the friction of actually applying it.

This experience doesn't just build skills. It also reveals how you think, how you approach problems, and what questions you ask. Joseph Devlin, Professor of Cognitive Neuroscience at UCL and co-founder of Applied Consumer Neuroscience, notes that even for those planning to stay in academia, real world exposure is invaluable. 'The complexity of the real world often means that our best-laid plans can go awry in unforeseen, but often interesting, ways', he says, and those surprises can lead to insights you won't find in a lab.

Even if you're early in your career or outside a formal role, your perspective can still be valuable. As Linnea Gandhi, Lecturer at the Wharton School and Adjunct Assistant Professor of Behavioral Science at the University of Chicago Booth School of Business, puts it: 'Behavioural concepts and the scientific method are just tools. Do you need permission to use Microsoft Excel? No? Then you don't need permission to use these tools either.' Some of the most impactful behavioural work happens when people use what they already have: access to a process, a product, or a team, and apply behavioural thinking to improve it.

In the end, the advice is consistent: start where you are, and begin doing the work. You don't need to master the field to contribute to it. You just need to engage with it directly. That's how most people got started, and how they continue to grow.

Follow, reach out, and talk

If you want to understand what behavioural science looks like in practice, not in textbooks or training programmes, but in actual day-to-day work, the best approach remains surprisingly simple: talk to people. Many in the field got started not by landing a perfect job, but by asking the right questions. What does a behavioural science team actually do? What methods do they rely on? How did others break in?

Charlie Nixon, Lead Behavioural Architect Manager at Cowry Consulting, is direct on this point: the worst thing that happens when you reach out is that you don't get a reply. And more often than not, people are generous with their time. Conversations with practitioners offer something job descriptions rarely provide: real insight in the day-to-day. They reveal how teams are structured, how decisions are made, what actually matters day-to-day, and how success is judged behind the scenes.

Some of the most important learning in the field still happens informally, through mentorships, peer networks, and hallway conversations. Vanessa Bohns, the Braunstein Family Professor and Chair of Organizational Behavior at Cornell University, credits these casual exchanges as central to her own understanding of the profession. She learned the most, she says, not in lectures or formal training, but in conversations with her graduate school cohort and mentors, whether between conference sessions or during long nights in the lab. It's in those unscripted moments that people often explain how the field really works: how to frame research for publication, how hiring decisions get made, how careers actually unfold.

And while those insights are valuable, they're not locked behind gates. You don't need insider access to stay connected. Following the right people, engaging with what they're reading, and joining the broader conversation can be just as powerful. Bri Williams, founder of People Patterns, recommends exactly that: use LinkedIn or Twitter to stay in touch with the field, set up alerts on the topics that interest you, and share what you find.

These small habits compound. They make it easier to spot emerging patterns: what topics are gaining traction, which organisations are growing, and how behavioral science is being applied in new spaces. They also make it easier to reach out with genuine curiosity, rather than generic questions. The behavioural science community is relatively small and often unusually open. Much of what matters is still passed along in conversation, and those conversations are easy to start if you're willing to ask.

Find your place in the field

Behavioural science is a single discipline, but it doesn't lead to a single job. Roles in the field vary dramatically, from academic research to product design, from public policy to behavioral strategy in the private sector. This diversity is part of what makes the field dynamic. But it can also make it hard to know where to begin, or what to aim for.

If you've already spoken to people in the field or taken on a side project, that variation becomes immediately clear. Behavioural science looks different depending on the setting, and so do the skills that matter. What you need to know to thrive in one role may be irrelevant in another. Roos van Duijnhoven, behavioural scientist and co-founder of Nuance Behavior, specializing in behaviour change and digital interventions, cautions against staying too broad in your goals. 'There are so many different directions that you can take', she says. 'I talk a lot about designing products, but you also have this whole field of international development or public policy – and that's a different game.' Her advice is to zoom in: figure out what kind of behavioural work you actually want to do. That clarity makes everything else easier to plan.

Zooming in not only clarifies the job you want, but it also sharpens the skills you'll need. If you want to run experiments, that comes with one set of requirements. If you're more drawn to behaviourally informed product decisions or to scaling programmes in global development, the demands shift. The more clearly you can define the space you're targeting, the better equipped you'll be to move towards it.

Daniel Connolly, postdoctoral researcher at Princeton, previously completed his PhD at Carnegie Mellon after several years designing large-scale field experiments at ideas42, argues that developing a subject-matter focus is one of the best ways to stand out, especially for those in applied roles. Cultivating expertise in a specific domain such as education, finance, or health creates a complementary skill set: not just behavioural science, but behavioural science grounded in context. That foundation makes you more credible and more valuable, whether you're aiming to be a generalist or a specialist in your field.

For others, behavioural science isn't the destination; it's a layer they add to an existing career. Eric Singler, Senior Adviser at Ipsos BVA, founder of BVA Nudge Consulting, as well as co-founder and President of NudgeFrance, draws the distinction between becoming a behavioural scientist outright and using behavioural insights to enhance another role. 'You could be a behavioural scientist and specialise through formal research', he explains. Or you could be a better marketer, UX designer, HR manager, leader, or entrepreneur by applying behavioural science in what you already do.

Both routes are valid. But each demands a different mix of skills. A consultant in behavioural science may need broad methodological fluency and strong communication skills to translate insights for clients. An academic, by contrast, is often rewarded for rigour and depth in a specific area of research. This is where models such as the 'T-shaped' skillset become especially useful.

Steven Johnson, former Chief Behavioural Officer and WPP behavioural science leader, puts it this way: he looks to hire people with a deep vertical specialism, grounded in behavioural science, and a wide crossbar of complementary skills. 'If you're going to go vertical on the science', he says, 'make sure you've got a range of other tools in your crossbar – starting with Design and Data.' The goal isn't to be good at everything. It's to be fluent enough across disciplines to work effectively in teams, which brings your own unique strength.

That team environment is worth preparing for. Whether you work in academia, tech, policy, or consulting, you'll probably be collaborating with designers, analysts, strategists, or engineers. Robert Meza, founder of Aim for Behavior, advising governments and global organisations on behavioural transformation and institutional change, stresses the importance of learning their languages and tools. Systems thinking, human-centred design, and adjacent disciplines can dramatically improve your ability to collaborate and to deliver work that sticks.

The clearer you are about the work you want to do, the more strategic you can be about preparing for it. Behavioural science has many doors in. Knowing which one you're aiming for helps you navigate the others with more focus and flexibility.

The pipeline problem: supply isn't meeting demand

Even as individuals work to define their place in behavioural science, the field still struggles with what Connor Joyce, Senior User Researcher at Microsoft, calls a 'pipeline problem'. As he explained to me, the challenge has two sides: supply and demand. Both are underdeveloped, and both make it harder for the next generation of behavioural scientists to thrive. This section is mentioned here because it's a key part of finding your place in the field to realize that this may be an incredibly hard thing to do. And possibly, you might be better off just on the outskirts of the field, or to approach behavioural science as an add-on to a different field/job specification, as mentioned by Eric Singler. Let's discuss this pipeline problem so we're on the same page about what this means.

On the demand side, organisations often don't know what they want. Joyce pointed out that unlike other professions, behavioural science lacks clear entry points and established credentials. 'You don't ask, how does someone become a good manager? Well, we have this thing called an MBA that does a pretty good job to do that. It's the CPA for accountants, the bar for lawyers', he noted. Those structures create legitimacy and signal competence. Behavioural science, by contrast, still lacks its equivalent at a scaled level. The result is that companies approach it with curiosity but little clarity, which makes it hard to create stable career tracks. Yes, there obviously are MSc and PhD degrees in behavioural science, but the pipeline to then immediately slot into a readily available Behavioural Scientist role is really not that likely.[a]

But the supply side is equally problematic. Organisations may build behavioural science teams with enthusiasm, but they rarely know how to sustain them. Joyce reflected that many of the best programmes 'are not placing at the same rate that equivalent programs are placing MBAs into management consulting', precisely because companies don't understand how to use the skills they're hiring for. Too often, the excitement fades when quick wins don't materialize. Teams get folded into product analytics, dissolved altogether, or rebranded as general 'insights' functions. As he put it, 'Every behavioral science team I've been on, even the most successful ones, are no longer in the same form than when I was on them.'

This constant churn discourages long-term investment. Skilled practitioners often move into consulting, where they can parachute into organisations without being trapped in structures that don't last. Joyce estimates that only 'maybe a hundred people' worldwide have truly built and maintained behavioural science teams inside organisations, and most of them now work independently. That's a strikingly small number for a field that aspires to influence policy, business, and design on a global scale.

The cycle is self-reinforcing: without a strong professional pipeline, companies don't know how to integrate behavioural science. Without companies that can sustain the work, talented practitioners leave. New entrants then face the same lack of investment and support, and the cycle continues. As Joyce observed, 'the new people struggle to get the investment and the organizational support to build out something that's lasting'.

For future behavioural scientists, recognizing this pipeline problem is crucial. It helps explain why pathways into the field feel less defined than in law, finance, or management, and why resilience, adaptability, and collaboration matter so much. The issue is not just what skills you bring, but how you navigate a system that has yet to fully know what to do with you. And this leads back to comments made by Kelly Peters and Sasha Tregebov, who have bountiful experience leading such teams: the remit of a behavioural scientist is really quite wide, as somehow, you'll need to consistently sell yourself and the field while maintaining scientific rigour. And that is unlikely to be sustainable for a single person in the long run, which brings us to the next piece of advice.

Collaborate

You can learn a lot by reading and observing, but you learn far more by working with other people. Collaboration accelerates skill development, exposes you to different ways of thinking, and offers insight into problems you wouldn't approach on your own. In behavioural science, this is not optional. It's a necessity.

John List, the Kenneth C. Griffin Distinguished Service Professor of Economics at the University of Chicago and Chief Economist at Walmart, reflecting on his own early years, encourages young researchers to work with as many co-authors as possible, both peers and more experienced colleagues. Each collaboration, he argues, teaches you something different: how to approach a question, how to write about it clearly, how to think about data. Although he's speaking to academics, the lesson applies just as well in applied work. You will always learn more and faster by solving real problems alongside others.

That's not just a matter of skills. It's about building meaningful relationships in the field. Following someone's work is one thing. Working with them is another. Early collaborations often create the loose connections that lead to jobs, research projects, or long-term partnerships. As Peter Slattery notes, people tend to undervalue these weak ties; however, they are often where the most important insights and opportunities come from. Success, in his view, rarely comes from a single network. It's built by integrating different ideas, disciplines, and resources.

That only works if the people you work with actually bring something different to the table. Angie Fagerlin, Associate Vice President for Faculty and Chair of Population Health Sciences at the University of Utah, is clear about this. In her experience, solving behavioural problems effectively requires teams that span multiple disciplines and perspectives. Too often, early career behavioural scientists default to only collaborating with people who share their training or worldview. But working only with other psychologists, economists, or designers limits the diversity of thinking a problem might need. For Fagerlin, real progress comes when team members bring contrasting methods, assumptions, and skills, and when you deliberately avoid surrounding yourself with people who look and think just like you.

The right collaboration can also evolve into mentorship. Many experienced behavioural scientists credit informal mentors with helping them see past early obstacles and make better decisions about their work. Arron Child, Senior Customer Experience (CX) Specialist at Resolution Life, describes this as one of the most valuable forces in his career. He's sought out mentors consistently and found their experience and guidance to be instrumental in his development.

But mentoring doesn't always flow top-down. Dan Benjamin, Professor of Behavioral Economics and Genoeconomics at UCLA, points out that seniority is not a requirement for learning. Some of the most valuable collaborators, he argues, are junior researchers; people who are immersed in current methods, steeped in the literature, and often full of unconventional ideas. What they may lack in experience, they make up for in creativity, focus, and proximity to the cutting edge.

Whether you're looking for feedback, project partners, or longer-term guidance, the principle is the same: behavioural science is best done together. Working with others isn't just a way to grow your skills. It's how the field itself advances.

Be flexible and adaptable

If there's one constant in behavioural science, it's change; and not just behavioural change. The field is still young. Methods are evolving, job titles are shifting, and the path into the profession looks different every few years. What feels cutting-edge today may look rudimentary five years from now. That shouldn't be a cause for anxiety; it's an invitation to stay curious, creative, and open.

Ruth Schmidt, Associate Professor of Behavioral Design at Illinois Institute of Technology, Institute of Design, after almost a decade at Deloitte as the Innovation Program Lead, reminds us not to focus too rigidly on where the field is right now. Instead, she encourages people to imagine what it could become. Until recently, most roles were defined by academic credentials and traditional research skills. But the next wave of behavioural science jobs may emerge in less expected places: marketing, design, communications, and data science. These roles may still rely on a strong understanding of behavioural insights, but they won't always be centred around research itself. Some professionals will bring behavioural science into other fields as specialists. Others will arrive from those fields and use behavioural thinking to deepen their own practice. Either way, Ruth suggests, the future will belong to people who can move fluidly between domains, people who are 'T-shaped', with both deep expertise and broad applicability.

This flexibility applies to career planning, too. Many people enter the field hoping for a clean job title: behavioural scientist, behavioural insights lead, or even Chief Behavioural Officer. But in reality, behavioural science often operates as a layer, not a role. Piyush Tantia, former Chief Innovation Officer of ideas42 and Managing Director of Corporate Strategy at Fifth Third Bank, advises looking beyond the obvious destinations. Instead of focusing exclusively on behavioural teams or specialist centres, he recommends considering roles in marketing, UX, product, HR, or communications; jobs where behavioural skills can be applied meaningfully, even if they're not the headline.

Colin Strong, Head of Behavioural Science at Ipsos UK and Professor of Practice at Nottingham University Business School, echoes this. 'The path into behavioural science', he says, 'can be tricky. For many, the better option is to find an adjacent role and bring behavioural thinking into it. It may not look like a textbook behavioural science career. However, the impact can be just as significant, and the learning just as rich.'

There's also a more personal kind of flexibility at play here. Even with the right skills and the right opportunities, behavioural science can be messy. Research fails. Interventions flop. Studies produce no clear outcome. And that's not a sign that you're doing it wrong. It's just a sign that you're doing it.

Dan Benjamin puts it bluntly: 'research is hard. Most ideas don't work the first time. Failure is not just normal; it's necessary. If you're not failing occasionally, you're probably not pushing far enough.' The scientific method, after all, is built on iteration. One setback doesn't disqualify the process. It's part of the process.

When things go wrong, because they will, what matters is how you respond. Some days, that might mean screaming, venting and throwing the whole research project out the window. Other days, it means going back to basics and rebuilding. Tara Austin, former Partner at Ogilvy and now Campaign Director at PAR.global, reminds us that this kind of flexibility is inseparable from creativity. The field is still growing. There are many more optimizations to be found. So try something different. Experiment. Adjust. Learn. The point isn't to do everything perfectly. It's to keep moving forward.

Flexibility isn't just a mindset. It's a strategy. The behavioural scientists who thrive aren't just rigorous. They're adaptive. They know the tools, and they know how to pivot. They're comfortable in uncertainty, curious about what comes next, and willing to keep learning as the field evolves. That's what gives this work its energy, and what keeps it exciting for the long haul.

Conclusion

There is still no single way to enter or grow within behavioural science; there never has been, and I'm not sure how likely it is that there will ever be a single way. The field has been shaped by people taking different routes, testing out ideas in unfamiliar places, and finding behavioural angles in roles that didn't always include the word 'behavioural'. That diversity isn't just a historical footnote. It's one of the field's greatest strengths.

The advice in this chapter reflects that diversity. It doesn't offer a checklist, but a set of principles: act before you feel ready, learn through others, understand the ecosystem you're stepping into, collaborate widely, and stay adaptable as the field shifts. Each of these is rooted in the lived experience of those performing the work, people who have navigated uncertainty, experimented, failed, and adjusted as they went.

This mirrors the broader theme of the book: behavioural science is not fixed. It's still being shaped by the work we choose to do, the problems we choose to solve, and the ways we choose to show up. Whether you're entering the field or helping to lead it, your contribution is part of that process. There is no perfect path. But there are plenty of meaningful ones. And if this chapter has done its job, you might now feel a little more equipped, and a little more energized, to find your own!

10

Towards the Future of Behavioural Science

Behavioural science has always carried with it a paradox: it is at once a young discipline and an old one, a field still defining itself yet also deeply indebted to psychology, economics, sociology, and the many foundational fields that came before it. Across this book, its story has been followed from its foundations through its promises, pitfalls, and possibilities. Each chapter has taken on a different vantage point: history, myth, sampling, methods, replication, ethics, skills, and careers. Together they form not a definitive account of what behavioural science is, but a roadmap of what it could become.

What behavioural science could become

From the very beginning, as Colin Camerer, the Robert Kirby Professor of Behavioral Economics at Caltech, reminded us, the success of behavioural economics and its sister fields was not accidental. It came from importing concepts across disciplines and demonstrating them through careful, cumulative experimentation. Yet, as Scott Rick, Associate Professor of Marketing at the University of Michigan's Ross School of Business, warned, 'elegant lab experiments will only take us so far'. Behavioural science today finds itself at an inflection point, pulled between the clarity of controlled studies and the messiness of lived reality. The chapters of this book have shown how behavioural science has grown, but also how it has sometimes faltered.

Chapter 1 traced the long lineage of ideas about human behaviour, showing how psychology and economics, once sceptical of one another, slowly converged into a shared enterprise. It was not inevitable that experiments would become central; it took pioneers such as Vernon Smith, Kahneman and Tversky, and Richard Thaler to show that studying behaviour empirically could illuminate economic decision-making in ways theory alone could not. That history matters because it set the stage for both the successes and the blind spots that followed.

Those blind spots became clear in Chapter 2, where the moments when the field went astray were examined. The pressure for novelty, the allure of eye-catching results, and the rush to publish left behavioural science vulnerable to fragility. Replication failures and methodological shortcuts undermined credibility. In many ways, this was the cost of success: as the field grew popular, its incentives bent towards speed over care, headlines over cumulative progress. Yet recognizing those mistakes is not an act of disavowal; it is a step towards building a science that can learn from its missteps.

The rise of nudge exemplified both the promise and the peril. As Chapter 3 showed, the seductive simplicity of choice architecture propelled behavioural science into governments, boardrooms, and living rooms around the world. Telling people that most of their peers pay taxes on time, or making pension enrolment the default, demonstrated that small changes could have outsized effects. These stories made behavioural science famous. But they also risked narrowing its identity, reducing it to a toolkit of tricks rather than a discipline attentive to context, ethics, and mechanism. The mythology of nudge simplified the field, at times to its detriment.

The question of who we study, and how, came next. Chapter 4 confronted the field's reliance on WEIRD samples; participants who are Western, Educated, Industrialized, Rich, and Democratic. For decades, findings drawn from narrow populations were treated as universal. Yet when interventions travelled across borders, they often faltered. Defaults that worked in London stumbled in Lagos; social norm messages that resonated in Boston fell flat in Bangalore. As Serene Koh, Director of the BIT in Singapore, reminded us, if behavioural science does not adapt to context, 'large populations of the world will not benefit from the good that behavioural scientists can do'. The task is not simply methodological diversity but inclusivity, ensuring the science represents the very people it seeks to serve.

Chapter 5 extended this critique to methods more broadly. The RCTs, celebrated as the 'gold standard', gave the field rigour and clarity, but also constrained its imagination. Too often, elegant lab experiments asked, 'what works?' while leaving 'why?' unanswered. The path forward, it was argued, is not to replace experiments but to situate them within a wider methodological repertoire: ethnography, narrative analysis, participatory workshops, data science, and increasingly, AI. As Henry Stott, co-founder and Managing Director at Decision Technology and Head of Research at Agio Ratings, observed, 'the decision environment is nearly everything', and capturing that environment requires methodological pluralism, not purity.

Replication brought the conversation to a breaking point. Chapter 6 showed how fragile results, opaque practices, and perverse incentives shook the credibility of the field. Fraud cases made headlines, but the deeper issue was systemic: universities rewarded novelty, journals favoured significance, and null results disappeared into file drawers. Yet here too we saw reform: preregistration, open data, registered reports, and multisite collaborations are now reshaping the culture of science. As Brian Nosek, co-founder and Executive Director of the Center for Open Science and Professor at the University of Virginia, put it, 'I want to flip that – so that science is always innovating on how it does its work, not just what questions it asks.' That shift, still underway, is what will determine whether behavioural science earns trust not only for its insights but for its integrity.

From there, the conversation turned explicitly to ethics in Chapter 7. Behavioural science does not operate in a vacuum; it intervenes in people's lives. The very tools that make it powerful, the ability to shift choices subtly, at scale, make it vulnerable to misuse. As Nick Chater, Professor of Behavioural Science at the Warwick Business School, warned, humans are resistant to being experimented on, especially when decisions feel imposed rather than co-created. For the field to be worthy of trust, ethics cannot be a side constraint; it must be the foundation. That means transparency, accountability, and reflexivity. It means recognizing that influence without responsibility is manipulation, not science.

Chapters 8 and 9 asked how to equip the next generation to carry this work forward. Skills are not just technical, although methodological rigour and data fluency are essential, but also relational and ethical skills are a must. Curiosity, creativity, communication, and reflection are as important as statistics. Advice for practitioners followed: how to find a place in the field, how to collaborate across sectors, how to remain flexible in a discipline still defining itself. What became clear is that behavioural science's future will not be secured by insights alone, but by people prepared to pair evidence with humility, influence with care, ambition with accountability.

Taken together, these chapters are not a fixed map of behavioural science but a record of its ongoing negotiation with itself. The field is still in motion, still asking what it wants to become. And perhaps that is its greatest strength: it is unfinished, and in that unfinishedness lies its potential.

The work already underway

If the first half of this book has been about identifying problems, the second half has been about recognizing the extraordinary work already being performed to solve them. Behavioural science is not a blank slate waiting for some future reinvention. It is already being pushed forward by hundreds of practitioners, teams, and organisations who are building the field's next chapter in real time.

Government behavioural units, once novel, are now a global network. The UK's BIT helped establish the model, proving that carefully designed field experiments could improve tax compliance, energy use, and public health. But the story has not stopped there. Today, behavioural teams are embedded across the world; from Singapore's Social and Behavioural Sciences Research Unit, which designs community interventions with citizens, to the eMBeD at the World Bank, which works alongside governments in low- and middle-income countries. Renos Vakis, Head of eMBeD at the World Bank noted that there are now 'over 600 behavioural science teams in the public sector alone', a staggering expansion that shows how mainstream the field has become.

Academia, too, is evolving. The Center for Open Science, among other academic initiatives, has pioneered registered reports, shifting incentives away from headline-grabbing results towards a transparent process. Many other academics have coordinated multisite replications that test robustness across contexts, showing the field how to design for replication rather than hope for it after the fact. And universities are slowly retooling curricula: embedding preregistration into training, teaching students qualitative as well as quantitative methods, and beginning to require intercultural competencies.

On the applied side, organisations such as the Busara Center in Kenya and Irrational Labs in the US are demonstrating that behavioural science can be both rigorous and context-sensitive. Busara's work on savings, gender equity, and climate adaptation exemplifies the importance of grounding interventions in local realities rather than assuming universality. As Emily Daniels, Senior Behavioural Researcher at Bupa, reminded us, 'Too often, behavioural science projects falter because the problem hasn't been clearly defined.' By starting with ethnography and participatory workshops, Busara shows what it looks like to define problems from the ground up.

Private sector firms are also changing practice. Instead of treating behavioural science as a bolt-on consultancy function, companies are embedding behavioural scientists directly into data and product teams. As Torben Emmerling argued, the real shift happens when behavioural hypotheses are tested alongside user experience changes, not in parallel. Google's use of A/B testing may be infamous for its scale: 41 shades of blue tested for advertising revenue. But the infrastructure behind it is now being used by behavioural scientists to test nudges, prompts, and choice architectures in real time. Integration, not isolation, is the new frontier.

Equally important is the work being performed to diversify the population's behavioural science studies. Scholars and practitioners across Africa, Asia, and South America are challenging the field's WEIRD bias by creating research hubs closer to the communities they serve. Serene Koh's call to ensure the field benefits 'large populations of the world' is being answered by initiatives such as the Global Behavioral Science Network, which supports collaborations across borders. Funders such as J-PAL are increasingly supporting replications outside the Global North, making it possible to distinguish local effects from true universals.

There is also innovation in methodology. AI is already being used to code large volumes of qualitative data, reducing bottlenecks that once made ethnography and interviews prohibitively slow. Pilot projects funded by universities and NGOs are showing that large language models can augment, not replace, the interpretive work of human researchers. Jez Groom, co-founder of Ogilvy Change and later founder of Cowry Consulting, cautioned that behavioural science must be 'holistically integrated into the building of these systems from inception', but if used well, AI can democratize methods that were once out of reach for smaller teams.

The ethical conversation, too, is no longer abstract. After high-profile cases of fraud and growing public scepticism about nudging, behavioural scientists are embedding ethics at the heart of their practice. Adversarial collaborations, preregistered protocols, and the publication of null results are becoming signs of credibility rather than vulnerability. Jason Collins, Senior Lecturer at the University of Technology Sydney, who previously led behavioural economics and data science teams at ASIC and PwC Australia, warned against presenting behavioural science as 'party tricks', and the field is listening, we are learning to tell better stories of process, not just of outcomes.

In short, the field is already reimagining itself. The replication crisis has not destroyed behavioural science; it has galvanized it. The criticisms of WEIRD samples have not paralyzed research; they have widened its ambition. The limitations of RCTs have not diminished their value; they have spurred methodological pluralism. Each critique has been met with creative responses from people and institutions who care deeply about getting this right.

As Philipe Bujold, formerly a Senior Behavioural Scientist at NGO Rare, said, 'Being a behavioural scientist means tackling tasks you never really prepared for. Some of my biggest successes started with me thinking, "I have no idea how to do this, but I can learn."' That spirit, one of curiosity, humility, and resilience, is what propels the field forward. Behavioural science is not waiting for permission to change. It is already changing, in labs and governments and companies around the world. What remains is to deepen, connect, and accelerate that work so that the field can live up to the promise that drew us in: to better understand people, and to build better systems.

Future challenges we haven't yet addressed

Despite the progress already underway, the field still faces challenges it has barely begun to confront. Some are technical, some are philosophical, and some are existential. Together, they will shape what behavioural science can become in the decades ahead.

Software versus hardware

One of the most important frontiers is the integration of neuroscience. For years, behavioural science has described human decision-making in terms of biases, heuristics, and nudges; the 'software' of the mind. Yet beneath those patterns lies the 'hardware': the neural systems that shape attention, motivation, and memory. Philipe Bujold, with a background in neuroscience, has seen this problem loom large for a while now: 'I touched on this in my PhD thesis years ago – that behavioral science was struggling to bridge the gap between idealized decision models and the way the brain actually works – and I haven't seen a significant push to move past that.'

Reconciling these layers is no small task. How do we link the activation of brain networks with the real-world behaviours that matter most? How do we avoid neuro-reductionism, the temptation to say, 'it lit up in the brain, therefore it is true'? And how do we ethically collect and use neural data in applied settings, where power imbalances are sharp? As Lasana Harris, Professor of Social Neuroscience and Vice Dean Global Engagement Faculty of Brain Sciences at UCL, has warned, the risk is not just methodological but moral: 'the biggest challenge to behavioural science is the lack of truly globally representative samples in experiments', and neuroscience risks compounding that problem if its datasets are drawn from the same narrow populations. The future will require behavioural scientists to collaborate with neuroscientists, ethicists, and clinicians, not to replace our current theories but to ground them in a more complete picture of the human organism.

AI, again

A second challenge is the deeper integration of AI. Already, LLMs are being used to code qualitative data and simulate participant responses. Sameer Munshi, Head of Behavioral Science & Simulation at EY, noted that 'there's a whole synthetic data world out there where you might not even need real consumers to run experiments'. This opens dazzling possibilities, but also troubling ones. If AI-generated participants become common, what happens to the richness of lived experience, the cultural specificity, the unexpected stories that only real people can tell us? Patrick Fagan's warning rings especially true here: 'data quality will likely take a hit with AI bots sneaking into datasets. It's cool, but it's also a bit shaky since you're relying on something artificial to mimic actual human behaviour.' The task ahead is to design ethical guardrails that ensure AI augments rather than erases the human dimension of behavioural science.

Standalone or embedded

A third unresolved question is whether behavioural science is a discipline of its own, or a lens to be embedded into others. Some argue that it should stand alongside psychology, economics, and sociology as a distinct field, with its own departments, degrees, and journals. Others argue that its strength lies precisely in being symbiotic: a way of seeing that enriches existing domains from health to education to finance. This debate is more than academic. It will determine how students are trained, how careers are structured, and how credibility is earned. If behavioural science insists on being its own silo, it risks becoming rigid and insular, and especially the topic of ethics has struggled with this. If it dissolves entirely into other fields, it risks losing coherence and identity. Navigating this tension will be one of the great strategic challenges of the next generation.

The universal theory of human behaviour

Related to this is the ambition, sometimes whispered, sometimes shouted, of building a universal theory of human behaviour. Can we ever distil the messiness of culture, context, and cognition into a single framework? Kahneman and Tversky's Prospect Theory[52] was one attempt. Gigerenzer's work on fast-and-frugal heuristics was another.[226] Today, with computational models such as BEAST-GB, researchers are embedding behavioural biases directly into machine learning systems, hoping to capture predictive universality. Yet as Henry Stott reminds us, 'the decision environment is nearly everything'. If environments vary endlessly, then universality may be more mirage than reality. Perhaps the future lies not in a grand unified theory, but in a federation of middle-range theories that are transparent about where they apply and where they do not. But is that good enough for a field of scientific inquiry?

Where supply meets demand

Another looming issue is the pipeline of talent. Universities around the world are training behavioural science students at unprecedented rates. Master's programmes proliferate, PhD cohorts expand, and short courses promise to 'make you a behavioural scientist' in weeks. This enthusiasm is exhilarating, but it risks producing more graduates than the field can realistically absorb. If career pathways are not diversified into government, NGOs, startups, and interdisciplinary research, the danger is disillusionment. As Connor Joyce, Senior User Researcher at Microsoft, has already warned us, we may be training more behavioural scientists than we can realistically place. To avoid this, the field must invest in expanding demand as well as supply, ensuring that behavioural insights are not a luxury for elite governments or firms but a common good accessible across sectors.

Trust

There are also challenges of legitimacy and trust. Experiment aversion may become increasingly more of a problem if trust in science, or government, continues to diminish. Meyer et al (2019) showed that people often prefer universal but untested policies over carefully designed trials, driven by suspicion that experts 'should already know' the answer.[112] As Jason Collins cautioned, if behavioural science continues to be communicated as 'party tricks', public trust will erode further. Building legitimacy requires more than good science. It requires storytelling that is humble, transparent, and attentive to power. At the risk of becoming nothing more than storytellers, one of Patrick Forscher's biggest concerns. There is an interesting tension to explore here. And a real challenge for current and future behavioural scientists.

And many more ...

And then there are the challenges we cannot yet name as they don't exist yet or will morph into new kinds of challenges. Climate change, pandemics, AI governance, demographic shifts; each will create behavioural puzzles that stretch current methods to the limit. Just as past generations of behavioural scientists could not have predicted the digital platforms that now shape attention and identity, we cannot predict what environments will dominate in 20 years. What we can do is train ourselves for adaptability: to be, in Robin Schimmelpfennig's words, 'context-ready'.

These challenges are daunting, but they are also opportunities. They are signs that behavioural science is alive, dynamic, and unfinished. They remind us that the future of the field will not be written by any single theory or institution, but by the collective curiosity and courage of its people.

What you can do now

If there is one lesson that emerges across all these chapters, it is that behavioural science is not finished. It is still in the making, still shaped by the choices of those who practice it, teach it, fund it, and communicate it. Which means the next steps are not abstract; they belong to all of us. This book is not intended as a final word, but as an invitation: a way of saying, 'Here is where we are; now let's decide together where to go.'

For researchers, the first step is to align incentives with integrity. As Hans Rocha IJzerman reminded us, 'who gets jobs, promotions, or grants still often depends on the number of papers published, not on the quality of the research or the robustness of the methodology'. You can push back against this by choosing transparency over novelty: preregistering your studies, sharing your code and data, publishing null results. These may not always bring immediate rewards, but collectively they change the culture of what counts as success. For mentors, it means modelling humility: showing students that being wrong is not shameful and that revising beliefs is part of the craft. For journal editors and funders, it means rewarding openness and replication, not just surprise.

For practitioners, the challenge is to embed rigour without losing relevance. As Helena Rubinstein, Head of Strategic Services and Behavioural Scientist at Innovia Technology, warned, 'until we are able to get more systematic evidence for what works and what doesn't … organisations will become cynical about the value of behavioural science'. That means not settling for one-off nudges or flashy pilots. Build lightweight testing pipelines; use discovery workshops to ensure you're solving the right problem; document failures as carefully as successes. Share white papers, even when the results are messy. When clients or policy makers demand certainty, offer them something better: clarity about what is known, what is not, and what is worth testing next. This honesty is not weakness; it is how trust is earned.

For students, the call is to train for adaptability. Robin Schimmelpfennig, postdoctoral researcher at the Max Planck Institute for Human Development and UN Behavioural Science, was right: 'practitioners must be context-ready'. That means saying yes to field placements, to learning languages, to immersing yourself in settings far from your comfort zone. It means treating every context as a teacher, every failed replication as an insight. As Philipe Bujold put it, 'Some of my biggest successes started with me thinking, "I have no idea how to do this, but I can learn."' If the future of behavioural science belongs to anyone, it belongs to those who are willing to learn in public, to fail openly, and to carry those lessons forward.

For institutions, the task is infrastructure. Imagine if every behavioural intervention, successful or not, were logged in a global context library, coded for population, outcome, and cultural setting. Imagine if null results were not buried in file drawers but shared as open resources. Imagine if funders earmarked a portion of every grant for replication, and if governments treated evaluation not as an afterthought but as a condition of policy. These are not distant dreams; they are feasible steps. The OECD, World Bank, J-PAL, and the BIT have already pioneered much of this. The next move is to make it the norm, not the exception.

For all of us, the responsibility is communication. As Jason Collins warned, behavioural science risks being dismissed as 'party tricks' if we only tell the easy stories. The alternative is not to abandon storytelling, but to tell deeper ones: stories of process, of failed predictions, of lessons learned the hard way. Prince Ghuman, Head of Marketing for Nurp, lamented that 'the communication of research behind behavioural science was not calibrated to the public at large'. We can fix that. Write blog posts about null results. Share the story of how your study design evolved. Teach students not only to run regressions, but to explain what those regressions mean to a neighbour, a policy maker, or a client. Communication is not an add-on; it is how science earns its social licence.

And finally, for anyone reading who feels overwhelmed, the next step can be as simple as staying curious. This book began with asking a handful of people what they thought behavioural science could become. That curiosity grew into hundreds of conversations, and those conversations became this book. You do not need a research centre or a government role to make a difference. You can start with a question, a conversation, or a small project. The future of behavioural science is not being decided somewhere else; it is being decided wherever people choose to do the work with integrity, humility, and imagination.

None of this will be easy. The incentives that reward flashy results will not change overnight. The gravitational pull of WEIRD samples will not vanish with one more call for diversity. The replication crisis will not be solved by good intentions alone. But every project, every class, every policy trial is a chance to do things differently. As Brian Nosek reminded us, 'Science as a system is very conservative. Peer review today looks like it did in the 1960s, even though everything else in the world has evolved. I want to flip that – so that science is always innovating on how it does its work, not just what questions it asks.' That spirit, of innovating not just what we study but how we study, is the spirit we need now.

So the invitation is simple: wherever you are, whatever role you occupy, take the next step. If you are a student, seek out diverse contexts. If you are a practitioner, build lightweight testing into your workflow. If you are a researcher, preregister your next study. If you are a policy maker, insist on evidence that is both rigorous and inclusive. If you are a communicator, tell the harder stories as well as the easy ones. The future of behavioural science will not be decided by slogans or by manifestos. It will be decided by the everyday choices of those who care enough to do the work well.

As Eric Singler reminded us, humility must come first: 'Context is so important … universal learnings can often be questioned. We still have a lot to learn.' That humility, combined with courage, is what will carry behavioural science forward. And if there is one thing that this book hopes to leave you with, it is not a set of answers, but a sense of possibility. Behavioural science could become more inclusive, more ethical, more cumulative, more impactful. It could become a field that not only studies behaviour, but models the best of it. That future is not guaranteed. But it is possible. And it starts with the next step you choose to take.

Closing reflections

When this project began, it was simply a PhD student's attempt to learn from others. In total, 12 interviews, 6 by me and 6 by Etinosa Agbonlahor, became over 250, and eventually, this book. Along the way, what emerged was not just a set of answers, but a set of questions; the questions that define a living, breathing discipline.

Behavioural science today is imperfect. It has been too quick to overclaim, too narrow in its samples, too slow to embrace replication and transparency. But it is also inspiring. It has helped governments design better policies, businesses create more human-centred products, and communities find new ways of working together. It has made a difference, and it can make much more.

The future of behavioural science will depend on whether we choose humility over hubris, inclusivity over insularity, and curiosity over complacency. It will depend on whether we see ourselves not as owners of insight but as stewards of trust.

As Hans Rocha IJzerman said, 'I hope we'll see an increased use of ethnographies and qualitative research methods to better understand how different populations experience the same concepts.' As Susan Michie noted, 'harnessing the power of machine learning and artificial intelligence has the potential to make much more progress'. As Eric Singler reminded us, 'context is so important'. And as Brian Nosek urged, 'science must innovate not just on what questions it asks, but how it does its work'.

Behavioural science is not finished. Neither are we. That is its challenge, and its gift.

Welcome, then, not to the end of this book, but to the beginning of the work it calls for. The future of behavioural science is not something we are waiting for. It is something we are building, project by project, paper by paper, conversation by conversation. And if this book has done its job, it has left you feeling a little more informed, a little more connected, and a lot more excited about the road ahead.

Afterword

This journey began with a question, not a plan. A handful of interviews with people further along the path gradually became hundreds of conversations across academia, government, and industry. At the time I was a PhD student, uncertain about where I fit, simply curious about what behavioural science was and what it could become. I did not imagine that those conversations would grow into this book. But over time, patterns revealed themselves: shared frustrations, repeated blind spots, and, above all, a collective hope that this field could be more than it currently is.

The answer cannot come from any single voice. It comes from the community. The practitioners who run small but vital pilots in schools or municipalities. The academics who dedicate years to patient, careful replications. The organisations building behavioural units within governments, firms, and NGOs. The students who arrive with fresh perspectives and challenge us to question our habits. Each has shaped this book, and each has a stake in the future it gestures towards.

One caution I would offer is this: too often we hear the same voices repeated on conference stages, in popular books, and in the media. They are often brilliant, but if we only listen to them, we risk mistaking a slice of the field for its entirety. Some of the most useful lessons I have learned came not from the keynote speakers but from the people doing the everyday work: policy officers trying to test an intervention in overstretched governments, NGO staff adapting behavioural tools in low-resource settings, or junior researchers running the replications that rarely make headlines. Their insights are grounded, practical, and hard-won. If behavioural science is to grow, it must make more room for those voices.

The truth is that we do not need more evangelism; we need more honesty about what works, what fails, and what sits in between.

We need to celebrate practical wisdom alongside theory, and to resist the temptation to inflate fragile findings into universal laws. Rigour matters, but so does relevance. And relevance only comes from engaging with the messy realities of people's lives, not just the elegance of controlled experiments.

So here is my invitation. Stay curious. Keep asking the uncomfortable questions. Seek out the voices that are not always heard. Share your failures as openly as your successes. Build bridges across disciplines, sectors, and cultures. Mentor someone who is just starting out. Join a replication project. Help create the infrastructures and context libraries we still lack. And if you want to keep the conversation going, please do reach out; I would love to continue that dialogue. The interview series that inspired this book will carry on, with new voices and new questions, because the work of defining this field will never be finished.

Behavioural science is not done. Neither are we. And that is a good thing, because the challenges ahead will demand our best curiosity, humility, and imagination. Let us meet them together.

Notes

Chapter 1

[a] There are many excellent, in-depth, summaries and analyses of the history of behavioural economics and behavioural science. My core recommendations would be:

- Camerer, C.F., Loewenstein, G. and Rabin, M. (eds) (2004) *Advances in Behavioral Economics*, Princeton University Press;
- Camerer, C. (1999) 'Behavioral economics: Reunifying psychology and economics', *Proceedings of the National Academy of Sciences*, 96(19): 10575–77;
- Angner, E. and Loewenstein, G. (2012) 'Behavioral economics', in U. Mäki (ed) *Handbook of the Philosophy of Science, Vol. 13: Philosophy of Economics*, Elsevier, pp 641–90.

Chapter 3

[a] Whether pension defaults can be justified by long-term welfare gains has come under debate: Laibson, D. (2020) 'Nudges are not enough: The case for price-based paternalism', [Conference presentation], *AEA/AFA Joint Luncheon, American Economic Association Annual Meeting*, San Diego, California, January 3, Available from: www.aeaweb.org/webcasts/2020/aea-afa-joint-luncheon-nudges-are-not-enough

[b] Cohen's d is a measure used in statistics to indicate the size of the difference between two groups. It tells us how much one group differs from another in terms of standard deviations. A Cohen's d of 0.2 indicates a small effect size (the groups are slightly different), 0.5 indicated a medium effect size (the groups are moderately different), and 0.8 indicates a large effect size (the groups are very different). Therefore, Cohen's d helps us understand whether the difference between two groups is trivial, noticeable, or substantial.

Chapter 4

[a] The current correct form is also to no longer address study participants as 'subjects', but as participants, signaling their active role in the study of behaviour.

[b] The SRQ-20 is a mental health screening tool developed by the WHO. It contains 20 yes/no questions designed to detect common mental disorders, such as depression and anxiety, in primary care or community settings.

Chapter 5

[a] A gradient boosting model is a machine learning method that improves its predictions by building many small decision trees, with each new tree learning from and correcting the mistakes of the ones before it. For example, if the model is predicting whether a customer will make a purchase, the first tree makes an initial prediction, the next tree focuses on the customers it got wrong, and each subsequent tree further improves the overall prediction accuracy.

Chapter 6

[a] I really recommend reading *I'm So Sorry for Psychology's Loss, Whatever It Is*, by Adam Mastroianni, it's fantastic. And somewhat depressing.

Chapter 7

[a] There is actually a huge body of literature on the consistent failure of disclosure in the financial domain. For example:

- Adams, P., Hunt, S., Palmer, C. and Zaliauskas, R. (2019) 'Testing the effectiveness of consumer financial disclosure: Experimental evidence from savings accounts', *NBER Working Paper No. 25718*, National Bureau of Economic Research, doi.org/10.3386/w25718

Chapter 8

[a] Dan's interview was conducted before large language models, such as ChatGPT and Claude, were a thing. Therefore, science communications, especially in the written form, have really undergone quite a transformation. We're still in the process of finding out whether it's been beneficial. But safe to say that a lot of people are using these tools to help them break down complex scientific constructs and communicate them to different audiences more effectively. I definitely have!

Chapter 9

[a] I myself am a Senior Product Manager and haven't had a professional title that includes the word 'behavioural' for years now.

References

1. Hubble, C. and Varazzani, C. (2023) 'Mapping behavioural insights', 'Mapping behavioural insights', Observatory of Public Sector Innovation, Available from: https://oecd-opsi.org/blog/mapping-behavioural-insights/
2. Behavioral Teams. (n.d.) 'Global behavioural teams – team table', [online], Available from: www.behavioralteams.com/team-table/
3. Behavioral Economics (n.d.) Graduate and undergraduate programmes in behavioural economics, *Behavioral Economics*, Available from: www.behavioraleconomics.com/resources/be-grad-programs/
4. Mertens, S., Herberz, M., Hahnel, U.J. and Brosch, T. (2022) 'The effectiveness of nudging: A meta-analysis of choice architecture interventions across behavioral domains', *Proceedings of the National Academy of Sciences*, 119(1): e2107346118, Available from: www.pnas.org/doi/10.1073/pnas.2107346118
5. Maier, M., Bartoš, F., Stanley, T.D., Shanks, D.R., Harris, A.J. and Wagenmakers, E.J. (2022) 'No evidence for nudging after adjusting for publication bias', *Proceedings of the National Academy of Sciences*, 119(31): e2200300119, Available from: www.pnas.org/doi/10.1073/pnas.2200300119
6. DellaVigna, S. and Linos, E. (2022) 'RCTs to scale: Comprehensive evidence from two nudge units', *Econometrica*, 90(1): 81–116.
7. Smith, A. (2010) *The Theory of Moral Sentiments*. Penguin.
8. Skinner, B.F. (1953) *Science and Human Behavior*. MacMillan Company.
9. Simon, H.A. (1957) *Models of Man: Social and Rational; Mathematical Essays on Rational Human Behavior in Society Setting*. Wiley.
10. Hallsworth, M., Egan, M., Rutter, J. and McCrae, J. (2018) 'Behavioural government: Using behavioural science to improve

how governments make decisions', Available from: www.bi.team/wp-content/uploads/2018/08/BIT-Behavioural-Government-Report-2018.pdf

11. Morris, N. (2013) 'How the authors of Nudge convinced David Cameron to change the way we are governed', *The Independent*, [online], Available from: www.independent.co.uk/news/uk/politics/first-obama-now-cameron-embraces-nudge-theory-2050127.html
12. Behavioural Insights Team. (n.d.) BIT website publications, Available from: www.bi.team/insights/publications/
13. Australian Productivity Commission (2008) 'Behavioural economics and public policy', [roundtable proceedings], Available from: https://webarchive.nla.gov.au/awa/20141010052517/http://pandora.nla.gov.au/pan/53654/20160428-1424/www.pc.gov.au/research/supporting/behavioural-economics/behavioural-economics.pdf
14. Afif, Z., Islan, W.W., Calvo-Gonzalez, O. and Dalton, A. (2019) 'Behavioral science around the world: Profiles of 10 countries', World Bank Group, Available from: https://apo.org.au/sites/default/files/resource-files/2019-03/apo-nid223781.pdf
15. NSW Government. (n.d.) 'Sludge toolkit', Behavioural Insights Unit, Available from: www.nsw.gov.au/departments-and-agencies/behavioural-insights-unit/sludge-toolkit
16. World Bank. (2015) 'World development report 2015: Mind, society, and behavior', Report No. 92863, World Bank, Available from: www.worldbank.org/content/dam/Worldbank/Publications/WDR/WDR%202015/WDR-2015-Full-Report.pdf
17. Behavioral Science.org. (n.d.) 'Behavioral science teams', Behavioral Science.org, Available from: www.behavioralscience.org/behavioral-science-teams
18. Polman, E. and Maglio, S.J. (2024) 'The problem with behavioral nudges', *The Wall Street Journal*, [online], 26 May, Available from: www.wsj.com/economy/consumers/decision-making-research-behavior-2e5060c1
19. *The Guardian*. (2024) 'The problem with the nudge effect: It can make you buy more carrots – but it can't make you eat them', *The Guardian*, [online], 28 May, Available from: www.theguardian.com/science/article/2024/may/27/the-problem-with-the-nudge-effect-it-can-make-you-buy-more-carrots-but-it-cant-make-you-eat-them
20. Young, S. (2024) 'Bridging the divide between the potential & practice of behavioral science in the private sector', *Behavioral Science & Policy*, doi.org/10.1177/23794607241263414

21. Bovens, L. (2009) 'The ethics of nudge', in T. Grüne-Yanoff and S.O. Hansson (eds) *Preference change: Approaches from Philosophy, Economics and Psychology*, Springer, pp 207–19.
22. Lades, L.K. and Delaney, L. (2022) 'Nudge FORGOOD', *Behavioural Public Policy*, 6(1): 75–94.
23. Dallacker, M., Appelius, L., Brandmaier, A.M., Morais, A.S. and Hertwig, R. (2024) 'Opt-out defaults do not increase organ donation rates', *Public Health,* 236: 436–40.
24. Ritchie, S. (2021) 'The Government's Covid comms failure The obsession with behavioural science is a classic case of over-promising and under-delivering', UnHerd, [blog], February, Available from: https://unherd.com/2021/02/behavioural-science-wont-save-us/
25. Sanders, J., Tosi, A., Obradović, S., Miligi, I. and Delaney, L. (2021) 'Lessons from lockdown: Media discourse on the role of behavioural science in the UK COVID-19 response', *Frontiers in Psychology*, 12: 647348.
26. Reicher, S. (2021) 'Human behaviour: What scientists have learned about it from the pandemic', *The Conversation*, [online], 1 July, Available from: https://theconversation.com/human-behaviour-what-scientists-have-learned-about-it-from-the-pandemic-163666
27. Banerjee, S. and John, P. (2024) 'Nudge plus: incorporating reflection into behavioral public policy', *Behavioural Public Policy,* 8(1): 69–84.
28. Banerjee, S., Galizzi, M.M., John, P. and Mourato, S. (2022) 'What works best in promoting climate citizenship? A randomised, systematic evaluation of nudge, think, boost and nudge+', *Journal of Behavioral Public Administration,* 5(1).
29. Liebman, J., Ludwig, J., Katz, L., Chetty, R., Kling, J., Sanbonmatsu, L. et al (2020) 'Evaluating the impact of moving to opportunity in the United States', *Poverty Action Lab*, Available from: https://www.povertyactionlab.org/evaluation/evaluating-impact-moving-opportunity-united-states
30. Shah, A.M., Osborne, M., Lefkowitz Kalter, J., Fertig, A., Fishbane, A. and Soman, D. (2023) 'Identifying heterogeneity using recursive partitioning: evidence from SMS nudges encouraging voluntary retirement savings in Mexico', *PNAS nexus,* 2(5): pgad058.
31. Schöning, C., Matt, C. and Hess, T. (2019) 'Personalised nudging for more data disclosure? On the adaption of data usage policies format to cognitive styles', *Business & Information Systems Engineering*, 61(6): 649–62.

32. Peer, E., Egelman, S., Harbach, M., Malkin, N., Mathur, A. and Frik, A. (2020) 'Nudge me right: Personalizing online security nudges to people's decision-making styles', *Computers in Human Behavior*, 109: 106347.
33. Brown, M.G., Schiltz, J., Derry, H. and Holman, C. (2019) 'Implementing online personalized social comparison nudges in a web-enabled coaching system', *The Internet and Higher Education*, 43: 100691.
34. Hertwig, R. and Grüne-Yanoff, T. (2017) 'Nudging and boosting: Steering or empowering good decisions', *Perspectives on Psychological Science*, 12(6): 973–86.
35. Grüne-Yanoff, T. and Hertwig, R. (2016) 'Nudge versus boost: How coherent are policy and theory?', *Minds and Machines*, 26(1): 149–83.
36. Van Roekel, H., Reinhard, J. and Grimmelikhuijsen, S. (2022) 'Improving hand hygiene in hospitals: comparing the effect of a nudge and a boost on protocol compliance', *Behavioural Public Policy*, 6(1): 52–74.
37. Franklin, M., Folke, T. and Ruggeri, K. (2019) 'Optimising nudges and boosts for financial decisions under uncertainty', *Palgrave Communications*, 5(1), doi.org/10.1057/s41599-019-0321-y
38. Chater, N. and Loewenstein, G. (2023) 'The i-frame and the s-frame: How focusing on individual-level solutions has led behavioral public policy astray', *Behavioral and Brain Sciences*, 46: e147.
39. Kirschbaum, C., Pirke, K.M. and Hellhammer, D.H. (1993) 'The "Trier Social Stress Test"–a tool for investigating psychobiological stress responses in a laboratory setting', *Neuropsychobiology*, 28(1–2): 76–81.
40. Silan, M., Zelkowitz, A., Titus, B., Forscher, P., Gennari, F., Hickler, B. and Terer, M. (2023) 'Behavioral insights in the Global South', *APS Observer*, 36, Available from: www.psychologicalscience.org/observer/gs-behavioral-insights-global-south
41. Henrich, J., Heine, S.J. and Norenzayan, A. (2010) 'The weirdest people in the world?', *Behavioral and Brain Sciences*, 33(2–3): 61–83.
42. Snibbe, A.C. and Markus, H.R. (2005) 'You can't always get what you want: Social class, agency, and choice', *Journal of Personality and Social Psychology*, 88: 703–20.
43. Stephens, N.M., Markus, H.R. and Townsend, S.S.M. (2007) 'Choice as an act of meaning: The case of social class', *Journal of Personality and Social Psychology*, 93: 814–30.

44. Haidt, J., Koller, S.H. and Dias, M.G. (1993) 'Affect, culture, and morality, or is it wrong to eat your dog?' *Journal of Personality and Social Psychology*, 65(4): 613–28.
45. Falk, C.F., Heine, S.J., Yuki, M. and Takemura, K. (2009) 'Why do Westerners self-enhance more than East Asians?' *European Journal of Personality*, 23(3): 183–203.
46. Henrich, N. and Henrich, J. (2007) *Why Humans Cooperate: A Cultural and Evolutionary Explanation*, Oxford University Press.
47. Kim, H. S. and Markus, H.R. (1999) 'Deviance or uniqueness, harmony or conformity? A cultural analysis', *Journal of Personality and Social Psychology*, 77: 785–800.
48. Grossmann, I., Na, J., Varunum, M.E.W., Kitayama, S. and Nisbett, R.E. (2010) 'Cultural differences in analytic and holistic thinking; Implications for attention, perception, and reasoning', in R.S. Wyer Jr., C. Chiu, and Y. Hong (eds) *Understanding Culture: Theory, Research, and Application*, Psychology Press, pp 215–36.
49. Carpenter, J., Burks, S. and Verhoogen, E. (2005) 'Comparing students to workers: The effects of social framing on behavior in distribution games', in J. Carpenter, G.W. Harrison and J.A. List (eds) *Field Experiments in Economics*, JAI.
50. Henry, P.J. (2009) 'College sophomores in the laboratory redux: Influences of a narrow database on social psychology's view of the nature of prejudice', *Psychological Inquiry*, 19: 49–71.
51. Kahneman, D. and Tversky, A. (1979) 'Prospect theory: An analysis of decision under risk', *Econometrica*, 47(2): 263–91.
52. Camerer, C. (2003) *Behavior Game Theory: Experiments in Strategic Interaction*. Princeton University Press.
53. Van Bavel, J.J.V., Baicker, K., Boggio, P.S., Capraro, V., Cichocka, A., Cikara, M. et al (2020) 'Using social and behavioural science to support COVID-19 pandemic response', *Nature Human Behaviour*, 4(5): 460–71.
54. IJzerman, H., Dutra, N., Silan, M., Adetula, A., Brown, D.M.B. and Forscher, P. (2021) 'Psychological science needs the entire globe, Part 1', *APS Observer, 34*, Available from: www.psychologicalscience.org/observer/global-psych-science
55. Silan, M., Adetula, A., Basnight-Brown, D.M., Forscher, P.S., Dutra, N. and IJzerman, H. (2021) 'Psychological science needs the entire globe, Part 2', *APS Observer*, 34.
56. Forscher, P.S., Basnight-Brown, D.M., Dutra, N., Adetula, A., Silan, M. and IJzerman, H. (2021) 'Psychological science needs the entire globe, Part 3', *APS Observer*, 35.

57. Crum, A.J., Akinola, M., Martin, A. and Fath, S. (2017) 'The role of stress mindset in shaping cognitive, emotional, and physiological responses to challenging and threatening stress', *Anxiety, Stress, & Coping*, 30(4): 379–95.
58. Crum, A.J., Salovey, P. and Achor, S. (2013) 'Rethinking stress: the role of mindsets in determining the stress response', *Journal of Personality and Social Psychology*, 104(4): 716.
59. Cole, S., Balcetis, E. and Dunning, D. (2013) 'Affective signals of threat increase perceived proximity', *Psychological Science*, 24(1): 34–40.
60. Serpell, R. (2017) 'Perspectives on African Indigenous knowledge of child development and socialization', in N.J. Cabrera and B. Leyendecker (eds) *Handbook on Positive Development of Minority Children and Youth*, Springer.
61. Lin, C.L. and Chang, C.Y. (2017) 'Personality and family context in explaining grit of Taiwanese high school students', *Eurasia Journal of Mathematics, Science and Technology Education*, 13(6): 2197–213.
62. Bae, S. and Wu, A.D. (2016) 'The role of grit in cross-cultural adjustment among international students', *Journal of International Students*, 6(3): 626–42.
63. Dowswell, T., Carroli, G., Duley, L., Gates, S., Gülmezoglu, A. M., Khan-Neelofur, D. et al (2010) 'Alternative versus standard packages of antenatal care for low-risk pregnancy', *Cochrane Database of Systematic Reviews*, 10(1): CD000934.
64. Kuhnlein, H. V. and Receveur, O. (1996) 'Dietary change and traditional food systems of indigenous peoples', *Annual Review of Nutrition*, 16(1): 417–42.
65. Sharma, S., Gittelsohn, J., Rosol, R. and Beck, L. (2010) 'Addressing the public health burden caused by the nutrition transition through the Healthy Foods North nutrition and lifestyle intervention programme', *Journal of Human Nutrition and Dietetics*, 23(S1): 120–7.
66. Jiang, L., Manson, S.M., Beals, J., Henderson, W.G., Huang, H., Acton, K.J. et al (2013) 'Translating the Diabetes Prevention Program into American Indian and Alaska Native communities: Results from the Special Diabetes Program for Indians Diabetes Prevention demonstration project', *Diabetes Care*, 36(7): 2027–34.
67. Esposito, K., Kastorini, C.M., Panagiotakos, D.B. and Giugliano, D. (2011) 'Mediterranean diet and weight loss: Meta-analysis of randomized controlled trials', *Metabolic Syndrome and Related Disorders*, 9(1): 1–12.

68. Goetz, A.M. and Gupta, R.S. (1996) 'Who takes the credit? Gender, power, and control over loan use in rural credit programs in Bangladesh', *World Development*, 24(1): 45–63.
69. MicroLoan Foundation. (2021) 'Annual impact report', Available from: www.microloanfoundation.org.uk/wp-content/uploads/2020/09/2021-MLF-Annual-Report-unsigned-FINAL.pdf
70. Lok Capital. (2022) 'Impact and innovation: Expanding access to financial services', Available from: www.lokcapital.com/impact
71. Omnivore. (2025) 'Impact report: Empowering smallholder farmers', Available from: https://omnivore.vc/uploads/oacsf_impact_report_2025_f03226b09d_2_3_d5bafa9007.pdf
72. Bolton, P. and Tang, A.M. (2002) 'An alternative approach to cross-cultural function assessment', *Social Psychiatry and Psychiatric Epidemiology*, 37(11): 537–43.
73. Summerfield, D. (2001) 'The invention of post-traumatic stress disorder and the social usefulness of a psychiatric category', *British Medical Journal*, 322(7278): 95–8.
74. Bolton, P. and Betancourt, T.S. (2004) 'Mental health in postwar Afghanistan', *Journal of the American Medical Association*, 292(5): 626–8.
75. Berthold, S.M., Mollica, R.F., Silove, D., Tay, A.K., Lavelle, J. and Lindert, J. (2019) 'The HTQ-5: Revision of the Harvard Trauma Questionnaire for measuring torture, trauma, and DSM-5 PTSD symptoms in refugee populations', *European Journal of Public Health*, 29(3): 468–74.
76. Tol, W.A., Komproe, I.H., Jordans, M.J., Thapa, S.B., Sharma, B. and De Jong, J.T. (2009) 'Brief multi-disciplinary treatment for torture survivors in Nepal: A randomized controlled trial', *BMC Psychiatry*, 9: 1–12.
77. Tay, A.K., Riley, A., Islam, R., Welton-Mitchell, C., Duchesne, B., Waters, V. et al (2019) 'The culture, context, and mental health of Rohingya refugees: A review for staff in mental health and psychosocial support programs for Rohingya refugees', *Intervention*, 17(2): 160–7.
78. Rasmussen, A., Ventevogel, P., Sancilio, A., Eggerman, M. and Panter-Brick, C. (2014) 'Comparing the validity of the self-reporting questionnaire and the Afghan Symptom Checklist: Dysphoria, aggression, and gender in transcultural assessment of mental health', *BMC Psychiatry*, 14: 206.
79. Bolton, P., Bass, J., Betancourt, T.S., Speelman, L., Onyango, G., Clougherty, K.F. et al (2007) 'Interventions for depression symptoms among adolescent survivors of war and displacement

in northern Uganda: A randomized controlled trial', *JAMA*, 298(5): 519–27.

80. Brockington, D. and Igoe, J. (2006) 'Eviction for conservation: A global overview', *Conservation and Society*, 4(3): 424–70, Available from: www.jstor.org/stable/26392837
81. Robalino, J. and Pfaff, A. (2013) 'Ecopayments and deforestation in Costa Rica: A nationwide analysis of PSA's initial years', *Land Economics*, 89(3): 432–48.
82. Schmink, M. and Perz, S.G. (2019) 'Forest peoples and protected areas: Social, ecological, and policy dimensions of conservation in the Amazon', *Annual Review of Anthropology*, 48: 395–412.
83. Mylek, M.R. and Schirmer, J. (2020) 'Understanding acceptability of fuel management to reduce wildfire risk: Informing communication through understanding complexity of thinking', *Forest Policy and Economics*, 113, 102120.
84. Western, D. and Waithaka, J. (2020) 'People, parks, and wildlife: The Kenyan experience', *Conservation Biology*, 34(4): 1065–74.
85. Mbaiwa, J.E. and Stronza, A.L. (2011) 'Changes in residents' attitudes towards tourism development and conservation in the Okavango Delta, Botswana', *Journal of Environmental Management*, 92(8): 1950–9.
86. Lewis, J., Schneegans, S. and Straza, T. (eds) (2021) 'UNESCO science report: The race against time for smarter development', Unesco Publishing, Available from: https://unesdoc.unesco.org/ark:/48223/pf0000377250
87. Mughogho, W., Adhiambo, J. and Forscher, P.S. (2023) 'African researchers must be full participants in behavioural science research', *Nature Human Behaviour*, 7(3): 297–9.
88. Paris, B., IJzerman, H. and Forscher, P.S. (2020) 'PSA 2020–2021 study capacity report', doi.org/10.31234/osf.io/v9zma
89. Society for the Improvement of Psychological Science. (2020) 'SIPS Demographics Report', Available from: https://improvingpsych.org/2020/06/16/sips-demographics-report/
90. Nielsen, M., Haun, D., Kärtner, J. and Legare, C.H. (2017) The persistent sampling bias in developmental psychology: A call to action', *Journal of Experimental Child Psychology*, 162: 31–8.
91. Amarante, V., Burger, R., Chelwa, G., Cockburn, J., Kassouf, A., McKay, A. et al (2021) 'Underrepresentation of developing country researchers in development research', *Applied Economics Letters*, 29(17): 1659–64.

92. Tindle, R. (2021) 'Improving the global reach of psychological research', *Discover Psychology*, 1(5), doi.org/10.1007/s44202-021-00004-4
93. Wundt, W. (1897) *Outlines of Psychology*. Wilhelm Engelmann.
94. Nobel Prize Outreach AB. (n.d.) 'Vernon L. Smith – Facts', Available from: www.nobelprize.org/prizes/economic-sciences/2002/smith/facts/
95. Engel, C. (2011) 'Dictator games: A meta study', *Experimental Economics*, 14(4): 583–610.
96. Papandrea, D., Shepard, D. and Martinez-White, X. (2021) '56% of Americans donated to charity in 2021, at average of $574', *LendingTree*, Available from: www.lendingtree.com/debt-consolidation/charitable-donations-survey-study/
97. GiveNow. (2022) 'Giving by individuals in Australia, the stats!', Available from: https://help.givenow.com.au/hc/en-us/articles/360001505255-Giving-by-individuals-in-Australia-the-stats
98. Germann, M. and Merkle, C. (2023) 'Algorithm aversion in delegated investing', *Journal of Business Economics*, 93(6): 1691–727.
99. Statista. (n.d.) 'Robo-advisors - United States', Available from: www.statista.com/outlook/dmo/fintech/digital-investment/robo-advisors/united-states
100. Mordor Intelligence. (n.d.) '*US Asset Management Market – Growth, Trends, COVID-19 Impact, and Forecasts (2024–2029)*, Available from: www.mordorintelligence.com/industry-reports/usa-asset-management-industry
101. Kinniry, F.M., Jr., DiJoseph, M.A., Jaconetti, C.M., Walker, D.J. and Quinn, M.C. (2022) 'Putting a value on your value: Quantifying Vanguard Advisor's Alpha®', The Vanguard Group, Available from: www.vanguardsouthamerica.com/content/dam/intl/americas/documents/latam/en/2022/08/mx-sa-2335954-putting-a-value-on-your-value-quantifying-vanguard-advisors-alpha.pdf
102. Behavioural Insights Team. (2012) *Applying behavioural insights to reduce fraud, error and debt*. UK Cabinet Office, Available from: https://assets.publishing.service.gov.uk/media/5a789ae740f0b62b22cbb536/BIT_FraudErrorDebt_accessible.pdf
103. Akbaş. M., Ariely, D., Robalino, D.A. and Weber, M. (2016) 'How to help poor informal workers to save a bit: Evidence form a field Experiment in Kenya', *IZA Discussion Paper*, No 10024, IZA Institute of Labor Economics, Available from: https://ssrn.com/abstract=2803856

104. Van den Broek, T. and Bos, K. (2018) 'Behavioural insights and job-seeking: Lessons from field experiments in the Netherlands', *Journal of Behavioural Public Administration*, 1(1): 1–11.
105. Allcott, H. (2011) 'Social norms and energy conservation', *Journal of Public Economics*, 95(9–10): 1082–95.
106. Karlan, D. and List, J.A. (2007) ‚Does price matter in charitable giving? Evidence from a large-scale natural field experiment', *American Economic Review*, 97(5): 1774–93.
107. Behavioural Economics Team of the Australian Government. (2022) 'Improving organ donor registration among young adults', Australian Government, Department of the Prime Minister and Cabinet, Available from: https://www.pmc.gov.au/sites/default/files/2025-06/ota-report-final.pdf
108. Banerjee, A., Duflo, E., Glennerster, R. and Kinnan, C. (2015), The miracle of microfinance? Evidence from a randomized evaluation', *American Economic Journal: Applied Economics*, 7(1): 22–53.
109. Behavioural Insights Team. (2016) 'The Behavioural Insights Team update report 2015–16: Lessons from the UK's behavioural insights team', Behavioural Insights Team, Available from: www.bi.team/wp-content/uploads/2016/09/BIT_Update_Report_2015-16-.pdf
110. Momsen, K. and Stoerk, T. (2014) 'From intention to action: Can nudges help consumers to save electricity?', *Energy Policy*, 74: 376–82.
111. Banerjee, A.V. and Duflo, E. (2011) *Poor economics: A radical rethinking of the way to fight global poverty*. PublicAffairs.
112. Meyer, M.N., Heck, P.R., Holtzman, G.S., Anderson, S.M., Cai, W., Watts, D.J. et al (2019) 'Objecting to experiments that compare two unobjectionable policies or treatments', *Proceedings of the National Academy of Sciences*, 116(22): 10723–8.
113. Mislavsky, R., Dietvorst, B.J. and Simonsohn, U. (2019) 'The minimum mean paradox: A mechanical explanation for apparent experiment aversion', *Proceedings of the National Academy of Sciences*, 116(48): 23883–4.
114. Mazar, N., Elbæk, C. T. and Mitkidis, P. (2023) 'Experiment aversion does not appear to generalize', *Proceedings of the National Academy of Sciences*, 120(16): e2217551120.
115. Hallsworth, M., Berry, D., Sanders, M. and Sallis, A. (2017) 'Stating appointment costs in SMS reminders reduces missed hospital appointments: Findings from two randomised controlled trials', *PLOS One,* 12(9): e0184731.

116. Haynes, L., Green, D.P., Gallagher, R., John, P. and Torgerson, D.J. (2013) 'Collection of delinquent fines: An adaptive randomized trial to assess the effectiveness of alternative text messages', *The Journal of Policy Analysis and Management*, 32(4): 718–30.
117. Holson, L.M. (2019, February) 'Putting a bolder face on Google', *The New York Times*, [online], Available from: https://www.nytimes.com/2009/03/01/business/01marissa.html
118. Levi, Y. and Benartzi, S. (2020) 'Mind the app: Mobile access to financial information and consumer behavior', doi.org/10.2139/ssrn.3557689
119. Plonsky, O., Apel, R., Ert, E., Tennenholtz, M., Bourgin, D., Peterson, J.C. et al (2019) 'Predicting human decisions with behavioral theories and machine learning', *arXiv* [preprint], Available from: https://arxiv.org/abs/1904.06866
120. *The Australian.* (2024) 'Insurer turns to AI to streamline application process', *The Australian,* [online], 24 May, Available from: www.theaustralian.com.au/business/financial-services/insurer-turns-to-ai-to-streamline-application-process/news-story/800c949d475a3f3899e5911b048302e3
121. Park, J.S., Zhang, Y., Smith, A. and Lee, M. (2024) 'Generative agent simulations of 1,000 people', *arXiv,* [preprint], Available from: https://arxiv.org/abs/2411.10109
122. Foster, I., Ghani, R., Jarmin, R.S., Kreuter, F. and Lane, J. (eds) (2016) *Big Data and Social Science: A Practical Guide to Methods and Tools*, Chapman and Hall/CRC.
123. Rosenthal, R. (1979) 'The file drawer problem and tolerance for null results', *Psychological Bulletin*, 86(3): 638–41.
124. Parry, D.A., Davidson, B.I., Sewall, C.J., Fisher, J.T., Mieczkowski, H. and Quintana, D.S. (2021) 'A systematic review and meta-analysis of discrepancies between logged and self-reported digital media use', *Nature Human Behaviour*, 5(11): 1535–47.
125. Bekkers, R. and Wiepking, P. (2011) 'Accuracy of self-reports on donations to charitable organizations', *Quality & Quantity*, 45(6): 1369–83.
126. Bornstein, E. (2012) *Disquieting Gifts: Humanitarianism in New Delhi*. Stanford University Press.
127. Bourgois, P.I. (2003) *In Search of Respect: Selling Crack in El Barrio,* Cambridge University Press.
128. Ho, K. (2009) *Liquidated: An Ethnography of Wall Street*, Duke University Press.

129. Morduch, J. and Schneider, R. (2017) *The Financial Diaries: How American Families Cope in a World of Uncertainty*, Princeton University Press.
130. Luo, X., Wang, Y., Lee, L. H., Xing, Z., Jin, S., Dong, B. et al (2023) 'Using a virtual reality interview simulator to explore factors influencing people's behavior', *Virtual Reality*, 28(1): 56.
131. Erle, L., Timm, L., Straßmann, C. and Eimler, S.C. (2023) 'Using focus group interviews to examine biased experiences in human-robot-interaction', *arXiv* [preprint], Available from: https://arxiv.org/pdf/2310.01421
132. Rubin, J. and Chisnell, D. (2008) *Handbook of Usability Testing: How to Plan, Design, and Conduct Effective Tests* (2nd edn), Wiley.
133. Guadagno, J., Chao, V. and Callison-Burch, V. (n.d.) 'Pomoting connection: Designing social media experiences to support people with eating disorders', [Facebook page], Facebook, Available from: https://scontent-syd2-1.xx.fbcdn.net/v/t39.8562-6/240842566_386930596155437_3891986093217265885_n.pdf
134. Frank, A.W. (2022) *The Wounded storyteller: Body, Illness & Ethics*, University of Chicago Press.
135. Bamberg, M. (2004) 'Form and functions of "Slut Bashing" in male identity constructions in 15-year-olds: "I know it may sound mean to say this, but we couldn't really care less about her anyway"', *Human Development*, 47(6): 331–53.
136. Watson, T.J. (2009) 'Narrative, life story and manager identity: A case study in autobiographical identity work', *Human Relations*, 62(3): 425–52.
137. Tuckett, D., Smith, R.E. and Nyman, R. (2014) 'Tracking phantastic objects: A computer algorithmic investigation of narrative evolution in unstructured data sources', *Social Networks*, 38: 121–33.
138. Silverman, D. (2013) *Doing Qualitative Research: A Practical Handbook* (4th edn), Sage Publications.
139. Rolfe, G. (2006) 'Validity, trustworthiness, and rigour: Quality and the idea of qualitative research', *Journal of Advanced Nursing*, 53(3): 304–10.
140. Ochieng, P.A. (2009) 'An analysis of the strengths and limitation of qualitative and quantitative research paradigms', *Problems of Education in the 21st Century*, 13: 13.
141. Bryman, A. (2012) *Social Research Methods* (4th edn), Oxford University Press.

142. Barbour, R.S. (2001) 'Checklists for improving rigor in qualitative research: A case of the tail wagging the dog?', *BMJ*, 322(7294): 1115–17.
143. Charmaz, K. (2014) *Constructing Grounded Theory* (2nd edn), Sage Publications.
144. Rasheed, Z., Waseem, M., Ahmad, A., Kemell, K.-K., Xiaofeng, W., Duc, A.N. et al (2024) 'Can large language models serve as data analysts? A multi-agent assisted approach for qualitative data analysis', *arXiv* [preprint], Available from: https://arxiv.org/pdf/2402.01386
145. Zhang, H., Wu, C., Xie, J., Rubino, F., Graver, S., Kim, C. et al (2024) 'When qualitative research meets large language model: Exploring the potential of QualiGPT as a tool for qualitative coding', *arXiv* [preprint] Available from: https://arxiv.org/pdf/2407.14925
146. Bryda, G. and Sadowski, D. (2024) 'From words to themes: AI-powered qualitative data coding and analysis', in A. Costa, L.P. Reis and A. Moreira (eds) *Computer Supported Qualitative Research*, Springer, pp 309–45.
147. Geiecke, F. and Jaravel, X. (2024) 'AI can carry out qualitative research at unprecedented scale', *London School of Economics Impact Blog*, [blog], 30 October, Available from: https://blogs.lse.ac.uk/impactofsocialsciences/2024/10/30/ai-can-carry-out-qualitative-research-at-unprecedented-scale/
148. Cornet, M. and Le Ludec, C. (2024) 'Humans are essential for training AI', *Le Monde*, [online], 25 June, Available from: www.lemonde.fr/en/science/article/2024/06/25/humans-are-essential-for-training-ai_6675713_10.html?utm_source=chatgpt.com
149. Rabbi, M., Philyaw-Kotov, M., Li, J., Klasnja, P. and Murphy, S.A. (2020) 'Translating behavioral theory into technological interventions: Case study of an mHealth app to increase self-reporting of substance-use related data', *Proceedings of the ACM on Interactive, Mobile, Wearable and Ubiquitous Technologies*, 4(1): 1–23.
150. Benavides, C., Benítez-Andrades, J.A., Marqués-Sánchez, P. and Arias, N. (2024) 'eHealth intervention to improve health habits in the adolescent population: Mixed methods study', *JMIR mHealth and uHealth*, Advance online publication, e20217, doi.org/10.2196/20217
151. Sun, X., Teljeur, I., Li, Z. and Bosch, J.A. (2024) 'Can a funny chatbot make a difference? Infusing humor into conversational agents for behavioral intervention', *Journal of Medical Internet Research*, Advance online publication.

152. Costa, J. (2024) 'Mixed methods in educational large-scale studies: Integrating qualitative perspectives', *Education Sciences*, 14(12): 1347.
153. Baumeister, R.F., Bratslavsky, E., Muraven, M. and Tice, D.M. (1998) 'Ego depletion: Is the active self a limited resource?', *Journal of Personality and Social Psychology*, 74(5): 1252–65.
154. Hagger, M.S., Chatzisarantis, N.L., Alberts, H., Anggono, C.O., Batailler, C., Birt, A.R. et al (2016) 'A multi-lab pre-registered replication of the ego-depletion effect', *Perspectives on Psychological Science*, 11(4): 546–73.
155. Open Science Collaboration. (2015) 'Estimating the reproducibility of psychological science', *Science*, 349(6251): aac4716.
156. Ranehill, E., Dreber, A., Johannesson, M., Leiberg, S., Sul, S. and Weber, R. A. (2015) 'Assessing the robustness of power posing: No effect on hormones and risk tolerance in a large sample of men and women', *Psychological Science*, 26(5): 653–6.
157. Klein, R.A., Ratliff, K.A., Vianello, M., Adams, R.B., Bahník, Š., Bernstein, M.J. et al (2014) 'Investigating variation in replicability: A "many labs" replication project', *Social Psychology*, 45(3): 142–52.
158. Klein, R.A., Vianello, M., Hasselman, F., Adams, B.G., Adams, R.B., Alper, S. et al (2018) 'Many Labs 2: Investigating variation in replicability across samples and settings', *Advances in Methods and Practices in Psychological Science*, 1(4): 443–90.
159. Cuddy, A.J., Wilmuth, C.A. and Carney, D.R. (2010) 'The benefit of power posing before a high-stakes social evaluation', *Psychological Science*, 21(10): 1363–8.
160. Bargh, J.A., Chen, M. and Burrows, L. (1996) 'Automaticity of social behaviour: Direct effects of trait construct and stereotype activation on action', *Journal of Personality and Social Psychology*, 71(2): 230–44.
161. Doyen, S., Klein, O., Pichon, C. L. and Cleeremans, A. (2012) 'Behavioral priming: It's all in the mind, but whose mind?', *PLoS One*, 7(1): e29081.
162. Johnson, D.J., Cheung, F. and Donnellan, M.B. (2014) 'Does cleanliness influence moral judgments? A direct replication of Schnall, Benton, and Harvey (2008)', *Social Psychology*, 45(3): 209–15.
163. Vohs, K.D., Mead, N.L. and Goode, M.R. (2006) 'The psychological consequences of money', *Science*, 314(5802): 1154–6.

164. Vicens, J., Perelló, J. and Duch, J. (2018) 'Citizen social lab: A digital platform for human behaviour experimentation within a citizen science framework', *PloS One*, 13(12).
165. Orquin, J.L. and Loose, S.M. (2013) 'Attention and choice: A review on eye movements in decision-making', *Acta Psychologica*, 144(1): 190–206.
166. Ceravolo, M.G., Fabri, M. and Polonara, G. (2019) 'Cash, card or smartphone: The neural correlates of payment methods', *Frontiers in Neuroscience*, 13: 1188.
167. Banker, S., Dunfield, D., Huang, A. and Prelec, D. (2017) 'Neural mechanisms of credit card spending', *Scientific Reports*, 11(1): 4070, Available from: www.nature.com/articles/s41598-021-83488-3.pdf
168. Ahn, S.J., Bailenson, J.N. and Park, D. (2014) 'Short- and long-term effects of embodied experiences in immersive virtual environments on environmental locus of control and behavior', *Computers in Human Behavior*, 39: 235–45.
169. Liu, Z., Han, T., Rubin, D.B. and Deng, K. (2023) 'Bayesian criterion for re-randomization', *arXiv*, [preprint], Available from: https://arxiv.org/pdf/2303.07904
170. Long, M.W., Tobias, D.K., Cradock, A.L., Batchelder, H. and Gortmaker, S.L. (2015) 'Systematic review and meta-analysis of the impact of restaurant menu calorie labeling', *American Journal of Public Health*, 105(5): e11–e24.
171. Petimar, J., Zhang, F., Rimm, E.B., Simon, D., Cleveland, L.P., Gortmaker, S.L. et al (2021) 'Changes in the calorie and nutrient content of purchased fast food meals after calorie menu labeling: A natural experiment', *PLoS medicine*, 18(7): e1003714.
172. Allcott, H. and Rogers, T. (2014) 'The short-run and long-run effects of behavioral interventions: Experimental evidence from energy conservation', *American Economic Review*, 104(10): 3003–37.
173. Loewenstein, G. and Chater, N. (2017) 'Putting nudges in perspective', *Behavioural Public Policy*, 1(1): 26–53.
174. Michie, S., West, R. and Harvey, N. (2020) 'The concept of "fatigue" in tackling COVID-19', *BMJ*, 371: m4171.
175. Dietvorst, B.J., Simmons, J.P. and Massey, C. (2015) 'Algorithm aversion: People erroneously avoid algorithms after seeing them err', *Journal of Experimental Psychology: General*, 144(1): 114–26.
176. Logg, J. M., Minson, J.A. and Moore, D.A. (2019) 'Algorithm appreciation: People prefer algorithmic to human judgment', *Organizational Behavior and Human Decision Processes*, 151: 90–103.

177. Forbes, A. (2013) 'Blinding in randomised clinical trials: Hiding who got what', *Evidence-Based Nursing*, 16(3): 70.
178. Holman, C., Head, M.L., Lanfear, R., Jennions, M.D. and Kokko, H. (2015) 'Evidence of experimental bias in the life sciences: Why we need blind data recording', *PLoS Biology*, 13(7): e1002190.
179. Simmons, J.P., Nelson, L.D. and Simonsohn, U. (2011) 'False-positive psychology: Undisclosed flexibility in data collection and analysis allows presenting anything as significant', *Psychological Science*, 22(11): 1359–66.
180. Levelt, W.J.M., Noort, E. and Drenth, P.J.D. (2012) *Flawed Science: The Fraudulent Research Practices of Social Psychologist Diederik Stapel*, Dutch Academy of Sciences.
181. Wansink, B. (2017) 'The grad student who never said "no."', *Brian Wansink: PhD Advice* [blog], Available from: web.archive.org/web/20170312041524/http:/www.brianwansink.com/phd-advice/the-grad-student-who-never-said-no
182. Van der Zee, T., Anaya, J. and Brown, N.J. (2017) 'Statistical heartburn: An attempt to digest four pizza publications from the Cornell Food and Brand Lab', *BMC Nutrition*, 3(54), doi.org/10.1186/s40795-017-0167-x
183. Oransky, I. and Marcus, A. (2018) 'Cornell finds that food marketing researcher Brian Wansink committed misconduct as he announces retirement', *Retraction Watch*, [online], 20 September, Available from: https://retractionwatch.com/2018/09/20/beleaguered-food-marketing-researcher-brian-wansink-announces-his-retirement-from-cornell/
184. Shu, L.L., Mazar, N., Gino, F., Ariely, D. and Bazerman, M.H. (2012) 'Signing at the beginning makes ethics salient and decreases dishonest self-reports in comparison to signing at the end', *Proceedings of the National Academy of Sciences*, 109(38): 15197–200.
185. Simmons, J.P., Nelson, L.D. and Simonsohn, U. (2021) 'The honesty of dishonesty: Revisiting Ariely's data on signing at the top', *Data Colada*, Available from: https://datacolada.org/98
186. Simmons, J.P., Nelson, L.D. and Simonsohn, U. (2023a) 'Data Colada [109]: Evidence of fraud in academic work by Francesca Gino: Study 1', *Data Colada*, Available from: http://datacolada.org/109
187. Simmons, J.P., Nelson, L.D. and Simonsohn, U. (2023b) 'Data Colada [110]: Evidence of fraud in academic work by Francesca Gino: Study 2', *Data Colada*, Available from: http://datacolada.org/110

188. Simmons, J.P., Nelson, L.D. and Simonsohn, U. (2023c) 'Data Colada [111]: Evidence of fraud in academic work by Francesca Gino: Study 3', *Data Colada*, Available from: http://datacolada.org/111
189. Simmons, J.P., Nelson, L.D. and Simonsohn, U. (2023) 'Data Colada [112]: Evidence of fraud in academic work by Francesca Gino: Study 4', *Data Colada*, Available from: http://datacolada.org/112
190. Baek, K. (2024) 'Judge dismisses Francesca Gino's defamation claims against Harvard', *The Harvard Crimson*, [online], 12 September, Available from: www.thecrimson.com/article/2024/9/12/gino-defamation-lawsuit-dismissed/
191. Vargas, R.A. (2025) 'Harvard fires professor of honesty for "being dishonest"', *The Guardian*, [online], 27 May, Available from: www.theguardian.com/education/2025/may/27/harvard-professor-on-leave-falsified-ethics-data
192. Subbaraman, N. and Woodward, A. (2025) 'Harvard revokes tenure of star professor accused of research misconduct', *The Wall Street Journal*, [online], 28 May, Available from: /www.wsj.com/us-news/education/harvard-tenure-revoked-francesca-gino-research-misconduct-2c17e3c7
193. Lee, G.W. (2025) 'Law firm withdraws from representing HBS Prof. Gino in suit against Harvard', *The Harvard Crimson*, [online], 15 February, Available from: https://www.thecrimson.com/article/2025/2/15/nesenoff-miltenberg-withdraws-gino/
194. Epstein, E.H.C. and Lee, G.W. (2025) 'Harvard sues ex-HBS professor Gino for defamation, accusing her of falsifying evidence,' *The Harvard Crimson*, [online], 12 September, Available from: https://www.thecrimson.com/article/2025/9/12/harvard-sues-gino/
195. Kerr, N.L. (1998) 'HARKing: Hypothesizing after the results are known', *Personality and Social Psychology Review*, 2(3): 196–217.
196. John, L.K., Loewenstein, G. and Prelec, D. (2012) 'Measuring the prevalence of questionable research practices with incentives for truth telling', *Psychological Science*, 23(5): 524–32.
197. Rubin, M. (2017) 'When does HARKing hurt? Identifying when different types of undisclosed post hoc hypothesizing harm scientific progress', *Review of General Psychology*, 21(4): 308–20.
198. Aguinis, H., Ramani, R.S. and Alabduljader, N. (2018) 'What you see is what you get? Enhancing methodological transparency in management research', *Academy of Management Annals*, 12(1): 83–110.

199. Ioannidis, J.P.A. (2005) 'Why most published research findings are false', *PLoS Medicine*, 2(8): e124.
200. Franco, A., Malhotra, N. and Simonovits, G. (2014) 'Publication bias in the social sciences: Unlocking the file drawer', *Science*, 345(6203): 1502–5.
201. Carter, E.C., Schönbrodt, F.D., Gervais, W.M. and Hilgard, J. (2019) 'Correcting for bias in psychology: A comparison of meta-analytic methods', *Advances in Methods and Practices in Psychological Science*, 2(2): 115–44.
202. Johnson, E.J. and Goldstein, D. (2003) 'Do defaults save lives?', *Science*, 302(5649): 1338–9.
203. Steffel, M., Williams, E.F. and Tannenbaum, D. (2019) 'Does presumed consent save lives?', *Behavioral Science & Policy*, 5(1): 70–81.
204. Mastroianni, A. (2023) 'I'm so sorry for psychology's loss, whatever it is', *Experimental History*, Available from: www.experimental-history.com/p/im-so-sorry-for-psychologys-loss
205. Cesario, J. (2014) 'Priming, replication, and the hardest science', *Perspectives on Psychological Science*, 9(1): 40–8.
206. Maxwell, S.E., Lau, M.Y. and Howard, G.S. (2015) 'Is psychology suffering from a replication crisis?', *American Psychologist*, 70(6): 487–98.
207. Nelson, L.D., Simmons, J.P. and Simonsohn, U. (2018) 'Psychology's renaissance', *Annual Review of Psychology*, 69: 511–34.
208. Bakker, M., van Dijk, A. and Wicherts, J.M. (2020) 'The rules of the game called psychological science', *Perspectives on Psychological Science*, 15(5): 1226–44.
209. Inzlicht, M. and Friese, M. (2019) 'The past, present, and future of ego-depletion', *Social Psychology*, 50(5–6): 370–8.
210. Turner, E.H., Matthews, A.M., Linardatos, E., Tell, R.A. and Rosenthal, R. (2008) 'Selective publication of antidepressant trials and its influence on apparent efficacy', *The New England Journal of Medicine*, 358(3): 252–60.
211. Begley, C.G. and Ellis, L.M. (2012) Raise standards for preclinical cancer research', *Nature*, 483(7391): 531–3.
212. Swanson, E.W., Johnston, S.S. and Ross, J.S. (2021) 'Selective registration, publication, and outcome reporting in pivotal clinical trials supporting FDA approval of high-risk cardiovascular devices: A cross-sectional analysis', *Trials*, 22(767), doi.org/10.1186/s13063-021-05790-9

213. Krumholz, H.M., Miller, J.D. and Ross, J.S. (2018) 'Registration, results reporting, and publication bias of clinical trials', *Trials*, 19(295), doi.org/10.1186/s13063-018-2957-0
214. Reinhart, C.M. and Rogoff, K.S. (2010) 'Growth in a time of debt', *American Economic Review*, 100(2): 573–8.
215. Herndon, T., Ash, M. and Pollin, R. (2014) 'Does high public debt consistently stifle economic growth? A critique of Reinhart and Rogoff', *Cambridge Journal of Economics*, 38(2): 257–79.
216. McIntyre, S. and McKitrick, R. (2005) 'Hockey sticks, principal components, and spurious significance', *Geophysical Research Letters,* 32(3): L03710.
217. National Research Council. (2006) 'Surface temperature reconstructions for the last 2,000 years', The National Academies Press.
218. Regalado, A. (2005) 'In climate debate, the "hockey stick" leads to a face-off', *The Wall Street Journal*, [online], 14 February, Available from: www.wsj.com/articles/SB110834031507653590
219. Institute of Physics. (2009) 'Lessons from Schön – the worst physics fraudster?', ScienceDaily, [online], 7 May, Available from: www.sciencedaily.com/releases/2009/05/090505111649.htm
220. Gilchriese, M. (2002) 'Report of the Committee on the formal investigation of alleged scientific misconduct by LBNL staff scientist Victor Ninov', Public Records Archive, Available from: https://archive.org/details/victor_ninov_report
221. Gray, C.M., Kou, Y., Battles, B., Hoggatt, J. and Toombs, A.L. (2018) 'The dark (patterns) side of UX design', in *Proceedings of the 2018 CHI Conference on Human Factors in Computing Systems* (pp 1–14). Montreal, Canada.
222. Brignull, H., Miquel, M., Rosenberg, J. and Offer, J. (2015) 'Dark patterns-user interfaces designed to trick people', in *Proceedings of the Poster Presentation, Australian Psychological Society Congress* (pp 21–3) Sydney, Australia.
223. Brignull, H. (2011) 'Dark patterns: User interfaces designed to trick people', *Dark Patterns*, Available from: www.darkpatterns.org
224. Mathur, A., Acar, G., Friedman, M.J., Lucherini, E., Mayer, J., Chetty, M. et al (2019) 'Dark patterns at scale: Findings from a crawl of 11K shopping websites', *Proceedings of the ACM on Human-Computer Interaction*, 3(CSCW): 1–32.
225. Hausman, D.M. and Welch, B. (2010) 'Debate: to nudge or not to nudge', *Journal of Political Philosophy*, 18(1).

226. Gigerenzer, G. (2015) *Risk Savvy: How to Make Good Decisions*, Penguin.
227. Rebonato, R. (2012) *Taking Liberties: A Critical Examination of Libertarian Paternalism*, Palgrave Macmillan.
228. Sunstein, C.R. (2016) *The Ethics of Influence: Government in the Age of Behavioral Science*, Cambridge University Press.
229. Bösch, C., Erb, B., Kargl, F., Kopp, H. and Pfattheicher, S. (2016) 'Tales from the dark side: Privacy dark strategies and privacy dark patterns', *Proceedings on Privacy Enhancing Technologies*, 2016(4): 237–54.
230. van den Akker, M. and Sunstein, C.R. (2025) 'Do people like financial nudges?', *Judgment and Decision Making*, 20: e2.
231. Loewenstein, G., Bryce, C., Hagmann, D. and Rajpal, S. (2015) 'Warning: You are about to be nudged', *Behavioral Science & Policy*, 1(1): 35–42.
232. Beshears, J., Choi, J.J., Laibson, D. and Madrian, B.C. (2018) 'Behavioral household finance', in *Handbook of Behavioral Economics: Applications and Foundations 1*, North-Holland, pp 177–276.
233. Abdel-Sater, R. and Chevallier, C. (2025) 'Can green nudges increase inequalities?', *Mind & Society*, Advance online publication, doi.org/10.1007/s11299-025-00332-1
234. Choi, J.J., Laibson, D., Madrian, B.C. and Metrick, A. (2004) 'For better or for worse: Default effects and 401(k) savings behavior', in D.A. Wise (ed) *Perspectives on the Economics of Aging*, University of Chicago Press, pp 81–126.
235. Ziv, S. (2025) 'The hidden flaw in 401(k) matches: Who is missing out?', *Forbes,* [online], 9 January, Available from: www.forbes.com/sites/shaharziv/2025/01/09/does-your-companys-401k-match-formula-exacerbate-pay-inequity/
236. Greig, F., Madamba, A., Carranza, G., O'Dea, C., Choukhmane, T., Schmidt, L.D.W. et al (2024) 'Are employers optimizing their 401(k) match?', Vanguard, Available from: https://aemdam.assets.vgdynamic.info/assets/corp/research/pdf/are_employers_optimizing_their_401k_match.pdf
237. European Data Protection Board. (2023) 'Report of the work undertaken by the Cookie Banner Taskforce', [online], 18 January, Available from: www.edpb.europa.eu/our-work-tools/our-documents/other/report-work-undertaken-cookie-banner-taskforce_en
238. Federal Trade Commission. (2021) 'FTC to ramp up enforcement against illegal dark patterns that trick or trap consumers into

subscriptions', [online], 28 October, Available from: www.ftc.gov/news-events/news/press-releases/2021/10/ftc-ramp-enforcement-against-illegal-dark-patterns-trick-or-trap-consumers-subscriptions

239. Sugden, R. (2018) *The Community of Advantage: A Behavioural Economist's Defence of the Market,* Oxford University Press.
240. Sánchez-García, I., Rodríguez-Insuasti, H., Martí-Parreño, J. and Sánchez-Mena, A. (2019) 'Nutritional traffic light and self-regulatory consumption: The role of emotions', *British Food Journal*, 121(1): 183–98.
241. Shaaban, A., Policzer, A., Wu, E., Lima, L.A., Kannan, A. and Fu, E. (2022) 'Shame on you: The positive & negative emotions associated with colour on climate-friendly labels', *Food Quality and Preference*, 99, 104561.
242. Loewenstein, G., Sunstein, C.R. and Golman, R. (2014) 'Disclosure: Psychology changes everything', *Annual Review of Economics*, 6: 391–419.
243. Hastings, G., Stead, M. and Webb, J. (2004) 'Fear appeals in social marketing: Strategic and ethical reasons for concern', *Psychology & Marketing*, 21(11): 961–86.
244. Goldenberg, J.L. and Arndt, J. (2008) 'The implications of death for health: A terror management health model for behavioral health promotion', *Psychological Review*, 115(4): 1032–53.
245. Schüll, N.D. (2012) 'Addiction by design: Machine gambling in Las Vegas', in *Addiction By Design*, Princeton University Press.
246. Ivanova, I. (2023) 'Unlimited vacation can save companies billions. But is it a bad deal … ?', CBS News, [online], 7 August, Available from: www.cbsnews.com/news/unlimited-vacation-bad-deal-companies-save-billions/
247. Fast Company. (2025) 'Why unlimited paid time off doesn't work', Available from: www.fastcompany.com/91329390/why-unlimited-pto-doesnt-work-unlimited-paid-time-off
248. Whalen, R. (2022) 'Biased, burdenous, and burnt out: The real story of unlimited paid time off', PTO Exchange, [online], 15 May, Available from: www.ptoexchange.com/blog/the-real-story-of-unlimited-paid-time-off
249. Penzavecchia, C., Todisco, P., Muzzioli, L., Poli, A., Marangoni, F., Poggiogalle, E. et al (2022) 'The influence of front-of-pack nutritional labels on eating and purchasing behaviors: A narrative review of the literature', *Eating and Weight Disorders-Studies on Anorexia, Bulimia and Obesity*, 27(8): 3037–51.

250. del Valle, C.A., García, F., Gómez, M.M., Parker, P.G., Ayuzo, B. and Kanan, G.S. (2022) 'Weight stigma in Mexico and front-of-package labeling. A systemic review', *Salud Mental*, 45(2): 81–7.
251. Acquisti, A., Brandimarte, L. and Loewenstein, G. (2015) 'Privacy and human behavior in the age of information', *Science*, 347(6221): 509–14.
252. Sunstein, C.R. (2016) 'People prefer System 2 nudges (kind of)', *Duke Law Journal*, 66: 121–68.
253. Chater, N. and Loewenstein, G. (2023) 'Where next for behavioral public policy?', *Behavioral & Brain Sciences*, 46.
254. Connolly, D.J., Loewenstein, G. and Chater, N. (2025) 'An s-frame agenda for behavioral public policy research', *Behavioural Public Policy*, 9(3): 593–613.
255. Hagmann, D., Siegrist, M. and Hartmann, C. (2019) 'Risk perception and preference for renewable energy: Nudges, taxes, and support for climate policy', *Nature Climate Change*, 9(7): 480–3.
256. Thaler, R.H. and Sunstein, C.R. (2008) *Nudge: Improving Decisions About Health, Wealth, and Happiness*, Yale University Press.
257. Benartzi, S., Beshears, J., Milkman, K.L., Sunstein, C.R., Thaler, R.H., Shankar, M. et al (2017) 'Should governments invest more in nudging?', *Psychological Science*, 28(8): 1041–55.
258. Deaton, A. and Cartwright, N. (2018) 'Understanding and misunderstanding randomized controlled trials', *Social Science & Medicine*, 210, 2–21.
259. Hertwig, R. (2017) 'When to consider boosting: Some rules for policy-makers', *Behavioural Public Policy*, 1(2): 143–61.
260. Alemanno, A. and Spina, A. (2014) 'Nudging legally: On the checks and balances of behavioral regulation', *International Journal of Constitutional Law*, 12(2): 429–56.
261. Clavien, C. (2018) 'Ethics of nudges: A general framework with a focus on shared preferences', *Review of Philosophy and Psychology*, 9(2): 427–45.
262. Rizzo, M.J. and Whitman, D.G. (2009) 'Little brother is watching you: New paternalism on the slippery slopes', *Arizona Law Review*, 51: 685–739.
263. Barocas, S., Hardt, M. and Narayanan, A. (2019) *Fairness and Machine Learning*, MIT Press.
264. Raghavan, M., Barocas, S., Kleinberg, J. and Levy, K. (2020) 'Mitigating bias in algorithmic hiring: Evaluating claims and practices', in *Proceedings of the 2020 Conference on Fairness, Accountability, and Transparency* (pp 469–81). Barcelona, Spain.

Index